The *best* punctuation book, period.

A Comprehensive Guide for Every Writer,
Editor, Student, and Businessperson

The *best* punctuation book, period.

June Casagrande

TEN SPEED PRESS
Berkeley

Published in the United States by Ten Speed Press, an imprint of the Crown Publishing
Group, a division of Random House LLC, a Penguin Random House Company, New York.
www.crownpublishing.com
www.tenspeed.com

Ten Speed Press and the Ten Speed Press colophon are registered trademarks of
Random House LLC

Library of Congress Cataloging-in-Publication Data

Casagrande, June.
  The best punctuation book, period : a comprehensive guide for every writer, editor,
student, and businessperson / June Casagrande. — First Edition.
     pages cm
   1. English language--Punctuation—Handbooks, manuals, etc. 2. English language—
Grammar—Handbooks, manuals, etc. 3. English language—Rhetoric—Handbooks,
manuals, etc. I. Title.
 PE1450.C47 2014
 428.2'3—dc23
                          2013030260

Trade Paperback ISBN: 978-1-60774-493-1
eBook ISBN: 978-1-60774-494-8

Printed in the United States of America

Design by Betsy Stromberg

10 9 8 7

First Edition

CONTENTS

INTRODUCTION: PUNCTUATION IS EASY, EXCEPT WHEN IT'S NOT

Punctuate this:

In general the writer who did well in college earning As and Bs knows that a young aspiring middle grade novelist has an equally good reason to join the writers group because what it is is a line up of super creative people who for conscience sake treat it like a sub group of their audience to gauge the readers sensibilities and practice copy editing something they started in the 1960s and 70s because it was in the founders words far out

Did you put a comma after *in general*? Did you put commas after *writer, college, Bs,* and *group*? Did you put apostrophes in *A's, B's, writers', conscience', readers', '70s,* and *founder's*? Did you put hyphens in *middle-grade, super-creative,* and *sub-group*? Did you put a dash before *something*? Did you put quotation marks around *far out* but insert a period between the word *out* and the closing quotation mark?

1

If so, your passage probably looks a lot like this:

> In general, the writer, who did well in college, earning A's and B's, knows that a young aspiring middle-grade novelist has an equally good reason to join the writers' group, because what it is is a line up of super-creative people who for conscience' sake treat it like a sub-group of their audience to gauge the readers' sensibilities and practice copy editing—something they started in the 1960s and '70s because it was, in the founder's words, "far out."

And you might think your polished, carefully punctuated passage is perfect. But you'd be wrong.

The *Los Angeles Times* would disagree with your apostrophes in *A's and B's*. Per that newspaper, it should be *A's and Bs*. The *Chicago Manual of Style* would disagree on different grounds: in that style, it should be *As and Bs*. Any book editor would swiftly change your *copy editing* to *copyediting*. Then there's your punctuation of *"far out."* Most editors outside the United States would swap the places of your period and closing quotation mark.

It gets worse: your punctuation marks could even be creating factual errors. *The writer, who did well in college* refers to someone different than does *the writer who did well in college*. That comma changes the identity of the subject and even the number of people it represents because *the writer who did well in college* can refer to every student who did well in college.

Are you really sure that just one founder called it *far out*? Or could those be the *founders'* words? How sure are you that you're talking about *the readers' sensibilities* and not *the reader's sensibilities*? Are you certain you want to leave *line up* as two unhyphenated words? Are you confident that an em dash is a better choice for setting off that final thought than parentheses or a colon? How would you explain your choice to leave a comma out of *what it is is*?

How would you feel if, after leaving a comma out of *young aspiring middle-grade novelist*, you saw a highly respected publication use the same phrase except with a comma after *young*?

On the surface, punctuation is simple stuff: a system of clear, well-documented rules we all learned in school. But when you sit down to write an article or a story or a business email or a blog post, suddenly it's not so simple. One after another, situations arise in which the basic rules you thought you knew are no help at all. If you start looking for answers, it can get even more confusing. One of the most well-respected and influential style guides in the country will tell you to put just one comma in *red, white and blue*. But if you take that as gospel, you'll be lost when you notice that nearly every book you pick up prefers to throw in another comma before the *and*, writing it *red, white, and blue*.

And heaven help you if you start paying attention to how professional editors use hyphens.

The truth is, punctuation can be very difficult. Professional writers don't know it all. Even professional editors look things up, debate them with colleagues, and are sometimes still left guessing.

No one knows everything there is to know about every punctuation mark, and no one is expected to. But that leaves any amateur or professional writer to ask: *So what am I expected to know? Will I look stupid if I put a comma here or an apostrophe there? Or do even professional editors share my confusion on this matter?*

A lot of people assume that there's a single correct answer for every punctuation conundrum. Either a comma belongs in a certain spot or it doesn't. Either the possessive of *James* is formed by adding an apostrophe plus an *s*, or it's formed by adding the apostrophe alone.

The good news here is also the bad news: often there's more than one right answer. Whether to use a certain punctuation mark can be a matter of choice—the writer's way of emphasizing his meaning, creating rhythm, or making the words more pleasing to the eye. Other times these questions boil down to a matter of style—the kind with a capital *S* that's laid down by one of the publishing world's official playbooks. Still other times, there is only one correct choice, and if you fail to choose it, you can inadvertently change your meaning.

The goal of this book is let you punctuate every sentence, even those that fall into the gray areas of punctuation rules or style differences, with complete confidence.

What Is Style?

In editing, *style* refers to the guidelines laid out by authorities like *The Associated Press Stylebook*, *The Chicago Manual of Style*, the Modern Language Association, the American Psychological Association, and any of the countless different in-house rules of specific publications and publishers. For example, large papers including the *New York Times* and the *Los Angeles Times* have their own in-house style guides. These style guides cover a broad range of issues, including grammar, word usage, and capitalization. But they also contain punctuation rules, and on these rules, the major guides often disagree. For example, for much of its history the *New York Times* put apostrophes in decades: *1970's, 1980's*. Most other publications do not, clearly stating it should be *1970s, 1980s*, and so on. The *Los Angeles Times* has its own rule for how to write *African-American*. Contrary to AP style and even the dictionary the newspaper follows, the *Los Angeles Times* dictates that its reporters write *African American* with no hyphen.

Book publishing often writes its own rules, too, and these can be even more specific than newspapers' in-house guides. Though most book editing follows *The Chicago Manual of Style*, book copy editors regularly create style sheets designed to govern a single book. These style sheets document the copy editor's decisions on highly specific matters of punctuation as well as spelling and word choice—matters that may not be mentioned in the dictionary or the style guide—to assure that they're handled consistently throughout the book. For example, a copy editor has to make a judgment call about whether a compound like *green farming procedures* requires a hyphen, and then note it in the style sheet to make sure it's handled the same way throughout the book. Similarly, a style sheet for a novel in George R. R. Martin's Song of Ice and Fire series would probably note that the books use the variant spelling *grey* to the preferred American spelling of *gray* and that *ser* and *pease* are to be used in place of *sir* and *peas*.

Dictionaries pile on another layer of complexity. They disagree on many matters, especially the age-old conundrum of whether a term like *underway* or *face-lift* should be hyphenated, one word, or two words. What most people don't know is that major style guides usually specify which dictionary users must follow. *The Chicago Manual of Style* suggests users refer to *Merriam-Webster's Collegiate Dictionary* for all matters not specifically mentioned in the style guide. AP tells followers to fall back on *Webster's New World College Dictionary*. The result? In book publishing a writer might use *health care policy*, whereas in newspaper publishing it's *healthcare policy*—unless, of course, a house style sheet or style guide overrules the dictionary.

For the writer, this can add up to some serious confusion. You could see *green-farming procedures* with a hyphen in one publication on the same day you see it without a hyphen in another. Unless you understand style differences and the subtle art of punctuation, you're left to assume that one must be wrong. Because you don't know which one, you don't know how you should write it.

This book attempts to provide answers for users in every punctuation situation in any of four major styles: book style, as reflected by *The Chicago Manual of Style* and its designated dictionary *Merriam-Webster's Collegiate*; news style, as indicated by *Associated Press Stylebook* and its designated dictionary, *Webster's New World College Dictionary*; science style, as influenced by the American Psychological Association and its preferred dictionary, *Merriam-Webster's Collegiate*; and academic style, as outlined by the Modern Language Association, which does not designate a dictionary.

Business writing often reflects news style, especially in press-release writing. For that reason it's recommended that business writers consider following news style.

Whenever a matter is so murky that the style guides and dictionaries provide no definitive answers, we turn to a Punctuation Panel—made up of professional copy editors working in news media and book publishing—for their opinions on how they would punctuate specific terms and sentences. Panel preferences are marked with the symbol ✚. The panelists were asked what they would do in each situation if they were editing the passage in question. As you will see, sometimes all the panelists agreed, sometimes a majority preferred a certain option, and sometimes the panel split, illustrating how professional editors respond when they have to rely on their own judgment. These Punctuation Panel decisions are offered as options, not recommendations. After you've seen what these working pros would do, feel free to decide for yourself.

The goal is to show you every possible way to do it right so you can feel confident that you're making the best choice for your own writing.

HOW TO USE THIS BOOK

This guide aims to be a comprehensive punctuation resource for all writers. Chapters discussing a single punctuation mark explain the basic rules of its usage. Rules that apply in all four of the major editing styles contain no symbol. Rules that vary from style to style use symbols to indicate the right choice for a specific type of writer:

Ⓑ Book-editing style, recommended for fiction writers, authors of nonfiction books, and writers of articles for popular magazines. These recommendations are based largely on the recommendations of *The Chicago Manual of Style* and its designated reference books, including *Merriam-Webster's Collegiate Dictionary*.

Ⓝ News media and business writing style, based primarily on the *Associated Press Stylebook* and *Webster's New World College Dictionary*.

Ⓢ Science style, based on the *Publication Manual of the American Psychological Association* and *Merriam-Webster's Collegiate Dictionary*. CSE

Ⓐ Academic style, recommended for college papers and academic articles and based on the *MLA Handbook for Writers of Research Papers*.

For example, you will see this in the discussion of the serial comma:

Ⓑ Ⓢ Ⓐ When the final item in the series of words or phrases is preceded by a coordinating conjunction, especially *and*, insert a serial comma before the conjunction.

They play football, basketball, and soccer.

Ⓝ When the final item in the series of words or phrases is preceded by a coordinating conjunction, especially *and*, do not insert a serial comma before the conjunction.

They play football, basketball and soccer.

These symbols are also used in the "Punctuation A to Z" section, where you will see notations like these:

half dollar	**Ⓑ Ⓝ**
half-dollar	**Ⓢ**

When a style guide contains no guidance on a subject, it is excluded, as academic style is excluded from the *half-dollar* example above. When a style guide does not state a guideline outright yet nonetheless reveals a preference (including when evidenced in how the guide itself was edited), it is noted.

Preferences of the Punctuation Panel are indicated with the **✚** symbol.

The punctuation guidelines in this book emphasize American style, which differs from British style most notably in that, in American style, a period or comma always comes before a closing quotation mark.

Part II, Punctuation A to Z, provides an at-a-glance reference for punctuating commonly confused words and terms, as well as glossary-type entries on terms relevant to punctuation.

Part I

Guidelines

1

Apostrophe

Apostrophes have two main jobs: they show possession, and they indicate omitted letters or numbers.

Further, some styles allow you to use an apostrophe to form a plural when failure to do so could create confusion. For example, book-editing style advocates using apostrophes when making plurals out of lowercase letters, as in *mind your p's and q's*.

Following are the basic rules for using apostrophes, followed by a list of style-specific exceptions.

Apostrophe to Show Possession

MOST SINGULAR NOUNS

To form the possessive of a singular noun not ending in *s*, including proper names, add an apostrophe plus an *s*. Follow this practice of adding apostrophe plus *s* even if the word ends in *x*, *z*, *ce*, *ch*, or *sh*.

the cat's tail	*Emily's grades*
the ax's blade	*mace's properties*
the hatch's handle	*the quiz's questions*

SINGULAR COMMON NOUNS ENDING IN *S*

To form the possessive of a singular common noun ending in *s*, add an apostrophe plus *s*.

> *the boss's house*
>
> *the hostess's job*

Ⓝ Exception: If the word that follows begins with an *s*, use apostrophe only.

> *the boss' sister*
>
> *the hostess' station*

SINGULAR PROPER NOUNS ENDING IN *S*

To form the possessive of a singular proper noun (name) ending in *s*

Ⓑ Ⓢ Ⓐ add apostrophe plus *s*.

> *James's house*
>
> *Serena Williams's victory*

Ⓝ add only an apostrophe.

> *James' house*
>
> *Serena Williams' victory*

PLURAL NOUNS ENDING IN *S*

To form the possessive of a plural noun ending in *s*, add only the apostrophe. (But see exceptions that follow.)

> *the cats' tails*　　　　*my grandparents' house*
>
> *the girls' grades*　　　　*the Smiths' yard*

PLURAL NOUNS NOT ENDING IN *S*

To form the possessive of an irregular plural noun that does not end in *s*, add an apostrophe plus *s*.

the children's nap time   *the geese's migration*

the women's restroom   *the data's implications*

PLURALS OF FAMILY NAMES

A note of caution about plurals of family names: though last names are subject to the same rules as those laid out above, they account for a surprising number of apostrophe errors. It's common to see such errors as *Happy holidays from the Smith's, We'll see you at the Miceli's house*, and *Have you met the Norris's daughter?*

There's no mystery to getting these right. The basic rules of plurals and possessives apply. So the errors, which likely occur as a result of confusion, can be avoided simply by proceeding with caution. First, identify whether you're referring to one person or more—that is, a singular or a plural.

Mr. Smith plus Mrs. Smith equals two Smiths.

Bob Wilson plus Sue Wilson together are the Wilsons.

Names that end in *s* and similar sounds are the same except that they often use *es* to form the plural (just as many common nouns do: *one boss, two bosses, one latch, two latches*).

one Norris, two Norrises

one Walsh, two Walshes

Bob Thomas and Sue Thomas are the Thomases

Venus Williams and Serena Williams are Williamses

Once you have identified whether you're dealing with a singular like *Smith* or *Williams* or a plural like *Smiths* or *Williamses*, simply apply the basic rules of possessive formation: add apostrophe plus *s* for a singular or add an apostrophe only for a plural.

The Smiths live in the Smiths' house.

I will visit Mr. Smith's house.

Bob and Sue Thomas live in the Thomases' house.

Bob Thomas's house is on the corner.

We're visiting the home of the Walshes, so we'll see you at the Walshes' house.

We'll see you at Ms. Walsh's house.

Two Williamses are together researching the Williamses' ancestry.

Apostrophes with Proper Names		
	NAME NOT ENDING IN S	**NAME ENDING IN S**
Singular Possessive	Brian's *That is Brian's hat.*	**B S A** James's *That is James's car.*
	Smith's *That is Mr. Smith's car.*	**N** James' *That is James' car.*
	Chavez's *That is Mr. Chavez's car.*	**B S A** Jones's *That is Mr. Jones's car.*
	Miceli's *That is Mr. Miceli's car.*	**N** Jones' *That is Mr. Jones' car.*
Plural	Brians *There are two Brians in my class.*	Jameses *There are two Jameses in my class.*
	Smiths *There are two Smiths in my class.*	Joneses *There are two Joneses in my class.*
	Chavezes *There are two Chavezes in my class.*	
	Micelis *There are two Micelis in my class.*	
Plural Possessive	Brians' *Both Brians' test scores were high.*	Jameses' *Both Jameses' test scores were high.*
	Smiths' *We visited the Smiths' house.*	Joneses' *We visited the Joneses' house.*
	Chavezes' *Both Chavezes' test scores were high.*	
	Micelis' *We visited the Micelis' house.*	

NO APOSTROPHE IN POSSESSIVE *ITS*

Perhaps the most common punctuation error stems from confusion about *it's* and *its*. People often erroneously assume that *it's* is possessive because other possessive forms take apostrophe plus *s*: *the dog's tail, the house's roof, the book's cover*. But the correct possessive form is *its*, with no apostrophe. Just as the possessives *hers, his, ours,* and *theirs* never take apostrophes, neither does the possessive *its*: *the dog wagged its tail*.

NO APOSTROPHE IN POSSESSIVE *HIS, HERS, YOURS, THEIRS,* OR *OURS*

These possessive forms never take an apostrophe: *The job is hers. Instead of my car, we will take yours or theirs.*

EXCEPTIONS TO THE BASIC RULES FOR FORMING POSSESSIVES

B A singular word that ends in *s* and that doesn't change in the plural, such as *politics*, forms the possessive with an apostrophe only in both its singular and its plural forms: *politics' repercussions, economics' failings, this species' peculiar traits, those species' peculiar traits*.

B A place, organization, or publication with a name that ends with a plural word ending in *s* takes only an apostrophe: *United States' boundaries, Chino Hills' location,* Better Homes and Gardens' *illustrations*.

B *For . . . sake* expressions that contain a singular noun ending in *s*, such as *goodness*, can take an apostrophe only: *for goodness' sake, for righteousness' sake*. (But note that words that end in *ce, x,* or other letters that create an *s* sound are punctuated normally, with an apostrophe plus an *s*: *expedience's sake, appearance's sake*.)

N *For . . . sake* expressions that contain a singular noun ending in *ce*, such as *convenience*, take an apostrophe only: *for conscience' sake, for appearance' sake*.

S If the final *s* in a singular word is silent, add apostrophe only: *Descartes' methods, Blanche Dubois' journey, Arkansas' policies* (but not if the *s* is pronounced: *Jesus's teachings*).

Ⓑ For all singular words ending in *s*, book style users can follow an alternative practice of applying the apostrophe only: *James' house*, *Serena Williams' victory*.

SHARED VS. INDEPENDENT POSSESSIVES

Whenever two or more nouns share possession of something, only the last noun takes the apostrophe and *s*.

> *Bob and Jane's house*
>
> *Bob and Jane's friends* (the friends belong to both Bob and Jane)

Whenever each noun possesses something independently, each gets its own apostrophe and *s*.

> *Bob's and Jane's jobs*
>
> *Bob's and Jane's friends* (Bob and Jane have different friends)

QUASI POSSESSIVES

Quasi possessives are terms like *a week's vacation*, *two days' notice*, *a dollar's worth*, and *your money's worth*. These expressions are punctuated as possessives, taking an apostrophe.

POSSESSIVES OF COMPOUND TERMS

In multiword units such as *anyone else*, *everyone else*, *teacher's aide*, *attorney general*, *brother-in-law*, *queen mother*, *major general*, and *student driver*, the possessive is applied to the last word.

> *anyone else's family*
>
> *everyone else's experience*
>
> *the attorney general's case*
>
> *my brother-in-law's attitude*
>
> *the teacher's aide's schedule*
>
> *the queen mother's duties*
>
> *the major general's quarters*
>
> *the student driver's experience*

The same rule applies if the compound is plural: simply put the possessive on the last word, regardless of which word takes the plural.

> *the major generals' quarters* (quarters belonging to two or more major generals)

> *the student drivers' experience* (the experience of two or more student drivers)

> *the attorneys general's responsibilities* (the responsibilities of two or more attorneys general)

> *my brothers-in-law's attitudes* (the attitudes of two or more brothers-in-law)

> *the teacher's aides' schedules* (schedules of two or more aides working for single teacher)

> *the teachers' aides' schedules* (schedules of two or more aides working for two or more teachers)

Note that *attorney general*, *brother-in-law*, and similar terms like *passerby* form the plural by adding *s* to the first part of the term: *one attorney general, two attorneys general; one passerby, two passersby*. But this does not change the method for making them possessive. Regardless of which part of the term was made plural, the possessive marker still is placed at the end of the term: *attorneys general's, passersby's*.

POSSESSIVE VS. ADJECTIVE FORMS

If you've ever noticed *teachers union, homeowners policy, couples massage, farmers market*, or a similar term without an apostrophe, you may have assumed it was an error. But it was likely deliberate. Especially in news style, publications often opt to interpret *teachers, farmers*, etc. not as possessors but as adjectives (also called attributive forms). This is as much for aesthetic reasons as logical ones: some editors feel that the apostrophe clutters up the page and disrupts visual flow.

Logically, the difference between *farmers' market* and *farmers market* is that the apostrophe suggests the market is owned by the farmers whereas the absence of the apostrophe suggests the market is about the farmers. In many of these cases, the writer is free to choose either interpretation. But for certain terms, including *farmers market*, *workers' compensation,* and *teachers college,* editing styles have special rules. See individual entries in "Punctuation A to Z."

Note that only plurals that end in *s* offer this option. Irregular plurals like *men, women, children, sheep,* and *deer* must take an apostrophe and *s* in these types of constructions:

Right: *A children's hospital*

Wrong: *A childrens hospital*

Wrong: *A children hospital*

Right: *The men's department*

Wrong: *The mens department*

Wrong: *The men department*

The indefinite articles *a* and *an* before a plural usually preclude the possessive.

Right: *a Cubs game*

Wrong: *a Cubs' game*

This is because indefinite articles usually modify the same word that a possessive is modifying. So writing *a Cubs' game* would pose the same logical problem as *a Dave's car* or *a Jane's house.*

The definite article *the,* however, leaves open both options. *The Cubs game* could refer to the game that's modified by *Cubs* as an adjective. But *The Cubs' game* suggests the game belongs to the Cubs. So either form could be used.

✛ Punctuation Panel preferences for singular possessive, plural possessive, or attributive forms varied depending on the exact term. The following panel choices can serve as guidelines.

Check your homeowner's policy.

Consult the owner's manual.

They had a girls' night out.

Ask about the chocolate lover's package. (majority preference)

Welcome to fashion lovers' paradise. (majority preference)

They got new logos for the boys' team. (majority preference)

They formed a teachers' union. (book style experts' preference)
They formed a teachers union. (news style experts' preference)

He joined a taxpayers' association. (book style experts' preference)
He joined a taxpayers association. (news style experts' preference)

We go to the weekly farmers' market. (book style experts' preference)
We go to the weekly farmers market. (news style experts' preference)

POSSESSIVE WITH GERUND

Choosing whether to use an apostrophe and *s* in a sentence like *I appreciated Bob's visiting* or instead write it *I appreciated Bob visiting* can be difficult. The form with the apostrophe and *s* is sometimes called the possessive with gerund. The form without has been called the fused participle.

The form with the apostrophe and *s* has historically been the preferred form of writing experts, many of whom have condemned the one without the apostrophe as incorrect. The major editing styles do not contain specific rules for choosing one of these forms, though book style does note that the possessive with gerund form is a legitimate choice.

For a simple, safe guideline that can help you avoid criticism, consider this policy: opt for the possessive form whenever possible.

I enjoyed Bob's visiting.

I appreciate your taking the time to meet with me.

I appreciate his helping me with my homework.

Jane's ascending to the CEO position will be good for the company.

Our getting along is important.

The teacher's shouting got their attention.

Terms structured like *a friend of Bob's* are called double possessives or sometimes double genitives. They're called *double* because the word *of* is serving the same function as the apostrophe plus *s*. They're both indicating possession. Compare *the friend of Sue* to *Sue's friend*. They mean the same thing. For this reason, some have assumed that *of* combined with an apostrophe *s* form must necessarily be wrong—a redundancy. But editing styles allow these forms in certain cases.

🅑 In book style, writers can use a possessive after the word *of* anytime "one of several" is implied. So in book style, *a friend of Sue's* is acceptable, as is *a friend of hers*.

🅝 News style permits the double possessive if it meets two conditions: (1) the word after *of* must be an animate thing, such as a person, and (2) the word before *of* has to refer only to a portion and not to all of the animate object's possessions. So you could say *friends of Sue's attended* only if you're referring to some of her friends. If all her friends attended, news style requires the form *friends of Sue attended*.

Apostrophes in Contractions and to Indicate Other Omitted Characters

Apostrophes form contractions, indicating missing letters or numbers. For example, *don't* is a contraction of *do not*, so its apostrophe is standing in for a missing *o*.

In *it's*, the apostrophe indicates a missing letter *i* in *it is*.

In *walkin'*, the apostrophe represents a missing letter *g*, likely dropped as a clue to pronunciation, especially when the writer wants to convey a speaker's accent.

In decades, the apostrophe is used to indicate omitted numerals: *The music of the '80s. The family emigrated in the '50s.* In both these examples, the apostrophe indicates the missing numerals *1* and *9*. In *Bob drove an '07 Camry*, the apostrophe indicates an omitted *2* and *0* in the year *2007*. Apostrophes are not used to form plurals of decades. The correct form in book, news, science, and academic styles is *1980s*, not *1980's*.

A few common contractions are irregular. For instance, *won't* means *will not* and *ain't* means *am not* or *is not*. For specific terms, including unusual expressions such as *dos and don'ts* and *rock 'n' roll*, see the alphabetized listings in "Punctuation A to Z."

Contractions are formed the same way in the major editing styles: they always take apostrophes. The styles vary only in their view of when to use contractions.

S A Academic and science writing tend to be more formal, so writers in these styles should avoid contractions. For example, opt for *Smith did not attend* instead of *Smith didn't attend*.

B N Contractions in news and book styles are more common and acceptable. Judgment calls on whether or not to use them are usually based on the general tone of the publication and the writer's voice.

CONTRACTED VS. POSSESSIVE 'S

Note that *'s* can have two meanings. It can show possession, as in *We took Bob's car*. Or it can be a contraction of *is* or *has*.

Bob's here means *Bob is here*. *Bob's been late twice this week* means *Bob has been late twice this week*.

The Direction of the Apostrophe

When an apostrophe comes at the beginning of a word, many word-processing programs assume that the writer meant to type an open single quotation mark. This creates an error, with the apostrophe curving with its opening to the right, like the letter C, instead of to the left, like a comma. Not all fonts use a curved apostrophe. But if an apostrophe curves, it must curve with the opening to the left.

The band was popular in the '80s.

In fonts that do not curve apostrophes or single quotation marks, this is not an issue. But in most fonts, the writer should take care that all apostrophes at the beginnings of words are not inadvertently changed to open single quotation marks.

Capitalizing a Sentence That Begins with an Apostrophe

When a sentence begins with an apostrophe, for example in a contraction like *'Twas* or *'Tis*, the first letter of the word should be capitalized: *'Tis the season to be jolly.*

Apostrophes to Prevent Confusion When Forming Plurals

An apostrophe used to form a plural is usually an error, with *Eat your carrot's* being an incorrect way to write *Eat your carrots.*

But, as the major style guides recognize, sometimes an apostrophe is the best way to form a plural, especially plurals of individual letters.

APOSTROPHES IN PLURALS OF LETTERS

When writing about lowercase letters as letters, as in *Mind your p's and q's*, an apostrophe to form the plural prevents confusion and is permitted in book, news, science, and academic styles. But styles disagree on how to form plurals of capital letters.

🅑 In book style, capital letters do not take apostrophes in the plural: *Rs, Ss, Ts.*

🅝 In news style, single capital letters take an apostrophe to form the plural: *A's and B's.* Multiple capital letters like *ABCs, IOUs, TVs,* and *VIPs* take no apostrophe.

🅢 🅐 Science and academic styles do not have rules for forming plurals of letters, indicating only that no apostrophe should be used in plurals of an abbreviation: *TVs, PhDs, IQs.*

NO APOSTROPHE IN PLURALS OF NUMBERS

Plurals of numerals do not take apostrophes: *His SAT score was in the 1500s. The company was founded in the 1980s.* Numbers written as words don't take an apostrophe in the plural form, either: *there are some fours and fives in his phone number.*

Proper Names Containing a Possessive Apostrophe

A number of trade names are written as possessives, such as *Macy's, Chili's, McDonald's, Denny's,* and *Friendly's.* To form the plural, singular possessive, or plural possessive of one of these names, the Punctuation Panel unanimously treated these names as invariant (unchanging).

PLURAL

To make one of these proper names plural, use same form as the singular.

+ *There are two Macy's in this county.*
+ *He worked at five different Denny's.*

SINGULAR POSSESSIVE

For the possessive of these proper names, use the same form as the nonpossessive.

+ *Macy's location is perfect.*
+ *Denny's menu changes often.*

PLURAL POSSESSIVE

To form the plural possessive of these proper names, the Punctuation Panel unanimously favored using the same form as the singular nonpossessive.

+ *The three Macy's staffs trained together.*
+ *The seven Denny's locations are equally convenient.*

Abbreviations as Verbs

When an abbreviation like *OK* is used as a verb, its past and progressive forms are formed with an apostrophe: *OK'd, OK'ing.* This is true regardless of whether the style calls for periods: *O.K.'d, O.K.'ing.*

Ⓝ When the abbreviation is used as a verb in the third-person singular present tense, news style omits the apostrophe: *I hope the boss OKs my raise.*

Apostrophes with Other Punctuation

An apostrophe can be confusing when it comes next to another punctuation mark:

> *"The suspects told me they were just 'walkin' and talkin','" the detective recalled.*

Notice that *talkin'* ends with an apostrophe, is in single quotation marks, and comes at the end of a larger quotation. To punctuate a sentence like this one, treat the apostrophe as part of the word or number in which it appears, as if it were the letter *g* in *talking.* Then, following the rules for using quotation marks and commas, place the single quotation marks around the word *talkin'*, then insert a comma to set off the quotation from *the detective recalled*, then end with a regular quotation mark around the entire quotation. Taking this step by step, you get *talkin'* followed by a comma, followed by a single closing quotation mark, followed by a regular closing quotation mark (*talkin','"*).

An apostrophe to indicate possession works the same way: it should be treated as part of the word and inseparable from it.

> *The phone number he called was the Wilsons'.*

The period comes after the apostrophe. Don't confuse the apostrophe with a closing single quotation mark, which would come after the period: *'the Wilsons.'*

2

—

Comma

Commas are separators. Often, a comma indicates a pause. But it's a mistake to think that the only guideline for using commas is to insert one in any place where a pause would go. For example, compare the following:

> *I talked to my brother Steve.* (I have more than one brother.)
>
> *I talked to my husband, Stan.* (I have only one husband.)

Both of these can be correct due to the comma's job of setting off nonrestrictive, that is, nonessential information (see "Comma to Set off a Nonrestrictive or Parenthetical Word, Phrase, or Clause," page 32). For sentences like these, thinking of a comma as merely a pause would lead to errors.

Though some uses of the comma follow rigid rules, others are subject to the writer's judgment and aesthetic considerations.

Minimal Style Variance

Unlike hyphens, commas don't cause much disagreement among style authorities. The only comma issue on which there is outright disagreement is the serial comma—the question of whether to put a comma before a conjunction like *and* in a series like *red, white, and blue*. All the major styles except news style say to include that comma. News style omits it, opting for *red, white and blue* instead.

With the exception of the serial comma, all the rules in this chapter can be considered good guidelines for writers in every style.

Comma to Separate Items in a Series

Words, phrases, and clauses in series of three or more can be separated by commas. (But see exceptions below.)

Ⓑ Ⓢ Ⓐ When the final item in the series of words or phrases is preceded by a coordinating conjunction, especially *and*, insert a serial comma before the conjunction.

> *They play football, basketball, and soccer.*

Ⓝ When the final item in the series of words or phrases is preceded by a coordinating conjunction, especially *and*, do not insert a serial comma before the conjunction.

> *They play football, basketball and soccer.*

Here's an example of phrases in series:

> **Ⓑ Ⓢ Ⓐ** *Ours is a government of the people, by the people, and for the people.*

> **Ⓝ** *Ours is a government of the people, by the people and for the people.*

Ⓑ Ⓝ Ⓢ Ⓐ When the final item in the series of clauses is preceded by a coordinating conjunction, especially *and*, all styles advocate a comma before the conjunction.

> *In the 1980s, music was loud, hair was big, and clubs were hopping along Sunset Boulevard.*

ⓝ When the last or second-to-last item in a series contains its own conjunction, use the serial comma.

> *Sandwiches on the menu include tuna, turkey, and peanut butter and jelly.*

> *Sandwiches on the menu include tuna, peanut butter and jelly, and turkey.*

EXCEPTION: NONCOORDINATE ADJECTIVES BEFORE A NOUN

Multiple adjectives before a noun may or may not have commas between them, depending on the adjectives' relationship to the noun. Coordinate adjectives, which each modify the noun independently, are separated by commas: *He wants to meet a kind, gentle, sweet girl.* Noncoordinate adjectives, which have different relationships to the noun, often take no commas between them. For example, in *He wore bright red wingtip shoes, wingtip* is more integral to the noun than the other adjectives and *bright* modifies not the noun *shoes* but the adjective that immediately follows it, *red.* So the adjectives in *bright red wingtip shoes* are not coordinate and not separated by commas.

The difference between coordinate and noncoordinate adjectives can be subtle and, at times, merely a matter of intent. These tests can help determine whether adjectives are coordinate and, thus, whether they should be separated by commas:

1. Coordinate adjectives make sense with *and* between them: *He wants to meet a kind and gentle and sweet girl.* This is, in fact, the basis of the term "coordinate adjectives"—these are adjectives that could be connected with a coordinating conjunction (*and*). If it helps, think of the commas as representing the word *and.* Noncoordinate adjectives do not make sense with *and* between them: *He wore bright and red and wingtip shoes.*

2. Coordinate adjectives can appear in any order: *He wants to meet a sweet, kind, gentle girl. He wants to meet a gentle, kind, sweet girl.* Noncoordinate adjectives can't be moved around without some loss of emphasis or meaning: *He wore red wingtip bright shoes. He wore bright wingtip red shoes.*

These guidelines, however, leave some determinations up to the writer.

Right: *A young single person*

Right: *A young, single person*

If the writer means a single person who happens to be young, it should take no comma. But if the writer has in mind a person who is single and young—that is, whose singleness is as relevant as his youth—a comma can be used.

EXCEPTION: SERIES WITH INTERNAL COMMAS AND OTHER UNWIELDY LISTS

Series of items that contain their own commas are sometimes best separated by a semicolon.

> *We visited Tucson, Arizona; Boise, Idaho; Savannah, Georgia; and Fargo, North Dakota.*

> *Decisions were handed down on January 1, 2015; September 1, 2014; February 15, 2013; and April 4, 2012.*

Similarly, when the listed items are long or unwieldy, consider semicolons instead.

> *Sandwiches on the menu include albacore tuna salad with pesto mayonnaise on toasted brioche; pan-roasted turkey breast and smoked gouda on sourdough; and organic crunchy peanut butter and grape jelly on white bread.*

For more on semicolons see chapter 5.

COMMA IN LIST WITH AMPERSAND IN PLACE OF *AND*

An ampersand is never preceded by a comma.

> *Special Today: Corned Beef, Cabbage & Potatoes*

Multiple or repeated adverbs modifying a verb, an adjective, or another adverb follow the same rules as adjectives and are usually separated with commas.

> *He happily, passionately, and energetically followed the instructions.*

> *He was an extremely, fully, and thoroughly dedicated public servant.*

> *He was a very, very, very wise man.*

> *He sang utterly, absolutely, completely beautifully.*

Comma After an Introductory Word or Phrase

An introductory word or phrase may or may not be followed by a comma, as the writer or editor judges best.

> Right: *On Tuesday there was a small earthquake.*

> Right: *On Tuesday, there was a small earthquake.*

Clarity and ease of reading are the most important factors in deciding whether a comma should follow an introductory phrase or word. In general, the longer the introductory phrase, the more likely it is that a comma will aid comprehension.

> Comma required: *On the second Tuesday of every month that has thirty days or fewer, Joe cleans the coffee maker.*

With short prepositional phrases, the writer's preference and intended rhythm are the main factors in deciding whether to use a comma.

> Right: *Without him, I'd be lost.*

> Right: *Without him I'd be lost.*

Participles and participial phrases as introductory matter usually require a comma.

Seething, she turned to face him.

Seething with contempt, she turned to face him.

Some introductory adverbs are frequently followed by a comma, especially when a pause is intended.

Frankly, I don't like him.

But other adverbs are less likely to be followed by a comma.

Recently I discovered sushi.

Whenever the absence of a comma after an introductory word or phrase could cause a misreading, include one.

On the ground below, the belt from the car's radiator fan lay melted and smoking.

Comma to Separate Clauses

The rules for using commas to separate clauses vary depending on the length of the clauses and on whether the clauses are dependent or independent.

INDEPENDENT CLAUSES

Independent clauses joined with a conjunction are normally separated by a comma. An independent clause is any unit that contains both a subject and a verb and could stand alone as a complete sentence.

I know that you're going skiing without me on Tuesday, and I found out who you're bringing instead.

I know that you're going skiing without me on Tuesday, but I don't care.

I know that you're going skiing without me on Tuesday, so I'm going without you on Wednesday.

However, note the following example:

*I know that you're going skiing without me on Tuesday,
so leave.*

Imperatives—that is, commands like *leave*—can be confusing because they appear to have no subject. They are, nonetheless, independent clauses because imperatives always contain the implied subject *you*: *(You) Leave. (You) Eat. (You) Look!* Thus, *leave* qualifies as an independent clause.

When independent clauses joined by a conjunction are short and clear, the writer has the option of not using a comma.

Jane likes pizza and she also likes pasta.

You could stay or you could go.

I walked there but I ran home.

Vegetables are packed with vitamins and that's important.

Pack your things and go.

COMPOUND PREDICATES, COMPOUND SUBJECTS, AND THE LIKE

When units joined by a conjunction are not independent clauses, do not place a comma between them.

Sentence with a single subject shared by two verbs

*I know that you're going skiing without me on Tuesday and
don't care.*

They brought wine but forgot the corkscrew.

*Houses in this area require flood insurance and have other
disadvantages.*

*He was admired in the business community but was admired
most for his work with children.*

Sentence with a single verb shared by two subjects

*A palm tree that appeared to be dying and some parched-
looking scrub brush came into view.*

Sentence with a single verb shared by two objects

> *He prepared a brief presentation on the new product line and a handout for all the attendees.*

Any other two sentence elements that attach to a single stem

> *The city is cracking down on parking scofflaws by adding supplemental fines for late payment and by putting boot locks on the tires of vehicles with excessive unpaid tickets.*

Because none of these subjects, objects, verbs, or other elements are independent clauses, no comma should appear before a conjunction that connects them.

DEPENDENT CLAUSE BEFORE A MAIN CLAUSE

A dependent clause contains a subject and verb but can't stand alone as a sentence, usually because it starts with a subordinating conjunction like *if*, *although*, *because*, *before*, *when*, *until*, or *unless*. A dependent clause is usually followed by a comma when it precedes a main clause.

> *If the mall is open, we will go shopping.*

> *When the levee breaks, things will go from bad to worse.*

> *Until I hear from you, I will continue to worry.*

> *Because Mary's computer is broken, she didn't get any work done.*

> *Unless you're looking for trouble, you should keep quiet.*

However, if the dependent clause is short and the sentence is clear without a comma, the writer can choose to omit the comma.

> *If you want me I'll be in my room.*

DEPENDENT CLAUSE AFTER A MAIN CLAUSE

When a dependent clause comes after the main clause, a comma is usually not called for.

> *We will go shopping if the mall is open.*

> *Things will go from bad to worse when the levee breaks.*

I will continue to worry until I hear from you.

Mary didn't get any work done because her computer is broken.

You should keep quiet unless you're looking for trouble.

However, if the dependent clause is less closely related to the main clause, a comma to indicate a pause can be used.

I donate to children's charities every year, because that's the kind of guy I am.

Please complete these forms, if you would.

He'll be there, whether he wants to or not.

Comma to Set Off a Nonrestrictive or Parenthetical Word, Phrase, or Clause

A word, phrase, or clause that adds extra description or a supplemental thought inserted into a sentence is often set off with commas. This includes nonrestrictive relative clauses, appositives, adjectives placed after nouns, sentence adverbs and adverbials, and inserted phrases like *by the way* and *it should be noted*. These terms are said to be parenthetical—extra information that is not integral to the core sentence's meaning and does not narrow down a noun.

Compare these sentence pairs:

The woman, who works hardest, will get the promotion.
The woman who works hardest will get the promotion.

The man, with great courage, went off to battle.
The man with great courage went off to battle.

The store, where I got these shoes, is on the corner.
The store where I got these shoes is on the corner.

The proverb, known to all, influenced the decision.
The proverb known to all influenced the decision.

My brother, Lou, has a nice house.

My brother Lou has a nice house.

Karen, happily, joined the army.

Karen happily joined the army.

The commas indicate that information is parenthetical—it's extra information that can be lifted out of the sentence without any loss of meaning or specificity. The examples without commas use the same information in ways more crucial to the core sentence's meaning. Each is explained below.

COMMAS TO SET OFF A NONRESTRICTIVE RELATIVE CLAUSE

A relative clause begins with one of the relative pronouns: *that*, *which*, or *who* (including in its related forms *whom* and *whose*). A relative clause modifies a noun that comes before it.

> *Spiders, which have eight legs, live in every region of the United States.*
>
> *The racket that I prefer is lighter.*
>
> *Barbara, who is my favorite stylist, is off on Mondays.*
>
> *The candidate, whom I considered perfect for the job, withdrew his application.*

Commas setting off a relative clause mean that the clause's information is not crucial to the sentence's meaning and is not intended to narrow down or specify the noun. These clauses are said to be nonrestrictive, also sometimes called nonessential or nondefining. They can be lifted from the sentence without harming the sentence's meaning or losing any specificity of the noun.

Conversely, restrictive clauses (also known as essential or defining clauses) are integral to the meaning of the noun or the sentence and so can't be removed from the sentence without harming it. Restrictive relative clauses are not set off with commas.

Commas are, at times, the reader's only clue as to how the information in a relative clause is functioning. In *The woman who works hardest will get the promotion*, the lack of commas around the *who* clause indicates that this information is meant to show which woman the writer is talking about—specifically, the one woman who works harder than all the others.

But in *The woman, who works hardest, will get the promotion*, the commas indicate that the *who* clause is just extra information. *The woman* is meant to be fully self-explanatory, suggesting the reader already knows who *the* woman is.

Relative clauses that begin with *that* are always restrictive and so never take commas (*The car that he was driving was red. The racket that I prefer is lighter.*). Clauses that begin with *which* are usually nonrestrictive so usually take commas (*The menu, which includes a wide selection of pastas, changes daily.*) Relative clauses beginning with *who* and *whom* may or may not be restrictive, depending on the writer's intent.

COMMA TO SET OFF AN APPOSITIVE

An appositive is any noun phrase placed next to another noun phrase to restate it. (Note that a noun phrase can be more than one word, *a great man*.)

> *The CEO, a great man, will speak.*

> *The car, a maroon Honda, sped from the scene of the crime.*

> *You'll get to work with the best in the business, a team that has won more awards than I can count, my sales staff.*

> *The cab driver, a gregarious Armenian, dropped us off out front.*

> *She was great person, the kind of woman you could confide in, a wonderful mother and a true friend.*

> *Lawson's book,* Voyage to Tomorrow, *came out earlier this year.*

> *I talked to my brother, Steve.*

> *The carpenter, Charlie Carson, designed the set.*

Appositives are set off with commas. But the last three examples illustrate a sometimes-difficult area of comma use. Nouns set next to each other can sometimes do different jobs. Compare:

> The carpenter, Charlie Carson, designed the set.
>
> The carpenter Charlie Carson designed the set.

In the first example, *the carpenter* is the subject of the sentence and *Charlie Carson* just restates it. So in this example *Charlie Carson* is an appositive. But in the second example, *Charlie Carson* is the subject of the sentence and *the carpenter* is functioning as a modifier. So the lack of commas indicates that this is not an appositive relationship. Either form could be correct, depending on which emphasis the writer intends.

When noun phrases are placed together in this way, writers should take care to note which is the head noun because that will indicate whether or not to use commas, which, in turn, can carry unintended meaning.

For example, in *I talked to my brother, Steve,* the comma indicates that *Steve* is an appositive. This cues the reader that this is nonrestrictive information that in no way narrows down *my brother*. Thus, the writer is indicating he has only one brother and is throwing in, as an aside, the fact that his name is Steve.

But in *I talked to my brother Steve,* the lack of a comma indicates that *Steve* is not appositive. It is the head noun in a single noun phrase: *my brother Steve*. This tells the reader that the name is crucial for understanding who *my brother* refers to. *Steve* narrows down *my brother* to a single person. So the absence of a comma indicates that the writer has more than one brother.

Similarly, *Lawson's book* Voyage to Tomorrow *came out earlier this year* could imply that Lawson has more than one book. But with commas the sentence indicates that Lawson has just one book: *Lawson's book,* Voyage to Tomorrow, *came out earlier this year*.

When an appositive is long or complex, the writer should take extra care to make sure it is followed by a comma. This helps the reader keep clear which noun is the subject of the verb.

Right: *Maracas, the world's best Venezuelan restaurant, is located in Phoenix.*

Wrong: *Maracas, the world's best Venezuelan restaurant is located in Phoenix.*

Note, however, the following:

A durable fabric, cotton is still widely used today.

A popular tourist destination, Hawaii is warm year-round.

In these examples it is clear that the second noun phrase, not the first, is the subject of the verb. In this structure, no comma should follow the second noun phrase.

COMMA TO SET OFF ADJECTIVES, ADVERBS, AND OTHER INSERTED DESCRIPTORS

Descriptive words and phrases are often set off with commas. These can include the following:

Adjectives inserted after the noun they modify

The roses, fragrant and beautiful, overwhelmed our senses.

Adverbs inserted after or before the verb they modify

The deer bolted, quickly and noiselessly, from the clearing.

The deer, quickly and noiselessly, bolted from the clearing.

Prepositional phrases inserted before or after a verb they modify

The patient, with great difficulty, learned to walk again.

The patient learned, with great difficulty, to walk again.

Note that in many cases the writer can omit the commas if less separation is desired.

The deer bolted quickly and noiselessly from the clearing.

The patient learned with great difficulty to walk again.

Terms like *for example, as a result, to say the least, it is true, in spite of (something), you should note, indeed, as we will see, for instance, therefore, if not (something,) then (something), it is often said, most among them being (something)*, and many similar phrases can be inserted parenthetically into a sentence. Normally, such terms are set off with commas, though occasionally the commas are optional.

> *Walter was fidgeting with the radio and, as a result, missed the freeway exit.*

The Latin abbreviations *i.e.* (meaning "that is") and *e.g.* (meaning "for example") primarily appear in parentheses and are followed by a comma. If appearing outside of parentheses, a comma should come before and after.

> *His prom date (i.e., his cousin) arrived late.*

> *His prom date, i.e., his cousin, arrived late.*

Comma to Indicate Direct Address

A direct address is a name or anything standing in for a name that one person calls another: *Joe, sir, Mom, lady, dude, friend, darling, jerk, bub, miss, professor, ma'am, copper, doctor, young man*, etc.

Direct addresses, including names used to address a person, should be set off with commas.

> *Hello, Joe.*

> *No, Mom, it wasn't like that.*

> *Tell me, lady, are you this nice to everyone?*

> *Dude, that's so wrong.*

> *Hello, friend, and welcome.*

> *Good to see you, darling.*

> *Step off, jerk.*

> *Hey, bub.*

> *Miss, can you tell me if the bus stops here?*

Excuse me, professor.

This way, ma'am, if you will.

Young man, go to your room.

A common comma error occurs when an e-mail or letter greeting is structured:

Hey Jane,

Hi Pete,

Hello everyone,

Howdy stranger,

Jane, *Pete*, *everyone*, and *stranger* here are direct addresses that should be set off with commas.

Right: *Hey, Jane.*

Right: *Hi, Pete.*

Right: *Hello, everyone.*

Right: *Howdy, stranger.*

Note that these greetings follow a different grammatical structure from the classic *Dear John*, or *Dear Sirs*, in which the word *dear* is an adjective and therefore part of the direct address (part of the noun phrase).

Unlike *hey* and *hello*, *dear* is not a complete thought. So it makes sense to follow *Dear John* with a comma, thereby integrating it into the first sentence of the e-mail or letter. But *Hey, Jane* and *Hi, Pete* are complete sentences that can be followed by periods or other terminal punctuation.

Comma to Set Off a Quotation

A comma is often used to set off a quotation from other parts of a sentence, especially quotation attributions like *Wilson said, Jane replied,* and similar phrases.

> *Wilson said, "Try the ignition."*
>
> *"That's not what I meant," Jane replied.*
>
> *"I think," whispered Allen, "that we're being followed."*

When a quotation that otherwise would end with a period comes before an attribution, a comma takes the place of the period.

> *"Don't go," he said.*

When a quotation that precedes an attribution ends with a question mark or an exclamation point, no comma is used:

> *"Are you going?" she asked.*
>
> *"Get out!" he screamed.*

Some sentences integrate quotations in such a way that commas are not required. This is especially true with the word *that.*

> *Lynne said it's true that "the place is swarming with mosquitoes."*
>
> *Barry replied that some people "are just cruel."*

In some cases, it can be unclear whether the quotation is integrated into the sentence or whether it should be set off with commas.

For example, a song title could be perceived as the object of a verb and not a quotation, so no comma would precede it after a verb like *sang.*

> *He sang "Burning Love."*

Note, however, that a song lyric or text from a written work could be punctuated differently from a title.

In *He sang "Burning Love,"* the song title is less a quotation than an object of the verb. So *sang* is not a quotation attribution and should not be set off with a comma. But a song lyric or line of text could be perceived as a quotation and thus introduced with a comma. The major style guides do not address this question.

✦ A majority of the Punctuation Panel favored putting a comma after *sang*:

> *He sang, "I feel my temperature rising."*

✦ The Punctuation Panel unanimously agreed that there should be no comma here:

> *We read "The Road."*

(For formatting book titles in all styles, see "Quotation Marks vs. Italics for Titles of Works," page 74.)

✦ A majority of the Punctuation Panel members favored putting a comma in this sentence:

> *He opened the book and read, "Call me Ishmael."*

In other words, though the title *The Road* was perceived as a direct object of the verb *read*, the sentence "Call me Ishmael" was more likely to be perceived as a quotation, which should be set off with a comma after a verb like *read*.

✦ After *titled*, Punctuation Panel members unanimously favored no comma:

> *We enjoyed the skit titled "Star Snores."*

For verbs like *read, sang, recited,* and so on, the writer should use personal judgment to determine whether the matter in quotation marks is integrated into the sentence or intended as a direct quotation.

When words, including unarticulated thoughts, are attributed to a person without quotation marks, commas are usually used in the same way as with quoted matter.

Wendy wondered, why is he so cruel?

Karl said to himself, this is going to be a problem.

EXCEPTION S

Ⓝ In news style, when the attribution precedes a quotation of two or more sentences, the comma should be replaced by a colon.

Wilson said: "Try the ignition. If that doesn't work, pop the hood."

Ⓑ Book style *also* allows colons in place of commas when they add desired emphasis to a quotation. (See "Colon to Introduce a Quotation, Dialogue, or Excerpt," page 64.)

Comma to Indicate Omitted Words in a Repeated Pattern

In certain structures, a comma can indicate missing words that are clear from the context, especially in part of a sentence that mirrors a previous part.

Harry ordered a scotch; Bob, a gin and tonic.

Comma Between Repeated Words Like *Is Is, In In*, and *That That*

Sometimes a noun phrase or verb phrase ends with the same word that begins the rest of the sentence. Under normal circumstances a comma should not separate a subject from its verb. However, when a subject that ends with *is* precedes a verb phrase that begins with *is*, style guides indicate that a comma should intervene whenever it aids comprehension. Similarly, with other repeated words, the style guides leave it up to the writer whether or not to insert a comma.

Right: *The reality that is is the reality he must accept.*

Right: *The reality that is, is the reality he must accept.*

Right: *I'll check in in the morning.*

Right: *I'll check in, in the morning.*

Right: *He found that that was best.*

Right: *He found that, that was best.*

✝ A majority of the Punctuation Panel opted for no comma in this sentence:

What it is is a good idea.

Commas in Location Addresses

In general, use commas between street and city when they appear on the same line, and between city and state. But do not place a comma between state and zip code or between a street and a compass point, such as *SE* in *43rd Ave. SE*. See "Street Addresses," pages 144–46.

Comma with Age, City of Residence, and Political Party Affiliation

Ⓝ In news articles, it is common to put age, city of residence, or, in the case of an elected official, a political party and state after the person's name. News style indicates these should be set off with commas.

John Doe, 43, Whittier, was among the attendees.

Sen. Al Franken, D-Minn., chaired the committee.

Comma in Measurements

In general, avoid using a comma between parts of measurements, including time measurements such as years and months, and physical measurements such as feet an inches.

Ⓑ *She is five feet nine* or *She is five foot nine.*

Ⓝ *He is 6 feet 2 inches tall.*

Ⓢ *11 years 3 months*

Ⓢ *20 min 40 s*

Commas with Specific Words and Terms

TOO, ALSO, AND EITHER

The major styles do not give express instructions on whether commas should set off *too*, *also*, *either*, and similar terms.

✚ The Punctuation Panel disagreed on whether to use commas in the following:

I like it, too. (majority preference)

I too saw that movie.

I, too, saw that movie. (panel split)

I didn't see that movie, either.

I didn't see that movie either. (panel split)

He wrote "Love Story," also.

He wrote "Love Story" also. (panel split)

HOWEVER, THEREFORE, AND INDEED

Sentence adverbs like *however*, *therefore*, and *indeed* may or may not be set off with commas, depending on whether the writer judges them to be parenthetical insertions or well integrated into the sentence. When uncertain, remember that most of modern publishing prefers a sparse punctuation style to aid sentence flow and ease of reading.

Right: *The parking garage, however, was almost empty.*

Right: *The parking garage however was almost empty.*

Right: *The solution, therefore, is simple.*

Right: *The solution therefore is simple.*

Right: *Sharon is indeed a lucky girl.*

Right: *Sharon is, indeed, a lucky girl.*

Right: *Joe is therefore the best candidate.*

Right: *Joe is, therefore, the best candidate.*

INCLUDING, *SUCH AS*, AND SIMILAR TERMS

A comma often precedes *including*, *such as*, and similar terms. But no comma should come after.

Right: *America has many great cities, including New York, Chicago, and San Francisco.*

Right: *America has many great cities including New York, Chicago, and San Francisco.*

Wrong: *America has many great cities including, New York, Chicago, and San Francisco.*

Right: *The store is having a sale on many items, such as clothes, books, and electronics.*

Right: *The store is having a sale on items such as clothes, books, and electronics.*

Wrong: *The store is having a sale on many items such as, clothes, books, and electronics.*

ETC.

Etc., the abbreviation for *et cetera*, is set off with commas.

Toiletries, linens, etc., can be purchased at your destination.

ET AL., *AND SO FORTH*, *AND THE LIKE*, AND SIMILAR TERMS

Ⓑ *Et al.*, *and so forth*, *and the like*, and similar terms are usually set off with commas (preceded with a comma and, unless at the end of a sentence, followed by a comma).

Johnson, Smith, Brown, et al., wrote the definitive article on that topic.

Bedding, linens, and so on, can be purchased upstairs.

Muffins, croissants, and the like, are served in the lobby.

YES AND *NO*

Ⓝ News style specifies that *yes* and *no* should be set off with commas.

> *Yes, I want some cake.*

Ⓑ Ⓢ Ⓐ In other styles, *yes* and *no* are often, but not necessarily, set off with commas. The writer can choose to omit commas if they do not aid readability.

> *Yes, there is a Santa Claus.*
>
> *No, coyotes don't come this far north.*
>
> *Yes I want some cake.*
>
> *No you don't.*

✚ The Punctuation Panel unanimously preferred a comma in *Yes, thank you.*

RESPECTIVELY

✚ The Punctuation Panel unanimously favored setting off *respectively* with commas.

> *Sandy, Colleen, and Mark went to Harvard, Yale, and Tufts, respectively.*

OH, UM, AH, AND *WELL*

Oh, um, ah, well, and similar terms are often, but not necessarily, set off with commas. The writer can choose to omit commas if they do not aid readability.

> *Oh, I see what you're up to.*
>
> *Ah, that's the ticket.*
>
> *Well, you're the one who wanted to come here.*
>
> *Oh you.*

INC., LTD., AND SIMILAR ABBREVIATIONS

In book and news styles, *Inc.*, *Ltd.*, and similar abbreviations are often omitted, as they convey information that is usually not relevant to the sentence. However when they are used, the following guidelines apply:

Ⓑ Commas around *Inc.*, *Ltd.*, and the like are not required. If a writer working in book style chooses to put a comma before abbreviations such as *Inc.*, a comma is required after it as well.

>Right: *He has worked for ABC Inc. for three years.*

>Right: *He has worked for ABC, Inc., for three years.*

>Wrong: *He has worked for ABC, Inc. for three years.*

Ⓝ Commas around *Inc.*, *Ltd.*, and the like are never used.

>*He has worked for ABC Inc. for three years.*

PHD, MD, MA, DDS, JD, AND OTHER ACADEMIC CREDENTIALS

Academic credentials denoted as initials after a name are to be avoided when possible. When it's necessary to use them, place a comma before and after the abbreviation.

>Ⓑ *Jason Wellsley, PhD, gave a presentation.*

>Ⓝ *Jason Wellsley, Ph.D., gave a presentation.*

(For when to use periods with academic credentials, see "Abbreviations of Generic Nouns," pages 57–58, and "Punctuation A to Z.")

JR., SR., II, III, AND THE LIKE

Ⓑ Commas are not necessary around *Jr.* and *Sr.* and should never be used with *II*, *III*, etc.

>*Dr. Martin Luther King Jr. spoke.*

Ⓝ Do not use commas to set off *Jr.*, *Sr.*, etc.

Dr. Martin Luther King Jr. spoke.

Ⓐ Academic style usually prefers commas around *Jr.*, *Sr.*, etc.

Dr. Martin Luther King, Jr., spoke.

STATES, COUNTRIES, PROVINCES, AND THE DISTRICT OF COLUMBIA

A state, country, or province mentioned after a city name should be preceded and, unless at the end of a sentence, followed by a comma.

They stopped in Bangor, Maine, on their way to Massachusetts.

Vancouver, B.C., is beautiful this time of year.

Lyon, France, is a popular tourist destination.

Ⓑ The abbreviation for the District of Columbia is normally set off with commas. But if the writer opts not to use periods in *DC*, commas to set it off are optional. For when to use periods in *DC*, see "Abbreviations of Canadian provinces and the District of Columbia," page 57.

Right: *Washington, DC, gets hot in the summer.*

Right: *Washington DC gets hot in the summer.*

Right: *Washington, D.C., gets hot in the summer.*

Ⓝ *D.C.* is set off with commas.

Washington, D.C., gets hot in the summer.

For commas in full addresses, see chapter 18, page 146.

DATE AND YEAR

A date that follows a day of the week should be preceded and, unless at the end of a sentence, followed by a comma.

Monday, Oct. 4, is when the meeting took place.

Monday, October 4, is when the meeting took place.

A year that follows a complete date should be preceded and, unless at the end of a sentence, followed by a comma.

Oct. 4, 2014, is when the meeting took place.

However, a year that follows a month or a season alone should not be set off with commas.

October 2014 is when the meeting took place.

Spring 2010 was a memorable time.

INSTITUTION NAME CONTAINING AN INTERNAL COMMA

When an institution, especially a school, includes a comma, it is usually appropriate to insert a comma afterward.

University of California, Riverside, has many commuter students.

COMPOSITION TITLE CONTAINING AN INTERNAL COMMA

A book, song, play, or other composition the title of which contains an internal comma should not be followed by an additional comma in running text.

God Bless You, Mr. Rosewater is one of his favorite books.

NOT PHRASES

Noun phrases that begin with *not*, when inserted into a sentence for contrast, are set off with commas.

The student with the best grades, not the most popular student, will be appointed.

It was Rick, not Alan, who cleaned the microwave.

NOT ONLY . . . BUT . . . PHRASES AND SIMILAR TERMS

No comma is generally needed before the *but* in phrases like this.

Not only children on vacation from school but also adults on vacation from work flocked to the theater.

PLEASE

Editing styles do not have express rules on when to set off *please* with commas.

+ A majority of the Punctuation Panel preferred a comma in *May I have your attention, please?*

THE MORE . . . THE LESS, THE MORE . . . THE MORE, AND SIMILAR TERMS

A comma is usually needed in structures like this one:

> *The more I go on blind dates, the more I appreciate my dog.*

For very short sentences with this structure, however, a comma can be omitted.

> *The more the better.*

Comma Placement Relative to Other Punctuation

QUOTATION MARK

A comma always comes before a closing quotation mark.

> *He said, "Get out," but I know he didn't mean it.*

> *She peppers her speech with words like "awesome," "neato," and "fantabulous."*

SINGLE QUOTATION MARK

Do not confuse a single quotation mark with an apostrophe. A comma always comes before a closing single quotation mark.

> *"Don't call me 'jerk,'" he yelled.*

> *"Teenagers of years gone by favored terms like 'neato,' 'far out,' and 'keen,'" he said.*

APOSTROPHE

An apostrophe representing a dropped letter comes before a comma.

"I know you were just talkin'," he said.

I've been thinkin', Dad.

PARENTHESIS

A comma never immediately precedes a closing parenthesis, though a comma may follow a closing parenthesis.

The siren was loud (the ambulance was close by), so he covered his ears.

ELLIPSIS

A comma usually is not used with an ellipsis, though the writer may opt to insert one if it aids comprehension.

"To question why, to ponder causes, . . . to try to change outcomes is usually futile," she said.

HYPHEN OR EN DASH

✚ A hyphen or en dash can preclude the need for a comma. In *The Washington, D.C.–based company*, a majority of the Punctuation Panel favored omitting the comma that would otherwise be necessary after *D.C.* (For when to use commas with *D.C.*, see "States, Countries, Provinces, and the District of Columbia," page 47.)

PRIME SYMBOL AND OTHER MEASUREMENT SYMBOLS

Do not confuse a prime symbol or other mark of measurement with a quotation mark. In the rare instances when such a symbol appears in running text, a comma would follow it.

The javelin went 22', then it fell.

Gray Areas of Comma Use

Often, editors disregard comma rules to improve readability of a sentence. Other times, the rules allow different choices on which professional editors might disagree.

ADDING A COMMA AS NEEDED FOR CLARITY

Sometimes even when rules do not call for it, a comma is nonetheless the best way to separate and group sentence elements. In many cases, when a sentence can't be recast, writers can use their judgment.

+ Though the rules say that coordinate items joined by *and* or *or* are not separated by commas, a majority of the Punctuation Panel said they would disregard this rule if items were so long that a comma could aid reader comprehension.

> *She yelled to the man who took her purse, and grabbed her cellphone to call the police.*

> *The dog chased the squirrel that ran through the park, but not fast enough.*

> *This Ford packs an I-4 rated up to 32 mpg through a smooth six-speed automatic transmission, or a supercharged 221-horsepower V-8.*

+ Similarly, panel members disagreed on how to punctuate coordinate items in which one of the items contains a coordinating conjunction.

> *The resort offers elegantly appointed rooms, casitas, and villas and four swimming pools, along with other exciting amenities.* (A majority preferred no comma after *villas*.)

COMMA AFTER A PROPER NAME ENDING IN
AN EXCLAMATION POINT OR QUESTION MARK

❸ Book style calls for a comma after a proper name ending in an exclamation point or question mark in any context that would otherwise require a comma.

> *Shows playing this week include* Greg London: Impressions that Rock!, Who's Afraid of Virginia Woolf?, *and* Jersey Boys.

✦ Other styles do not have rules for these situations. News style experts on the Punctuation Panel were split on whether to put a comma after an exclamation point or question mark that was part of a proper name.

OMITTING A COMMA TO AVOID EXCESSIVE PUNCTUATION

✦ In the following example, strict adherence to rules would require commas after *husband* and *dog* and semicolons after *Tim* and *Bruno*. But a majority of the Punctuation Panel said that they might disregard those rules and instead punctuate as follows:

> *She lives with her husband Tim, her dog Bruno, and two cats, Bella and Charlie.*

✦ In the following example, the Punctuation Panel was split on whether to disregard the rule that would normally require a comma before *which* (if recasting the sentence were not an option).

> *Starting at less than $50,000, the Spider-12 is a classy and capable midsize SUV which, with its 7-seat Comfort Package, becomes a flexible family friend.* (half favored)

> *Starting at less than $50,000, the Spider-12 is a classy and capable midsize SUV, which, with its 7-seat Comfort Package, becomes a flexible family friend.* (half favored)

The need for a comma in some cases is subject to interpretation of the rules as well as personal taste.

A majority of the panel agreed that a comma should not come between the preposition *for* and its object, which in the following example is *what Jones lacks in age*. But because the object comes at the beginning of the sentence, and because that object is somewhat long and abstract, some might interpret it more as an introductory clause, which is often set off with a comma.

> *What Jones lacks in age she makes up for in energy.* (majority preference)

> *What Jones lacks in age, she makes up for in energy.* (minority preference)

Prepositional phrases like *at a variety of prices* are usually not preceded by a comma. However, in the following sentence that phrase could be momentarily misconstrued as modifying *women* instead of the store. A comma here reduces that potential for confusion.

> *Centrally located on Main Street, La Jolla Timepieces displays a carefully chosen selection of watches for men and women at a variety of prices.* (majority preference)

> *Centrally located on Main Street, La Jolla Timepieces displays a carefully chosen selection of watches for men and women, at a variety of prices.* (minority preference)

Normally, a verb and its object are not separated by a comma. But when a long, wordy object, in this case *some of the technology coming in the next few years*, is moved to the beginning of the sentence, writers sometimes insert a comma after it. In this case, however, all the Punctuation Panel members agreed they would not insert a comma.

> *Some of the technology coming in the next few years most people can't even imagine.*

3

—

Period

Periods end sentences and are used in certain abbreviations and initialisms.

Period to End a Sentence or Sentence Fragment

Use periods to end declarative sentences (statements) and imperative sentences (commands) in which an exclamation point would be too strong.

Joe works here.

Eat.

Leave now.

You can also use a period to form a sentence fragment. A sentence fragment is a unit that, though it does not qualify as a complete sentence, is used and punctuated as a sentence. The minimum criterion for a declarative sentence to be complete is that it contain both a subject and a verb (*Joe slept*). Because an imperative sentence (command) leaves the subject *you* implied, it can be complete with just one word: *Leave. Eat.*

A sentence fragment does not meet that minimum criterion. In formal and academic writing, sentence fragments may be considered inappropriate, or even errors. But in casual and literary contexts, fragments are standard.

Makes you think.

Another gloomy day.

Probably.

The reason? A girl.

Spacing After a Period

Ⓑ Ⓝ Do not double space between sentences. Use just one space after the terminal period.

Ⓢ Science style does not specify the number of spaces to use between sentences but notes that double spacing after a terminal period in a draft manuscript is helpful to editors and other readers.

Ⓐ Academic style prefers using just one space between sentences but also allows two spaces if the writer prefers. In either case, the writer should space consistently throughout the document.

Periods in Initials, Abbreviations, and Acronyms

INITIALS OF A PERSON'S NAME

Ⓑ Ⓢ Ⓐ In book, science, and academic styles, initials in names are followed by a period and separated by spaces. *H. L. Mencken*, *W. E. B. DuBois*. Initials representing full names, such as *JFK* and *FDR* take no periods or spaces.

Ⓝ In news style, initials representing names are followed by a period but not separated by spaces: *H.L. Mencken, W.E.B. DuBois*. Initials representing full names such as *JFK* and *FDR* take no periods or spaces.

Ⓑ Ⓢ Ⓐ Initials of nonhuman proper nouns take no periods: *US, USA, AA, UK.*

Ⓝ Two-letter initialisms of proper nouns usually take periods but no spaces: *U.S., U.K., U.N., B.C.* Initialisms of three or more letters do not take periods or spaces: *USA, FBI, CIA, GOP.*

Exceptions

Ⓑ Book style allows periods in *U.S.* in any context in which traditional state abbreviations (as opposed to two-letter postal codes) are being used.

Ⓝ In news headlines, the periods are omitted. *AA* never takes periods.

Ⓢ In science style, *U.S.* takes periods when used as an adjective: *the U.S. Army.*

ABBREVIATIONS OF STATES, CANADIAN PROVINCES, AND THE DISTRICT OF COLUMBIA

When referring to a state without a city or other address information, the state name is usually spelled out: *New Jersey, Arizona, Georgia.* When a state is mentioned with a city name or in an address, the state is sometimes abbreviated. Note that state names used with cities and addresses are set off by commas, including a comma after the state: *Springfield, Ill., is nearby. Findlay, Ohio, gets cold.* (For more about abbreviating state names in addresses, see "Abbreviation of states," pages 145–46.) However, *District of Columbia* is almost always abbreviated after *Washington* as *DC* or *D.C.* Style rules on when to use periods in these abbreviations are outlined in the following two sections.

Abbreviations of state names

Ⓑ In book style, state names are usually spelled out. When states are abbreviated, book style prefers using postal codes, which are written without periods: *AL, MD, NH, SC.* But news-style abbreviations are also allowed: *Ala., Md., N.H. S.C.*

Ⓝ In news style, states are spelled out when they stand alone but are usually abbreviated when they follow a city name or are part of an address. (See also "Street Addresses," page 144, for state abbreviations.) The abbreviations take periods, whether they're upper- and lowercase abbreviations like *Ala.* for *Alabama* or *Md.* for Maryland or two-letter initials like *N.H.* for *New Hampshire* or *S.C.* for *South Carolina.* In headlines, however, two-letter state abbreviations take no periods.

Ⓢ In many instances, including reference list entries, science style calls for states to be abbreviated as US postal codes, which take no periods: *AZ, IL, NY, TN.*

Ⓐ In academic style, two-letter state abbreviations and *DC* take no periods: *NJ, NY, FL.*

Abbreviations of Canadian provinces and the District of Columbia

Ⓑ Book style prefers no periods in *DC* or Canadian provinces. However, periods in *D.C.* are allowed in contexts in which the writer has chosen to use other US state abbreviations with periods. Two-letter postal abbreviations are preferred for Canadian provinces: *BC, ON, QC.*

Ⓝ News style calls for periods in *D.C.* Canadian provinces should not be abbreviated.

Ⓐ Academic style does not use periods in *DC* or in the abbreviations of Canadian provinces.

ABBREVIATIONS OF GENERIC NOUNS

Ⓑ Ⓢ Ⓐ When an abbreviation of a generic noun ends in a capital letter, customarily it takes no periods: *CPR, CT scan, CD, DVD, DVR, BC, BB, DNS, GPA, IM, IQ, IP address, GI.*

Ⓝ In news style, two-letter abbreviations usually take periods: *A.D., B.C., M.A., B.A., M.S.* However, a number of well-known two-letter terms are exceptions: *CD, CT scan, IM, IQ, IP address.*

(See "Punctuation A to Z" for specific entries.) Abbreviations of three or more letters take no periods: *CPR*, *DVD*, *GPA*.

Ⓑ Ⓝ Ⓢ Ⓐ Abbreviations that end in lowercase letters usually take periods: *Dr., Gov., Jr., e.g., i.e., etc., Inc., et al., Mr., Mrs.,* and so on.

Exceptions

Ⓝ In news style, *aka* takes no periods.

Ⓢ In science style, abbreviations of routes of administration and measurements do not take periods: *iv, icv, im, ip, cd, cm, ft, lb, kg,* except for the abbreviation for inches, *in.,* which could be confused for the word *in* without a period.

PERIODS WITH ACRONYMS

Acronyms such as *NAFTA*, *radar*, *GLAAD*, *laser*, and *AIDS* customarily do not take periods.

Periods After URL Addresses

Ⓑ A URL address (website) at the end of a sentence can be followed immediately by a period. There's no need to insert a space before the period.

> *Visit the company at www.companyname.com.*

Ⓢ In science style, a sentence that ends with a URL does not end in a period.

> *Visit the company at www.companyname.com*

However, to avoid the awkwardness of a sentence without terminal punctuation in science style, it is recommended that in running text, writers put URLs in parentheses, which can be followed by a period.

> *Visit the company at its website (www.companyname.com).*

Period Placement Relative to Other Punctuation

A period may come after or before another punctuation mark, depending on the mark and the meaning of the sentence.

QUOTATION MARK

A period always comes before a closing quotation mark.

Right: *He said, "Get out."*

Wrong: *He said, "Get out".*

Right: *She peppers her speech with words like "fantabulous."*

Wrong: *She peppers her speech with words like "fantabulous".*

SINGLE QUOTATION MARK

A period always comes before a closing single quotation mark.

He said, "Don't call me 'jerk.'"

According to Jones, "Teenagers of years gone by favored terms like 'neato.'"

APOSTROPHE

Do not confuse a single quotation mark with an apostrophe. An apostrophe representing a dropped letter comes before a period.

He said, "I know you were just talkin'."

PARENTHESIS OR BRACKET

A period comes before a closing parenthesis or bracket when the parenthetical item is a complete sentence standing on its own.

The siren was loud. (The ambulance was close by.)

But when the parenthetical is inserted into another sentence, no period goes before the closing parenthesis or bracket.

The siren was loud (the ambulance was close by).

(The siren was loud [the ambulance was close by].)

PRIME SYMBOL AND OTHER MEASUREMENT SYMBOLS

Do not confuse a prime symbol or similar mark used to indicate a measurement with a quotation mark. In the rare instances when such a symbol appears in running text, a period would follow it.

The javelin went 22'.

DASH

A period never precedes or follows a dash.

There is something you should know—it's something crucial.

ELLIPSIS

If an ellipsis comes after a complete sentence, a period is placed before the ellipsis.

"I have a dream. . . . I have a dream today."

But if words right before the ellipsis do not constitute a complete sentence, do not insert a period.

"This dream . . . still rings true today."

OMITTING A PERIOD TO PREVENT DOUBLE PUNCTUATION

When an abbreviation or an initialism that ends with a period comes at the end of a sentence, there is no need to add another period to end the sentence.

Talk to J.D.

They studied biology, chemistry, etc.

I know Hal Adams Sr.

When a sentence is structured in such a way that a question mark, or exclamation point is placed where a terminal period would otherwise go, the period is omitted.

Alfred E. Neuman's catch phrase is "What, me worry?"

He read the book What Color Is Your Parachute?

The company bought a thousand shares of Yahoo!

When a sentence that would normally end with a period is used as a quotation, and the attribution for that quotation follows as part of the same sentence, the period is replaced with a comma.

"Pizza is wonderful."

"Pizza is wonderful," Joe said.

When a quotation that would normally end with a period is used as a quotation within a larger sentence that ends with a question mark or exclamation point, the period is omitted.

Do you agree that, as Joe says, "Pizza is wonderful"?

Rhetorical Questions

Ⓝ Sentences that are interrogative in form (questions) but declarative in meaning (statements) can end in a period instead of a question mark if the writer prefers.

How about that.

Well, what do you know.

Really.

Why don't you just go.

4

Colon

The colon has several jobs.

The colon can introduce text that illustrates or underscores the sentence. It can introduce a list. It can introduce certain quotations. It can be used with direct address, as in a greeting in formal correspondence. And it is used in certain formatted and numbered items like times of day, ratios, and books of the Bible. It is also sometimes used between titles and subtitles and between some types of sources in academic citations.

Some of the colon's uses overlap with other punctuation. For example, instead of using a colon for emphasis between two independent clauses, a writer could in some cases use a period to make two sentences or use a semicolon.

I want to tell you something: you're awesome.

I want to tell you something. You're awesome.

I want to tell you something; you're awesome.

The colon, however, is usually the best choice for creating a sense of anticipation. The major editing styles have very similar rules for using colons, which follow.

Colon to Illustrate or Underscore a Prior Statement

Use a colon to introduce text that illustrates or underscores text before the colon.

> *Refrigerator temperature is critical: if it's not cold enough, food will spoil.*

Ⓑ Ⓢ A colon should usually follow a complete independent clause. If the text before the colon could not stand alone as a complete sentence, do not use a colon.

> Right: *The point I want to make is important: never mix acids and bases.*

> Wrong: *The point I want to make is: never mix acids and bases.*

Colon to Introduce a List

A colon can introduce a list of words, phrases, or clauses.

> *The pizza came with three toppings: pepperoni, onion, and mushrooms.*

Ⓑ Ⓢ A colon introducing a list should follow a complete independent clause. If the text before the colon could not stand alone as a complete sentence, do not use a colon.

> Right: *The pizza came with three toppings: pepperoni, onion, and mushrooms.*

> Wrong: *The pizza came with: pepperoni, onion, and mushrooms.*

NO COLON AFTER *INCLUDING* TO INTRODUCE A LIST

When the word *including* introduces a list, do not use a colon (even if each listed item falls on a separate line).

> Right: *They have many toppings available, including garlic, pepperoni, and onions.*

> Wrong: *They have many toppings available, including: garlic, pepperoni, and onions.*

Colon to Introduce a Quotation, Dialogue, or Excerpt

A colon can introduce a quotation.

Ⓑ In book style, a colon can be used instead of a comma to introduce a quotation when the writer wants to add extra emphasis.

> *Carlyle got straight to the point: "You're fired," he said.*

Ⓝ In news style, a colon introduces quotations of two or more sentences within the paragraph. But a one-sentence quotation within a paragraph is introduced with a comma.

Ⓑ Ⓝ In book and news styles, dialogue and question-and-answer interviews use colons to introduce text attributed to a speaker.

> *Claudia: I see you brought the new girlfriend.*
>
> *Larry: She's nobody, really.*

> *Village Herald: You've been busy this year.*
>
> *Williams: Yes, I've had a lot on my plate.*

Colon with *As Follows*, *The Following*, and Similar Expressions

In formal contexts, terms like *as follows* and *the following* usually call for a colon.

> *The schedule is as follows: roll call at 9:00 a.m., calisthenics at 9:15, breakfast at 9:45.*

> *The following items are not permitted: liquids, matches, and lighters.*

Colon After a Greeting

A colon may also be used after a greeting at the beginning of correspondence. A colon is considered more formal than a comma.

Dear Bob,

Dear Mr. Roberts:

Colon in a Ratio

B **S** In book and science styles, colons are sometimes used in ratios.
No space should precede or follow the colon.

2:1

(News style, however, uses hyphens in ratios: *2-to-1.*)

Colon in Other Numeric Terms

Colons are also used in other types of numeric terms:

times: *8:30 p.m.*

time elapsed: *His finish time was 1:58:22*

books of the Bible: *Genesis 22:10*

legal citations: *Fayetteville Municipal Code 3:282*

Colon Between a Title and a Subtitle

B **A** In running text and in bibliographies, a colon separates a title
from a subtitle.

My Last Year: A Memoir of Illness and Recovery

Tough Guys 2: The Final Conflict

Colon in Source Citations

When citing a source of information, such as a book or periodical, colons are used as follows.

Ⓑ In book style, a citation that includes a volume number and a page number uses a colon with no space on either side.

Journal of English Language Learning 15:220–29

Ⓑ Ⓢ In book and science style, a colon is used in citations between a place of publication and the name of the publisher.

New York, NY: Random House

Ⓑ Ⓝ Colons are used in other types of citations, such as books of the Bible and legal citations.

Genesis 22:10

Fayetteville Municipal Code 3:282

Spacing After a Colon

Do not double space after a colon.

Capital or Lowercase Letter After a Colon

Ⓑ Ⓝ Ⓢ If the text after a colon does not make up a complete sentence, it should begin with a lowercase letter unless it begins with a proper noun or is a quotation.

The climate is perfect: sunny days, warm nights, little rain.

They had a motto: "All for one and one for all."

Ⓑ Ⓝ Ⓢ If the colon introduces two or more complete sentences, dialogue or a proper noun, it begins with a capital letter.

The climate is perfect: The days are sunny. The precipitation is very low.

⒝ If text introduced by a colon could stand alone as a single sentence, book style nonetheless usually considers it to be part of the same sentence as the text before the colon and therefore requires it begin with a lowercase letter.

They put it in terms everyone there could understand: just as people used to write letters, young people today write e-mails.

⒩ If the text introduced by a colon makes up a complete sentence, it begins with a capital letter.

They put it in terms everyone there could understand: Just as people used to write letters, young people today write e-mails.

Colon with Other Punctuation

A colon usually precludes the need for other punctuation, so it seldom appears next to other punctuation marks. There are a few exceptions.

PARENTHESIS

A colon may come after a closing parenthesis, but never before one.

The truth was simple (almost too simple): Dan was guilty.

QUOTATION MARK

A colon can come after a closing quotation mark but never before one.

The truth, she said, was "simple": Dan was guilty.

EXCLAMATION POINT OR QUESTION MARK
AS PART OF A PROPER NAME OR TITLE

If a proper name or title ends with an exclamation point or quotation mark, a colon can follow.

Here's what makes up the costumes in Jubilee!*: rhinestones, sequins, and little else.*

Semicolon

The semicolon has two jobs. It connects closely related independent clauses, and it separates items in lists too unwieldy to be made sense of with commas.

Semicolon to Connect Closely Related Independent Clauses

When a writer wants to indicate a degree of separation that is weaker than a period and that falls between two independent clauses not joined with a conjunction, a semicolon can be used.

> *He hated vegetables; peas were the worst.*

BEFORE *HOWEVER, THEREFORE, INDEED,* AND SIMILAR CONJUNCTIVE ADVERBS

Ⓑ When a conjunctive adverb such as *however, therefore, indeed, accordingly, thus, hence,* or *besides* connects two closely related independent clauses, book style calls for a semicolon.

> *Rebecca had no compunctions about speaking her mind; therefore, John was about to get an earful.*

BEFORE *THAT IS, NAMELY, FOR EXAMPLE,* AND SIMILAR EXPRESSIONS

B *That is, namely, for example,* and similar expressions can be preceded by a semicolon if they connect closely related clauses.

John was just being helpful; that is, he was trying to be helpful.

BETWEEN CLAUSES CONTAINING EXTENSIVE PUNCTUATION

N When a conjunction joins independent clauses that contain extensive punctuation, news style permits a semicolon to connect the clauses but recommends breaking up the sentence instead.

Acceptable: *The man runs on the treadmill, uses the elliptical machine and lifts weights; but, even with all those efforts, plus a low-carb diet consisting mostly of vegetables, he still hasn't lost weight.*

Better: *The man runs on the treadmill, uses the elliptical machine and lifts weights. But, even with all those efforts, plus a low-carb diet consisting mostly of vegetables, he still hasn't lost weight.*

Semicolon to Separate Items in Lists

Semicolons can separate items in otherwise unwieldy lists, especially when the items listed contain their own internal commas.

The company has retail locations in Charlottesville, Virginia; Shreveport, Louisiana; and New Haven, Connecticut.

The case worker, trying to paint a favorable picture of her client, noted that Johnny had done charity work for a local soup kitchen, a senior center, and animal shelter; had gone to school every day; and had not gotten in trouble with the law for two years.

However, items that are clearly distinguished by commas require no semicolons.

The reading materials in the dentist's office included a copy of Newsweek, which I hate, a two-week-old newspaper, and a pamphlet on gingivitis.

Ⓑ Index entries, text citations, and similar lists in which commas would not clearly delineate items often use semicolons, especially (but not exclusively) in book style.

Butter, baking with, 150–155, 162, 188–204; sautéing with, 81–83, 97, 99–102.

(Carter and Johnstone 2002; Garnick 1986; VanDuren 1980)

Quotation Mark

"

Quotation marks always work in pairs. They have several jobs.

Quotation marks indicate direct quotations—text represented exactly as it was spoken or written, including dialogue of fictional characters (but see also "Em Dashes for Dialogue," page 119). Quotation marks are also used to highlight words and call them into question, for example, when casting doubt, using irony, or pointing out that a word itself is being referred to. Quotation marks also surround titles of certain works such as movie titles in news style and article titles in book style.

In most cases, the major editing styles use quotation marks the same way. The following rules apply to all four major styles unless otherwise indicated with style symbols.

Quotation Marks to Indicate
a Direct Quotation or Dialogue

Use quotation marks to indicate words used exactly as they were spoken or written. This includes quotations that are complete sentences, which are usually set off from the rest of the sentence with a comma, and quotations that are sentence fragments.

Senator Jones said, "I will work with both parties to reach an agreement."

Senator Jones vowed to "work with both parties to reach an agreement."

Quotations that continue into subsequent paragraphs are also placed in quotation marks as follows: the beginning of each new paragraph within a single quotation begins with an opening quotation mark, but only the very last word of the whole quotation—not the last word of each paragraph—ends in a quotation mark.

"Years ago, this land was covered with cornfields as far as the eye could see," Grant recalled. "Directly or indirectly, farming supported everyone in town.

"Today, most of the farms have been replaced with factories. The local economy is completely changed."

❸ In book style, unspoken thoughts can be placed in quotation marks or not, as the writer prefers. (When quotation marks aren't used, book style lowercases the first word of the thought, unless it is a long sentence.)

He wondered, "Will it rain?"

He wondered, will it rain?

ALTERNATIVE METHOD FOR LONGER QUOTATIONS

Longer quotations and excerpts, usually of one hundred or more words, are sometimes formatted as block quotations, also called extracts. Block quotations do not take quotation marks. A block quotation always starts as a new paragraph, all of which is usually indented to clearly set it off from preceding text.

If the extract contains internal quotations, those are set in regular double quotation marks.

Quotation Marks to Indicate Unusual
or Ironic Meaning

Quotation marks can indicate that a word or phrase is being used in a questionable or nonstandard manner. These quotation marks, sometimes called scare quotes, can indicate irony.

Lucy is a real "winner."

They can indicate that a term is being used in someone else's sense (not the writer's) or as slang.

The process, which experts call "spaghettification," affects objects in outer space.

Or quotation marks can indicate that a term is being made up by the writer or speaker.

By watering the plants more often, I'm "juicifying" the fruit they will produce.

Quotation Marks for Words Discussed as Words

Ⓝ In news style, quotation marks set off a word or phrase being discussed within the passage.

The word "hip" is becoming less common.

The expression he used, "right on," did not win over his listeners.

Ⓑ Ⓢ Ⓐ Book, science, and academic styles, however, recommend italics when a word or phrase is being discussed within the passage.

The word hip *is becoming less common.*

Ⓑ Ⓝ Ⓐ Quotation marks are also used to indicate English translations of foreign terms.

The Spanish expression ay Dios mío *means "Oh, my God."*

No Quotation Marks with *So-Called*

B N A Terms introduced with *so-called* are not put in quotation marks.

My so-called friend didn't show.

The so-called child protection act would actually put children in harm's way.

Quotation Marks vs. Italics for Titles of Works

Styles disagree on whether quotation marks or italics should be used for titles of written, produced, and performed works and works of art such as paintings. News style uses quotation marks for most titles, while book, science, and academic style more frequently prefer italics for titles of works.

N QUOTATION MARKS AROUND COMPOSITION TITLES IN NEWS STYLE

News style puts quotation marks around the titles of almost all created works. These include books, plays, poems, movies, TV shows, radio programs, works of art, computer games, operas, songs and albums, and titles of lectures and speeches.

Exceptions: The Bible and reference books such as dictionaries, handbooks, almanacs, and encyclopedias are not set in quotation marks.

S ITALICS INSTEAD OF QUOTATION MARKS AROUND COMPOSITION TITLES IN SCIENCE STYLE

Science style specifies that italics should be used for titles of books, periodicals, movies, videos, and TV shows.

B A ITALICS VS. QUOTATION MARKS FOR TITLES IN BOOK AND ACADEMIC STYLES

The following chart shows book and academic style guidelines on which titles should be set in quotation marks and which should be in italics. No entry means the style does not have a rule for the specific type of work.

Quotation Marks vs. Italics for Titles of Works

TITLE OF . . .	**Ⓑ** BOOK STYLE	**Ⓐ** ACADEMIC STYLE
Book other than Bible, Koran, or Talmud	italics	italics
Bible, Koran, or Talmud	no quotation marks or italics	no quotation marks or italics
Book series	no quotation marks or italics	
Chapter of a book	quotation marks	quotation marks
Movie	italics	italics
TV or radio show	italics	italics
Individual episode of a TV or radio show	quotation marks	quotation marks
Periodical	italics	italics
Article in a periodical	quotation marks	quotation marks
Play	italics	italics
Story	quotation marks	quotation marks
Poem	quotation marks	quotation marks
Long poem published as a book	italics	italics
Song	quotation marks	quotation marks
Opera or other long musical performance	italics	italics
Record album	italics	italics
Compact disc		italics
Pamphlet	italics	italics
Visual artwork such as a painting or sculpture	italics	italics
Website	no quotation marks or italics	italics
Individual page of a website	quotation marks	quotation marks
Blog	italics	
Individual blog post	quotation marks	
Online database		italics
Report	italics	
Ship, aircraft, or spacecraft	italics	italics
Regularly occurring column or department in a periodical	no quotation marks or italics	
Essay		quotation marks
Unpublished work such as a lecture or speech	quotation marks	quotation marks

Quotation Marks with Other Punctuation

Some of the most common punctuation errors occur when a writer puts a quotation mark in the wrong place relative to another punctuation mark. The following rules apply to all the major editing styles.

PERIOD

A period always comes before a closing quotation mark.

> *Joe hates it when people call him "pal."*
>
> *Lincoln's speech began, "Four score and seven years ago."*
>
> *Maria said, "That's not my car."*

COMMA

A comma always comes before a closing quotation mark.

> *When people call him "pal," Joe gets annoyed.*
>
> *"Four score and seven years ago," the president began.*
>
> *"That's not my car," Maria said.*

QUESTION MARK

A question mark may come before or after a closing quotation mark, depending on whether it modifies the whole sentence or only the quoted portion.

> *Can he pronounce the word "nuclear"?*
>
> *Alfred E. Neuman's catch phrase is "What, me worry?"*

EXCLAMATION POINT

An exclamation point may come before or after a closing quotation mark, depending on whether it modifies the whole sentence or only the quoted portion.

> *I'm outraged he can't pronounce "nuclear"!*
>
> *Every time you see her, Paula screams, "Hello!"*

SINGLE QUOTATION MARK

Single quotation marks are used to indicate a quotation within a quotation. As such, they appear inside of regular quotation marks.

Joe said, "Don't call me 'buddy.'"

In theory, quotations could appear within quotations that in turn are within other quotations. In the rare cases when these awkward nesting structures are unavoidable, alternate use of double and single quotation marks.

Mark reported, "Joe said, 'Don't call me "buddy."'"

Note that every open double or single quotation mark requires a closing double or single quotation mark and that these could all appear next to each other, as above.

Do not insert a space between a single and double quotation mark.

COLON

A colon can come after a closing quotation mark but never before one.

The truth, she said, was "simple": Dan was guilty.

SEMICOLON

A semicolon can come after a closing quotation mark but never before one.

A conviction, she said, was "inevitable"; Dan would go to jail.

ELLIPSIS

It is unnecessary to use an ellipsis at the beginning or end of a quotation. The reader generally understands that quoted text may not have been the first or last thing a person said. Ellipses often do appear in the middle of quotations. (See "Ellipsis," pages 88–90.)

ⓑ In the rare cases when a quotation ends with an ellipsis, book style recommends that a comma follow the ellipsis to introduce the quotation attribution.

> *"Um . . . um . . . ," said Charles.*

Forming the Plural of Text in Quotation Marks

ⓑ To make a plural of a term in quotation marks, the plural *s* is placed inside the quotation marks. No apostrophe is used. (*Note:* book style is the only style that explicitly rules on this.)

> *The act drew a lot of "wows."*
>
> *How many "happy birthdays" were uttered that day?*
>
> *Is it possible that the Beatles wrote two different "All You Need Is Loves"?*

Forming the Possessive of Text in Quotation Marks

✚ The major style authorities do not give instructions on how to form the possessive of text in quotation marks. When posed with a scenario in which a movie title would appear in quotation marks (that is, in news style), the Punctuation Panel was split on whether to place the apostrophe and possessive *s* inside the quotation marks in the following example.

> *"Casablanca's" best scene*
>
> *"Casablanca"'s best scene*

Direction of Quotation Marks

Most fonts use curved quotation marks, also sometimes called "smart" or "curly" quotation marks, creating a difference between an opening quotation mark and a closed quotation mark.

An opening quotation mark curves with its opening to the right, like the letter *C*, and indicates the beginning of quoted matter.

A closing quotation mark curves with its opening to the left and signifies the end of a quotation.

"This is fabulous," she said.

Quotation Mark as Distinct from Double Prime Symbol

The quotation mark should not be confused with a double prime symbol.

The rules governing placement of quotation marks relative to other punctuation do not apply to the double prime symbol. For example, a period or a comma would come before a closing quotation mark, but it would come after the double prime.

The ruler is 12".

7

Single Quotation Mark

Single quotation marks usually indicate quotations within quotations.

Quotation Within a Quotation

Single quotation marks are used to indicate a quotation or a word referred to as a word within a quotation. As such, they appear inside of regular quotation marks.

Joe said, "Don't call me 'buddy.'"

In theory, quotations could appear within quotations that in turn are within other quotations. In the rare cases when these awkward nesting structures are unavoidable, alternate use of double and single quotation marks.

Mark reported, "Joe said, 'Don't call me "buddy."'"

Note that single quotation marks work in pairs, so every open single quotation mark requires a closing single quotation mark. A single quotation mark can be placed immediately next to a double quotation mark. The writer should not insert a space between a single and double quotation mark, though typesetters and word processing programs may do so.

Single Quotation Marks Not for Words As Words

It is a common mistake to think of single quotation marks as milder alternatives to regular quotation marks, especially by using them for words being discussed or introduced.

Wrong: *Often called 'superbugs,' these germs resist antibiotics.*

Right: *Often called "superbugs," these germs resist antibiotics.*

Single Quotation Marks in Article Titles

Many newspapers and journals use single quotation marks in headlines in place of double quotation marks. This style convention is specific to each publication and is usually documented in the house style guide.

Single Quotation Marks with Other Punctuation

Single quotation marks work with other punctuation according to the same rules that govern double quotation marks. For guidelines, see "Quotation Marks with Other Punctuation," page 76.

Single Open Quotation Mark as Distinct from Apostrophe

In many fonts, an open single quotation mark curves with its opening to the right, like the letter C. This is the opposite direction from the apostrophe, which curves with its opening to the left. Word-processing programs often presume that an apostrophe at the beginning of a word should be changed to an open single quotation mark. The writer should note and correct any wrong changes made by word-processing programs.

A closing single quotation mark, however, is indistinguishable from an apostrophe. So closing single quotation marks do not pose the problem created by open single quotation marks.

Single Quotation Mark as Distinct from Prime Symbol

The single quotation mark should not be confused with a prime symbol.

The rules governing placement of single quotation marks relative to other punctuation do not apply to the prime symbol. For example, a period or comma would come before a closing single quotation mark, but it would come after the prime.

The room's length is 12'.

Question Mark

A question mark indicates a question.

Does the bus come by here?

Why?

How many times did you call?

What does the chef recommend?

Spacing After a Question Mark

Do not double space after a question mark.

Question Mark to Replace a Comma

A quotation that ends with a question mark is not followed by a comma.

Right: *"Are the sandwiches good here?" he asked.*

Wrong: *"Are the sandwiches good here?," he asked.*

ⓑ However, if the question mark is part of a proper name, it does not preclude a comma.

"Why Can't We Be Friends?," her favorite song, was on the radio.

Question Mark to Replace a Period

At the end of a sentence, a question mark always precludes a period, regardless of whether the question mark is within quotation marks, not in quotation marks, or part of a proper name.

> *The officer asked, "Do you know how fast you were going?"*
>
> *You should read* Which Way to My Bright Future?
>
> *You should read "Which Way to My Bright Future?"*

(For how to format book titles, see "Quotation Marks vs. Italics for Titles of Works," page 74.)

The only time a period can appear next to a question mark is when the last word of a sentence is an abbreviation or initialism.

> *Do you think he'll mind if I call him J.D.?*

Question Mark with an Exclamation Point

A question mark can immediately precede or follow an exclamation point when both marks are essential to the meaning of the sentence.

> *Why did you scream* charge!?

Question Mark to Preclude Another Question Mark

When a question ends with an internal question mark, such as in a title, the internal question mark can serve as terminal punctuation.

> *Do you know the song "Why Can't We Be Friends?"*

The practice of using multiple question marks or exclamation points (or both) for effect, which is common in casual correspondence, is discouraged in professional publishing.

> Right: *Are you crazy?*
>
> Not recommended: *Are you crazy???*
>
> Not recommended: *Are you crazy?!?!*

Question Mark in the Middle of a Sentence

When a question not in quotation marks comes in the middle of a sentence, it can be followed by a question mark even though the sentence does not end there.

Has there ever been a better time to try? he wondered.

✦ The Punctuation Panel favored this internal question mark.

The question Why? comes up a lot.

Question Mark After a Statement

A sentence that is grammatically structured as a statement can be followed by question mark if the writer intends it as a question.

You're 23 years old?

The cost of living is high where you're from?

He prefers coffee?

Question Mark Omitted in Rhetorical Questions

Sentences that are interrogative in form (questions) but declarative in meaning (statements) can end in a period instead of a question mark if the writer prefers.

How about that.   *Well, what do you know.*

Really.   *Why don't you just get out of here.*

Question Mark Not Preferred in *Guess What*

The majority of the Punctuation Panel favored punctuating *guess what* as a statement and not a question:

✦ Preferred: *Guess what.*

✦ Less popular: *Guess what?*

9

Exclamation Point

An exclamation point indicates high emotion, as in a shouted command or interjection.

No! he yelled.

You've gone completely mad!

Careful!

Spacing After an Exclamation Point

Do not double space after an exclamation point.

Exclamation Point to Replace a Comma

A quotation that ends with an exclamation point is not followed by a comma.

Right: *"This sandwich is fantastic!"* he said.

Wrong: *"This sandwich is fantastic!,"* he said.

However, if the exclamation point is part of a proper name, it does not preclude a comma.

"Mamma Mia!," her favorite play, was on Broadway.

Yahoo!, headquartered in Silicon Valley, is an international company.

Exclamation Point to Replace a Period

At the end of a sentence, an exclamation point always precludes a period, regardless of whether the exclamation point is within quotation marks, not in quotation marks, or part of a proper name.

The troops' battle cry was "Remember Jimmy!"

The only time a period can appear next to an exclamation point is when the last word of a sentence is an abbreviation or initialism.

But he said I could call him J.D.!

Exclamation Point with a Question Mark

An exclamation point can immediately precede or follow a question mark when both marks are essential to the meaning of the sentence.

Why did you scream charge!?

Exclamation Point to Preclude Another Exclamation Point

When an exclamation ends with an internal exclamation point, such as in a title, the internal exclamation point can serve as terminal punctuation.

I really hated "Jubilee!"

The practice of using multiple exclamation points or combining them with question marks for added emotion is discouraged in professional publishing.

Right: *You're crazy!*

Not recommended: *You're crazy!!!*

Not recommended: *Are you crazy?!?!*

Ellipsis

The term *ellipsis* can refer to omitted words or to the three-dot punctuation mark used where words have been omitted or where speech has been interrupted. The plural is *ellipses*. Some style authorities use the term *ellipsis points* for the punctuation. Some distinguish between ellipsis points and what are called *suspension points*, which indicate trailing or faltering speech (see page 90).

An ellipsis is used primarily in quotations to indicate the writer is leaving out something the speaker said.

Spacing Between Dots

🅑 🆂 🅐 In book, science, and academic styles, the ellipsis is typed as three periods with spaces in between them.

> *"I consider myself lucky . . . to still be alive."*

🅝 In news style, there are no spaces between the dots.

> *"I consider myself lucky ... to still be alive."*

✚ Punctuation Panel members differed on whether the spaces between dots were necessary. Some said that the rule requiring spaces between the dots seemed antiquated and that they do not insert spaces after the first and second dot.

Spacing Before and After the Ellipsis

The major style guides indicate that there should be one space before the first dot and one after the last dot.

Ellipses and Line Breaks

The writer should take care to ensure that all three ellipsis points appear on the same line of text.

No Ellipsis Needed at Beginning or End of a Quotation

It is understood that a quotation may begin well after a speaker first started talking and that it may end long before the speaker stopped talking. As such, there is almost never a need to begin or end a quotation with an ellipsis. However, in rare cases in which the writer determines that an ellipsis at the beginning or end of a quotation better conveys the meaning, the ellipsis can be used.

Right: *"Our fathers brought forth on this continent a new nation."*

Not recommended: *"... our fathers brought forth on this continent a new nation ..."*

Ellipsis After a Complete Sentence

When words before an ellipsis form a grammatically complete sentence, retain the period, question mark, or exclamation point that would normally conclude the sentence. In news style, writers should insert a space after a terminal punctuation mark and before the ellipsis. In book, science, and academic styles, there is no added space.

B S A *"They rode into town in a Sherman tank. . . . It was the most beautiful sight I had ever seen."*

N *"They rode into town in a Sherman tank. ... It was the most beautiful sight I had ever seen."*

B S A *"Did you know that Jenny is on her way? . . . This will be interesting."*

N *"Did you know that Jenny is on her way? ... This will be interesting."*

Note that when an ellipsis follows a complete sentence, the text that follows the ellipsis begins with a capital letter regardless of style.

Ellipsis with Other Punctuation

An ellipsis usually precludes the need for a comma, colon, semicolon, or dash. However, in rare cases in which the extra punctuation can aid comprehension, the writer may choose to include it.

Ellipsis to Indicate Interrupted or Faltering Speech

An ellipsis can also indicate a trailing off or stuttering effect. These dots are sometimes referred to as suspension points.

It's not that he finds her unattractive, it's just, well . . .

You . . . you . . . you monster!

✦ For a majority of the Punctuation Panel, this is different from speech interrupted by another person. Most members of the panel said they prefer em dashes instead of ellipses for speech interrupted by someone other than the speaker.

Martin was livid: "If I've told you once I've—"

"Stop right there," Pete yelled.

11

Hyphen

Hyphenation is hardly an exact science. The rules are complex, they vary by writing style, and they often leave much room for personal preferences and judgment calls. In some cases, it's entirely up to the writer or editor whether to hyphenate a term. In other cases, the rules are clear and inflexible.

Detailed guidelines for hyphenation follow. Many specific terms are also found in "Punctuation A to Z." Writers who need to hyphenate as professionally as possible should follow these guidelines closely. But writers who need an easy system more than they need to be "perfect" should consider the following three-point approach.

1. Hyphenate any compound that could create confusion without the hyphen: *small-business loans*. (Note that, because *ly* adverbs clearly modify a word that follows, compounds with *ly* adverbs are not hyphenated: *a happily married couple*.)

2. Do not hyphenate prefixes or suffixes unless the term looks odd without a hyphen (*antiviral* but *anti-American*).

3. For nouns and verbs, check a dictionary.

Good hyphenation begins by asking: what part of speech will this compound be?

Noun or verb. If the compound is a noun or verb, hyphenation is often determined by the dictionary. For example, *water-ski* contains a hyphen as part of its official spelling when it's a verb, according to the major dictionaries used in publishing. But the noun *water ski* takes no hyphen. These idiosyncrasies cannot be determined by applying any rule or formula. They must be looked up. The writer can also create compound nouns and verbs that are not found in the dictionary, called temporary compounds. Guidelines for hyphenating these temporary compound nouns and verbs are discussed in this chapter (see page 108 for nouns and page 110 for verbs).

Adjective or adverb. Adjectives and adverbs (that is, modifiers) that appear hyphenated in the dictionary are hyphenated before a word they modify. But in book style, compound adjectives that appear after a noun can, at the writer's or editor's discretion, be written without a hyphen even if they are hyphenated in the dictionary. Compound adjectives and adverbs that don't appear in the dictionary can be assembled by the writer according to basic hyphenation rules. These rules are often loose, sometimes leaving it up to the writer to determine whether a hyphen aids comprehension.

Prefix or suffix. Prefixes and suffixes require a different hyphenation strategy. Here it's important to note the difference between a dictionary-sanctioned word like *worldwide*, a suffix or prefix such as *-wide* that attaches to another word to create a term not found in the dictionary, like *communitywide*, and a distinct word that is not a prefix or suffix, like *adjacent* in *park-adjacent*. (See "Prefixes," page 111, and "Suffixes," page 115, for details.)

In all styles, modern publishing shuns excessive hyphenation. Writers who want to emulate professional publishing should use hyphens sparingly and with reader comprehension in mind.

Compound Modifiers

A compound modifier is a unit of two or more words working together to modify another term.

Frequently, compound modifiers are adjectives, like *vitamin-rich* in the sentence *Eat a vitamin-rich diet.* Compound modifiers can also be adverbs that modify verbs, like *full time* in the sentence *She works full time.* They can also be adverbs modifying adjectives, like *jaw-droppingly* in *That is a jaw-droppingly gorgeous sunset.*

Some compound modifiers are in the dictionary, for example, *good-looking.*

COMPOUND MODIFIERS LISTED IN THE DICTIONARY

Compound modifiers listed in the dictionary are often called *permanent compound modifiers* or just *permanent compounds.* They can be styled differently depending on where they fall in a sentence.

Permanent compound modifier before a noun

B N S A Compounds that are hyphenated in the dictionary retain their hyphens when placed before a noun: *a good-looking man.*

Permanent compound modifier after a noun

B In book style, a compound that is hyphenated in the dictionary and that comes after a noun is usually written without the hyphen, unless the sense would be unclear.

> *That documentary is award winning.* (Hyphen not necessary for clarity.)

> *That lawyer is really good-looking* (Hyphen prevents momentary misreading as *That lawyer is really good.*)

N S A In news, science, and academic styles, compounds found in the dictionary usually retain the hyphen when they appear after the noun they modify.

Writers may use compound modifiers not found in the dictionary, including terms of their own creation, called *temporary compounds*. These compounds are hyphenated according to the rules below.

Temporary compound adjective before a noun

B N S A Hyphenate a compound adjective that comes before a noun whenever the absence of a hyphen could create confusion (*a man-eating fish*) or even a momentary misreading *(That hole in the ground is a well-documented hazard)*. When the meaning is immediately clear, no hyphen is needed: *a crab cake recipe*. (But see "Exceptions and Special Circumstances for the Basic Compound Modifiers Rule," opposite page.)

Temporary compound adjective after a noun

Temporary compounds may or may not be hyphenated after a noun according to the following guidelines.

B S Do not hyphenate a compound adjective that comes after the noun it modifies if the meaning is clear: *Money well spent. The man is family oriented. This news is heaven sent.*

N Hyphenate a compound adjective that comes after a noun if it's connected with a form of the verb *to be* (*is, am, are, was, were, being, been*).

> *The mayor is donation-obsessed.*

> *The man was quick-thinking.*

> *The service is family-style.*

✦ News style is unclear on whether to hyphenate compound adjectives that follow other linking verbs (verbs of being), such as *seem, appear, become,* and *act*. The Punctuation Panel split on the question of whether to hyphenate a compound adjective after a linking verb, but a majority indicated a preference for using a hyphen in these situations.

> *This dessert seems guilt-free.*

> *The target looks bullet-riddled.*

This meat tastes hickory-smoked.

He feels honor-bound.

She appears quick-thinking.

Ⓐ Do not hyphenate a compound adjective that comes after a noun it modifies: *the man was quick thinking.*

EXCEPTIONS AND SPECIAL CIRCUMSTANCES FOR THE BASIC COMPOUND MODIFIERS RULE

Every editing style has its own hyphenation idiosyncrasies. For the exceptions and special circumstances that follow, the style icons indicate a preference for the style indicated. If the icon for your style does not appear, it means that your style does not take this circumstance into consideration and that you should follow the basic hyphenation rules and your own judgment instead.

The most important exception is that *ly* adverbs are not hyphenated as part of compound modifiers: *a happily married couple*, not *a happily-married couple*. For more on this, see "Compound containing an *ly* adverb," page 99.

COMPOUND ADJECTIVES CONTAINING SPECIFIC WORDS

Compounds containing specific words are hyphenated as outlined below.

Compound adjective with *best*
Ⓑ Ⓐ Hyphenate before but not after a noun: *The best-known restaurant. The restaurant that is best known.*

Compound adjective with *better*
Ⓐ Hyphenate before but not after a noun: *A better-known restaurant. That restaurant is better known.*

Compound adjective with *elect*

B N Hyphenate a temporary compound containing *elect* that modifies a noun (including a proper noun) regardless of whether the compound comes before or after the name: *Mayor-elect Joe Brown. Councilwoman-elect Jane Murphy. Pete Taylor, senator-elect.* (See also "Compound noun with *elect*," page 108.)

Compound adjective with *ever*

B Hyphenate before but not after a noun: *The ever-golden skies. My ever-wise grandfather. The skies are ever golden. My grandfather is ever wise.*

Compound adjective with *free*

B Hyphenate before or after a noun: *A hassle-free vacation. Free-beer Tuesdays. Leaves hair tangle-free.*

Compound adjective with *full*

B Hyphenate before but not after a noun: *A full-size sedan. The job is full time.*

N Hyphenate before or after a noun: *A full-page advertisement. A full-size sedan. A full-time job. A job that is full-time.* (But also see "Compound Adverbs," page 106.)

Compound adjective with *half*

B N Hyphenate before or after a noun: *A half-eaten breakfast. The report was half-finished.*

Compound adjective with *ill*

A Hyphenate before but not after a noun: *An ill-conceived idea. The idea was ill conceived.*

Compound adjective with *less* or *least*

B Do not hyphenate unless necessary to prevent confusion: *The less understood reason. The least known fact.*

Compound adjective with *little*

Ⓐ Hyphenate before but not after a noun: *A little-known fact. That fact is little known.*

Compound adjective with *lower*

Ⓐ Hyphenate before but not after a noun: *Lower-level employees. Those employees are lower level.*

Compound adjective with *more* or *most*

Ⓑ Do not hyphenate unless necessary to prevent confusion: *The more popular choice. The most traveled roads.*

Compound adjective with *much*

Ⓑ Hyphenate before but not after a noun: *A much-needed rest. Rest that was much needed.*

Ⓐ Do not hyphenate: *A much needed rest. Rest that was much needed.*

Compound adjective with *near*

Ⓑ Hyphenate before or after a noun: *a near-death experience.*

Compound adjective beginning with *odd*

Ⓑ Ⓝ Hyphenate: *odd-number days.*

Compound adjective ending with *odd*

Ⓑ Hyphenate: *I've told you a thousand-odd times.*

Compound adjective with *percent*

Ⓑ Ⓝ Do not hyphenate: *there's an 88 percent chance.*

Compound adjective with *quasi*

Ⓑ Usually hyphenated: *a quasi-successful venture.*

Compound adjective with *self*

🅑 🅝 🅢 Temporary compound adjectives with *self* should be hyphenated in all uses: *A self-aware robot. A robot that became self-aware.* (See also "Compound noun with *self*," page 110, and "Punctuation A to Z.")

Compound adjective with *super*

Super can be a word or a prefix. As a word, it can be hyphenated to form a compound adjective (*He is a super-busy man*) or it can form a compound adjective without a hyphen (*He is a super busy man*). In prefix form, it can be attached to another word without a hyphen (*He is a superbusy man*).

✦ The major style authorities discuss *super-* as a prefix, indicating that it is often closed, but do not discuss whether to hyphenate it if the writer chooses to interpret it as a word. A majority of the Punctuation Panel favored open forms in: *I've been super busy. She is super nice. He is super smart. They are super organized.* A minority of the panel preferred to hyphenate *super-busy, super-nice, super-smart,* and *super-organized.* None favored closed forms.

Compound adjective with *too*

🅑 Hyphenate before but not after a noun: *A too-steep road. A road too steep.*

🅐 Do not hyphenate: *A too steep road. A road that was too steep.*

Compound adjective with *very*

🅑 Compounds with the adverb *very* are usually not hyphenated, though they can be if the hyphen aids readability: *A very nice day. A very-little-known fact.*

🅐 Do not hyphenate compounds with the adverb *very*.

Compound adjective with *well*

🅑 🅢 🅐 Hyphenate before but not after a noun: *the well-known man is also well loved.*

🅝 Hyphenate before or after a noun: *the well-known man is also well-loved.*

Compounds of certain specific types and forms are hyphenated as shown below.

Compound containing an *ly* adverb

B **N** **S** **A** Adverbs ending in *ly* are not customarily hyphenated as part of compound modifiers.

That is a happily married couple.

The couple is happily married.

The blindingly bright sun made her blink.

The sun is blindingly bright.

Avoid the common error of mistaking the nouns that end in *ly*, such as *family* and *homily*, or adjectives that end in *ly*, such as *lovely* and *likely*, for adverbs.

a family-run business

a likely-voter response

Compound adjective indicating nationality

B Do not hyphenate unless "between" is implied: *Spanish Italian descent. Mexican American heritage. An African American man. A Spanish-Italian summit.*

N Hyphenate compound adjectives indicating dual nationality: *Spanish-Italian descent. Mexican-American heritage. An African-American man.* Otherwise, do not use a hyphen: *A French Canadian tourist. A Middle Eastern tradition.*

Compound adjective containing a comparative or superlative

Comparatives are forms of adjectives that normally end in *er: slower, faster, longer.* Superlatives normally end in *est: slowest, fastest, longest.*

S Do not hyphenate before or after a noun: *A slower burning fuel. A fuel that is slower burning. The fastest moving vehicle. The longest lasting battery.*

Compound adjective indicating age with *year* and *old*

Ⓑ Ⓝ Hyphenate before a noun, regardless of whether numeric or written out: *An eight-year-old child. An 8-year-old child.* Note, however, there are no hyphens in the forms *He is eight years old. He turned 101 years old.* As discussed in the "Compound Nouns" section, when terms with *year* and *old* are used as nouns, the forms always take hyphens: *she has a five-year-old and an eight-year-old.*

To determine whether to use numerals or write out numbers in each style, see chapter 18.

Date used as an adjective

Ⓑ Ⓝ Do not hyphenate a date used as an adjective: *a March 12 meeting.*

Compound adjective that includes an *ing* verb form

Before a noun, form a compound adjective that includes an *ing* verb form as follows:

Ⓑ Ⓢ Ⓐ Hyphenate a compound adjective ending in an *ing* form (a participle or a gerund) when it comes before the noun: *a high-achieving student, an all-knowing parent.*

Ⓝ In news style, include the hyphen only if it improves readability.

After a noun, form a compound adjective that includes an *ing* verb form as follows:

Ⓑ In book style, do not put a hyphen in a compound adjective that contains a present participle or gerund and appears after the noun: *Those students are high achieving. Some parents seem all knowing.*

Ⓝ In news style, hyphenate a compound modifier ending in an *ing* form when it comes after the noun only if it follows a form of the verb *be: Those students are high-achieving. Some professors aren't teaching-focused. Some parents seem all-knowing.*

Ⓢ Ⓐ In science and academic styles, a hyphen in a compound that appears after the noun and contains a present participle or gerund is usually discouraged, though the writer may opt to use it.

Compound adjective that includes a past participle

Past participles most commonly end in *ed* (*baked*, *ticketed*) or *en* (*eaten*, *given*, *driven*). But there are also many irregular past participles, such as *made*, *known*, and *brought*.

Before a noun, form compound adjectives with a past participle as follows:

Ⓑ Ⓢ Ⓐ Hyphenate a compound adjective containing a past participle when it comes before the noun: *A moth-eaten sweater. A little-known fact.*

Ⓝ Hyphenate only if it aids comprehension: *A little known fact. Chicken-fried steak.*

After a noun, form compound adjectives with a past participle as follows:

Ⓑ Do not hyphenate a compound adjective that contains a past participle and appears after the noun: *That sweater is completely moth eaten. Here's a fact that's little known.*

Ⓝ Hyphenate after the noun only if the compound adjective follows a form of the verb *be*: *that sweater is moth-eaten.*

Ⓢ Ⓐ In science and academic styles, a compound that contains a past participle and appears after a noun is usually not hyphenated, though the writer has the option of hyphenating it: *That sweater is completely moth eaten. Here's a fact that's little known.*

Working with phrasal verbs

A number of terms are two words as a verb (phrasal verbs) but one word as a noun, according to dictionaries. These include *back up/ backup*, *break up/breakup*, *cut off/cutoff*, and *take out/takeout*.

This poses a dilemma for writers who want to use one of these terms as an adjective because not only can two-word verbs be hyphenated to create adjectives but nouns can also function attributively as adjectives (think: *a paint store*, *a beach day*). So it's not clear whether you should hyphenate the verb to create an adjective (*a back-up plan*, *shut-down procedures*) or use the noun form (*a backup plan*, *shutdown procedures*). Style guides do not indicate which approach to take.

✛ In these circumstances, the Punctuation Panel preferred using the one-word form for the adjective (*a backup plan*, *shutdown procedures*, *the breakup king*, *a cutoff date*, *takeout pasta*) rather than hyphenating the two-word form.

Compound adjective formed from a familiar multiword noun

🅐 Do not hyphenate adjectives formed of familiar multiword terms such as *middle school* and *political science* and *systems analyst*: *A middle school student. A political science major. A systems analyst meeting.*

Proper noun of two or more words used as an adjective

🅑 🅝 🅐 Do not hyphenate proper nouns of two or more words when used to modify another noun: *A United States custom. A Jerry Seinfeld joke.*

🅑 Note that when a proper noun of two or more words is used as part of a larger compound adjective, book style uses an en dash: *a Jerry Seinfeld–like humor.*

Compound adjective with *socio*, *electro*, or other combining form

Terms like *socio* and *electro* that are derived from a word (*social*, *electric*) can combine with another word to create an adjective.

🅑 Do not hyphenate: *socioeconomic, electromagnetic.*

🅝 Hyphenate: *socio-economic, electro-magnetic.*

Compound adjective using a common multiword phrase

Before a noun, form a compound adjective using a common multi-word phrase as follows:

Ⓑ Ⓝ Ⓢ Phrases like *matter of fact*, *up to date*, *live for today*, *state of the art*, and *best of all worlds* may be hyphenated for use as adjectives before nouns: *A matter-of-fact tone. A best-of-all-worlds scenario. A live-for-today mentality. A state-of-the-art facility.*

After a noun, form a compound adjective using a common multi-word phrase as follows:

Ⓑ Do not hyphenate unless necessary for comprehension: *the report is up to date.*

Ⓝ Hyphenate if preceded by a form of *be*: *the report is up-to-date.*

Compound adjective using chemical terms
Ⓑ Ⓢ Do not hyphenate chemical terms used as modifiers: *A hydrogen peroxide reaction. An amino acid study.*

Compound adjective of two or more colors
Ⓑ Ⓐ Hyphenate before but not after a noun: *A brownish-red coat. The coat was brownish red. An orange-gold sunset. The sunset was orange gold.*

Compound adjective containing a color modified by an adjective or noun
Ⓑ Book style generally calls for hyphenating all compound color terms that come before nouns: *A pitch-black sky. Milky-white skin. A blood-red gemstone.*

+ However, book style experts on the Punctuation Panel split on whether to hyphenate *light*, *dark*, *soft*, *bright*, and similar terms when combined with a color to form an adjective. Half said to hyphenate *dark-red car*, *light-blue dress*, *bright-yellow lights*, and *soft-white glow*. Half said not to hyphenate unless ambiguity would result (for example, a *light blue dress* without a hyphen could indicate that the dress itself, not the color, was light).

Compound adjective indicating direction

Ⓑ Hyphenate only terms indicating three or more directions: *north-northeast, south-southwest,* but *northeast, southwest. We took the west-southwest route.*

Compound adjective containing a number

Ⓑ In book style, number-plus-noun compounds and times of day functioning as adjectives are usually hyphenated before a noun. This includes cardinal numbers (*a thousand-mile journey, a forty-meter drive, a three-time loser*), ordinal numbers (*a third-rate burglary, a fifth-place finish, the tenth-largest city*), simple fractions used as adjectives (*a two-thirds majority*), fractions combined with other words (*a half-hour massage*), and time of day (*a three-thirty appointment*). Two notable exceptions are mentioned below.

Percentages are not hyphenated as compound modifiers, regardless of whether the number is a numeral (strongly preferred) or spelled out: *A 60 percent majority. Sixty percent majorities are rare.*

Compounds in which a noun is followed by a numeral aren't hyphenated: *a category 4 hurricane, type 2 diabetes, lane 1 collision.*

Ⓝ Though news style does not have express rules on whether to hyphenate numeral-plus-noun combinations used as adjectives, the style shows a preference for hyphenating compounds like *a 10-year sentence* and *an 8-ounce serving.*

Percentages, which are always expressed in numerals in news style, are not hyphenated as compound modifiers: *a 60 percent majority.*

Fractions used as adjectives and fractions combined with other words to form adjectives are hyphenated: *a two-thirds majority, a one-fifth share, a half-hour massage, a quarter-hour break.*

Ⓢ Science style calls for hyphenating a compound that begins with a number when the compound precedes the term it modifies: *a four-way stop, a 10-point scale.* But when a numeral is the second element in a compound, do not hyphenate: *type 3 error, trial 1 performance.*

Fractions used as adjectives and fractions combined with other words to form adjectives are hyphenated: *a two-thirds majority, a one-fifth share, a half-hour massage, a quarter-hour break.*

Ⓐ In academic style, a hyphen is used in any compound adjective that contains a number and a noun and comes before another noun.

A late-twelfth-century painting.

✦ The Punctuation Panel unanimously favored a hyphen in *a 4-carat diamond* and *a 360-degree view.* But they split on how to hyphenate a *$25-million-losing project/a $25 million-losing project/a $25 million losing project*; each of these forms received support among the panel members.

(For more on when to use numbers vs. numerals, see chapter 18.)

Compound adjective containing individual letters

Ⓑ Ⓢ When a letter is the second element in a compound, do not hyphenate: *He has a type A personality. Group A researchers.*

SUSPENSIVE HYPHENATION

Ⓑ Ⓝ Ⓢ When two or more hyphenated terms share a word, the shared word does not need to be repeated. The hyphens are retained.

a family-owned and -operated business

a Grammy- and Emmy-award-winning actor

a mid- to late-1980s phenomenon

Ⓑ When closed terms share a second part, that element can be dropped and replaced with a hyphen.

Both over- and underachieving students applied.

✦ Style guides don't clearly address whether suspensive hyphenation should be used with an internal *ly* adverb, but Punctuation Panel members unanimously said they would use no hyphens in *an electronically monitored and controlled system.*

✦ Some terms are not clearly addressed by official hyphenation rules. For the following examples, members of the Punctuation Panel indicated how they would hyphenate if recasting the sentence were not an option.

Compound adjective of three or more terms including an *ly* adverb

✦ Half the Punctuation Panel said they would use one hyphen in *a too-widely known fact.* Half said they would use two: *a too-widely-known fact.* (None opted for no hyphens: *a too widely known fact.*) However, panel members said they would not hyphenate the adverb in a *nicely put-together woman.*

Compound adjective of uncertain scope

✦ At times, a writer must decide whether words preceding a noun form a single adjective that should be hyphenated as one modifier or whether some terms within are functioning independently. For example, in choosing between *a discriminating-but-value-conscious shopper* and *a discriminating but value-conscious* shopper, the writer can decide based on whichever best captures the intended meaning. In this case, the Punctuation Panel unanimously preferred just one hyphen: *a discriminating but value-conscious shopper.*

The panel split, however, on the following example:

> *They serve only thirty-day dry-aged beef.* (majority preference)

> *They serve only thirty-day-dry-aged beef.* (minority preference)

COMPOUND ADVERBS

Compound adverbs usually modify verbs and adjectives.

Compound adverb after a verb

The major styles do not expressly indicate whether to hyphenate a compound adverb after a verb. Examples from book and news styles give some clue to styles' individual preferences on a few very specific matters. For example, news style leans toward not using a hyphen in *She works full time.* Book style appears to prefer hyphenation of *style* in adverb compounds: *they dined family-style.* Yet all the styles are unclear on whether you should put a hyphen in a compound adverb like *tax free* in *You can donate tax free.*

✚ The Punctuation Panel split on whether to hyphenate compound adverbs in the following examples:

> *The combatants fought gladiator-style/gladiator style.*
>
> *You can donate tax-free/tax free.*
>
> *Enjoy treats guilt-free/guilt free.*
>
> *They were talking all drunk-like/drunk like.*
>
> *He only works part-time/part time.*
>
> *We're surviving day-to-day/day to day.*
>
> *She always flies first-class/first class.*
>
> *Drive extra-carefully/extra carefully.*
>
> *He dances old-school/old school.*
>
> *They sell it over-the-counter/over the counter.*
>
> *He gets paid under-the-table/under the table.*

However, the Punctuation Panel was unanimous in the view that *They walked arm in arm* should not be hyphenated.

Compound adverb indicating direction

Ⓑ Hyphenate only terms indicating three or more directions: *north-northeast, south-southwest,* but *northeast, southwest.*

> *They trudged north-northwest through the desert.*

Compound adverb before an adjective

Compound adverbs that come before an adjective are hyphenated according to the same rules as for compound adjectives: hyphenate all compounds, whenever doing so helps clarity or readability: *a jaw-droppingly gorgeous car, a dead-on accurate portrayal.*

Compound Nouns

Generalized guidelines for forming compound nouns do not exist in the major editing styles. Except in the specific cases that follow, the writer can decide whether a hyphen in a compound noun aids the reader.

RECOMMENDED GUIDELINES AND STYLE-SPECIFIC RULES

Here are some guidelines for forming compound nouns of certain structures or with certain terms.

Compound made of "co-equal" nouns
Ⓑ Ⓐ When combining nouns of equal weight, use a hyphen: *importer-exporter, writer-director.*

Compound noun containing a gerund
Ⓑ In book style, when combining a gerund (an *ing* verb form functioning as a noun) with another noun to create a term not found in the dictionary, do not hyphenate in noun form: *Hat making is a lost art. Dog walking is a good way to earn extra money.*

✚ News style experts on the Punctuation Panel preferred no hyphen in compounds formed with gerunds, including *hat making, dog walking,* and *people pleasing.*

Compound noun with *socio, electro,* or similar combining form
Terms like *socio* and *electro* that are derived from a word (*social, electric*) can combine with another word to create a noun.

Ⓑ Do not hyphenate: *socioeconomics, electromagnetism.*

Ⓝ Hyphenate: *socio-economics, electro-magnetism.*

Compound noun with *elect*
Ⓑ Ⓝ Hyphenate a temporary compound containing *elect: Joe Brown is mayor-elect. Consult the councilwoman-elect.*

Compound noun with *great* indicating a family relationship
Ⓑ Ⓝ Hyphenate: great-grandmother, great-great-grandmother.

Compound noun with *maker*

N Hyphenate compounds not found in the dictionary: *chip-maker*. Exception: *drugmaker*.

Compound formed with other *-er* noun (*giver, watcher, etc.*)

Style authorities offer no clear instructions for forming compound nouns when the second word is an *-er* form and the first word functions as an object of the second (*gift giver, hat maker*).

+ Punctuation Panel members favored no hyphen in compound nouns formed with *er* nouns, unanimously opting for no hyphen in the following:

She is a regular market watcher.

He is a great gift giver.

That ride is a real nausea inducer.

That subject is quite an argument starter.

She is a known chocolate and cheese lover.

Don't be a crowd follower.

Similarly, three-quarters of the panel opted for no hyphen in *She is a frequent compliment giver.*

Compound noun indicating color

B Do not hyphenate: *bluish green, blue green.*

What do you think of the bluish green in this painting?

Compound noun indicating direction

B Hyphenate only terms indicating three or more directions: *north-northeast, south-southwest,* but *northeast, southwest. West-southwest was the best direction, they agreed.*

Compound noun indicating time of day

B Do not hyphenate in noun form: *It's three thirty. I'll see you at four twenty.* (But see also "Compound adjective containing a number," page 104.)

Compound noun using chemical terms

Ⓑ Ⓢ Do not hyphenate multiword chemical terms unless listed as hyphenated compounds in the dictionary: *hydrogen peroxide, amino acids.*

Fractions as nouns

Ⓑ Ⓝ Hyphenate spelled-out fractions: *his brother got four-fifths, but he only got one-fifth.*

Ⓢ No hyphen in spelled-out fractions used as nouns: *his brother got four fifths, but he only got one fifth.*

Compound noun indicating nationality

Ⓑ Do not hyphenate: *An African American. A group of Mexican Americans.*

Ⓝ Hyphenate compound nouns indicating dual nationality or heritage: *A Mexican-American. A group of African-Americans.* But note: no hyphen in *French Canadian* or *Latin American.*

Compound noun with *self*

Ⓑ Ⓝ Ⓢ Many compound nouns with *self* are permanent compounds listed in the dictionary and spelled with hyphens. Temporary compound nouns with *self* should be hyphenated in all uses: *self-government, self-love.*

Compound noun indicating age with *year* and *old*

Ⓑ Ⓝ Hyphenate age terms that stand in for individuals regardless of whether numeric or written out: *she has an eight-year-old.*

(But see also "Compound adjective indicating age with *year* and *old*," page 100.)

To determine whether to use numerals or write out numbers in each style, see chapter 18.

Compound Verbs

The major editing styles do not have generalized rules for forming compound verbs not found in the dictionary. News style indicates a preference for hyphenating compound verbs, but leaves much up to the writer. In all styles, writers should follow the general guidelines of clarity and readability when determining whether to hyphenate a temporary compound verb. A number of common compound verbs are listed in "Punctuation A to Z."

Prefixes

In general, do not hyphenate a prefix unless it precedes a capital letter (*pre-Victorian*) or a number (*post-1917*), the hyphen prevents confusion (*re-create* vs. *recreate*), or the prefix ends with the same letter that also begins the following word and would therefore be awkward without a hyphen (*anti-inclusive, ultra-apathetic, intra-arterial*). Similarly, any prefix that without a hyphen could cause an awkward or difficult-to-read compound can usually be hyphenated: *pro-life, anti-geneticist*. Also hyphenate any prefix that would result in a doubling or tripling of the same prefix: *sub-subpar, pre-prewar*. Prefixes often create compounds not recognized by spell-checkers or listed in the dictionary. They are nonetheless correct.

STYLE-SPECIFIC EXCEPTIONS

Style-specific exceptions to these general rules and instructions for special terms follow. (Also see "Punctuation A to Z" for specific terms.)

Prefix with another hyphenated term

🅑 Hyphenate a prefix attached to another hyphenated term: *non-self-cleaning, un-co-opt, anti-pro-war*. (But use an en dash to attach a prefix to an open compound: *non–South American, post–World War I, anti–high school*).

anti-

🅝 For terms not listed in the dictionary, hyphenate most words with *anti-* with these exceptions: *antibiotic, antibody, anticlimax, antidepressant, antidote, antifreeze, antigen, antihistamine, antiknock, antimatter, antimony, antiparticle* (and similar physics terms like *antiproton*), *antipasto, antiperspirant, antiphon, antiphony, antipollution, antipsychotic, antiseptic, antiserum, antithesis, antitoxin, antitrust,* and *antitussive*.

co-

Ⓝ Hyphenate terms formed with *co-* when *co-* indicates occupation or position: *co-author, co-chairman, co-defendant, co-host, co-owner, co-pilot, co-signer, co-sponsor, co-star, co-worker.*

✦ *For other styles, the Punctuation Panel advocates hyphenating many nouns formed with co-*, including *co-defendant* and *co-chairman.*

Ⓑ Ⓝ Ⓢ Ⓐ Do not hyphenate *cooperate, cooperation, coordinate,* and *coordination.*

eco-

Editing styles have no specific guidelines for when to hyphenate *eco-*. Some terms have official spellings with or without hyphens.

Ⓑ Ⓝ Ⓢ *ecotourism, eco-friendly, eco-conscious, ecosystem*
The rules for hyphenating prefixes as well as dictionary entries for the combining form *eco-* show a preference for not hyphenating *eco-*, including in awkward constructions like *ecohero* and *ecocatastrophe.*

✦ However, the Punctuation Panel showed a strong preference for hyphenating *eco-* in most adjectives (*eco-smart*) and nouns (*eco-smarts*).

ex-

Ⓑ Ⓝ Hyphenate *ex-* when it means *former: ex-partner, ex-girlfriend, ex-convict, ex-soldier.* (Exception: In book style, an *ex-* placed before a multiword term such as *insurance salesman* or *New Kid on the Block* is connected with an en dash.)

extra-

In compound adjectives, *extra* can be a prefix or an adverb. As an adverb, it can modify a following adjective without a hyphen (*He is an extra nice person*), though like many other words it can also form a compound adjective through hyphenation (*He is an extra-nice person*). As a prefix, standard rules of hyphenation apply, usually requiring a closed form with no hyphen (*He is an extranice man*).

ⓑ To create terms not listed in the dictionary, the writer can choose whether *extra* is an adverb or a prefix. But in general, book style opts for closed forms with *extra* whenever appropriate: *extramural, extrafine,* but *extra-articulate.*

Ⓝ When *extra* means "beyond the usual size, extent, or degree," hyphenate: *an extra-large room, an extra-dry martini, extra-spicy sauce.* When *extra* means "outside of," the standard rules of prefixes apply: *extramarital, extrasensory, extracurricular, extra-articulate.*

Ⓢ Ⓐ For terms not listed in the dictionary, the writer can choose whether *extra* is functioning as a freestanding adverb (*an extra dry martini*), a hyphenated adverb (*an extra-dry martini*), or a prefix (*an extradry martini*).

✚ Punctuation Panel book style experts preferred hyphenating compounds with *extra* when the compound comes before a noun but not after.

> *He ordered an extra-dry martini.*
>
> *He is an extra-smart guy.*
>
> *Zach is extra nice.*

in-

ⓑ Ⓝ Ⓢ Ⓐ Be careful not to confuse the prefix *in-*, which means "not," with the preposition *in.* Most terms that use the negative prefix *in-* are listed in the dictionary and are customarily not hyphenated: *insufferable, inaccurate, indecision, indecisive, intolerable, indiscreet, indiscretion, indirect, infallible.*

Compounds formed with the preposition *in* follow the rules for forming compounds: *An in-depth study. An in-house recruitment effort.*

non-

Ⓝ Hyphenate only when necessary to prevent awkwardness, such as repeated letters (*non-nuclear*) or compounds formed of other hyphenated compounds (*non-wine-drinking*) or open compounds (*a non-Elvis Presley set*).

Ⓑ Hyphenate only when necessary to prevent awkwardness (*non-mnemonic*) or to form compounds with other hyphenated compounds (*non-wine-drinking*). If *non-* precedes an open compound, such as a proper name consisting of two or more words, an en dash, not a hyphen, is used (*a non–Elvis Presley set*). (See chapter 13.)

out-

Ⓝ Hyphenate *out-* in the meaning "to do better" or "exceed" in any term not listed in *Webster's New World College Dictionary*: *out-jump, out-mambo, out-calculate*. Terms listed in the dictionary customarily take no hyphen: *outbid, outdance, outdo, outdrink, outeat, outfox, outflank, outgrow, outgun, outlast, outperform, outscore, outspend, outstrip, outtalk, outthink*.

pan-

Ⓝ Hyphenate and capitalize before a proper noun: *Pan-African, Pan-American, Pan-Asiatic*.

post-

Ⓝ Hyphenate unless the term appears in the dictionary: *post-mortem, post-convention, post-picnic, post-breakup*. Two exceptions: *postelection, postgame*.

pre-

Ⓝ Hyphenate if the word that follows begins with an *e*, regardless of whether the compound appears unhyphenated in the dictionary: *pre-election, pre-eminent, pre-empt, pre-establish, pre-exist*.

pro-

Ⓑ Ⓢ Hyphenate only when necessary to aid readability: *pro-life, pro-choice, pro-American, pro-organic*.

Ⓝ Hyphenate all compounds in which *pro-* indicates support for something: *pro-labor, pro-business, pro-war*.

✦ A majority of the Punctuation Panel preferred hyphenated forms: *She is pro-labor. He is pro-peace.* A minority preferred open forms: *She is pro labor. He is pro peace.* None opted for the closed forms.

re-

Ⓝ Hyphenate if the word that follows begins with an *e*, regardless of whether the compound appears unhyphenated in the dictionary: *re-enter*, *re-entry*, *re-examination*.

Suffixes

Most compounds formed with suffixes are not hyphenated. The most common exceptions are compounds that would triple consonants (*bill-less*) and compounds formed with proper nouns (*Austin-wide*).

It is helpful to note that, in many cases, a term may be both a standalone word and a suffix, for example *less* and *able*. But other words the writer might wish to affix to the end of another term are not suffixes, for example *full* and *odd*. If the dictionary indicates that a term is a suffix, usually by giving it a separate entry that begins with a hyphen (*-less*), the writer can usually combine it to a root word without a hyphen. However if a term is not designated as a suffix by the dictionary, it follows the hyphenation rules for whichever part of speech it will form, such as a compound adjective, compound adverb, or compound noun. These terms are often hyphenated: *half-full*, *twenty-odd*.

Working with suffixes often creates compounds that are not found in the dictionary and are objected to by computer spellcheckers. Though sometimes awkward, these terms are nonetheless valid: *coffeeless*, *singable*, *eightyfold*.

STYLE-SPECIFIC EXCEPTIONS

Exceptions to these general rules follow. (Also see "Punctuation A to Z" for specific terms including *-ache*, *-borne*, *-elect*, *-free*, *-odd*, and *-style*.)

-fold

Ⓑ Do not hyphenate unless it follows a numeral (*125-fold*) or follows another hyphenated term (*twenty-eight-fold*).

-in-law

Ⓑ Ⓝ Ⓢ All forms hyphenated: *mother-in-law*, *mothers-in-law*, *brother-in-law*, *daughters-in-law*.

-like

Ⓑ Hyphenate all forms not listed in the dictionary: *genius-like*, *dog-like*, *freak-like*, *California-like*, *hall-like*.

Ⓝ News style in general calls for no hyphen in compounds formed with -*like* (*geniuslike*, *doglike*, *freaklike*), except with proper nouns and compounds that would put three l's in a row: *California-like*, *hall-like*. Exception: *flu-like*.

Ⓐ In most cases, do not hyphenate compounds formed with -*like*: *geniuslike*, *doglike*, *freaklike*. Academic style does not have express rules for adding suffixes to proper nouns. In determining whether to hyphenate -*like* with a proper noun, writers in academic style may note MLA's style rule calling for hyphenating prefixes with proper nouns (*pre-Freudian*) and extend it to suffixes (*California-like*).

-wide

Ⓑ Hyphenate compounds not found in the dictionary: *university-wide*, *office-wide*, but *worldwide*.

Ⓝ Do not hyphenate: *universitywide*, *officewide*, *industrywide*.

-wise

Ⓝ In the meaning "in the direction of" or "regarding," do not hyphenate: *clockwise*, *lengthwise*, *moneywise*, *conversationwise*. The form of *wise* that means "smart" or "savvy" is not a suffix but a distinct word. Compounds containing this form of *wise* are often found in the dictionary: *penny-wise*, *street-wise*. Temporary compounds using *wise* in the sense of "smart" follow the general rules in this chapter.

Ratios

Ⓝ News style uses hyphens in ratios (unlike book, science, and academic styles, which use colons). When the numerals appear before the word *ratio*, a hyphen replaces the word *to*.

> *They won by a ratio of 2-to-1.*
>
> *It was a 2-1 ratio.*

Betting Odds

Ⓝ News style uses hyphens in betting odds.

They're giving him 50-1 odds in Vegas.

Ranges

In running text, ranges of numerically valued things like ages, money, and time are usually written out with the word *to*, *through*, or *until*: *The job pays $50,000 to $55,000 a year. The park is open 5 to 7. Children ages 11 through 15 can enroll.*

Ⓝ Ⓢ Ⓐ In casual contexts and graphic elements (like tables), news, science, and academic styles allow hyphens instead: *The job pays $50,000-$55,000 a year. The park is open 5-7. Children 11-15 can enroll.*

Ⓑ In casual context and graphic elements, book style uses en dashes instead: *children 11–15 can enroll.*

Spelled-out Words

Use a hyphen to separate letters in a word being spelled out: *J-O-B. We said N-O.*

Hyphenated Names

Compound personal names use hyphens, not dashes.

Carolyn Howard-Johnson

Em Dash

An em dash is twice as long as a hyphen. It is used to indicate breaks in a sentence and, in certain styles, a change of speakers in dialogue and items in a list. In news style it is also used in datelines and lists.

Breaks in Sentence Flow

Em dashes are used to indicate breaks in sentence flow.

PARENTHETICAL INSERTIONS

Em dashes set off parenthetical insertions.

> *When you get the job—and I know you will—put in a good word for me.*

INSERTIONS OF ADDITIONAL INFORMATION

Additional "that is"–type information can be inserted between dashes.

> *The many departments that worked on the handbook—human resources, accounting, risk management—brought unique perspectives to the finished product.*

> *He wanted to try something new—namely, skydiving.*

A CHANGE OF SENTENCE STRUCTURE OR THOUGHT

Dashes can indicate a change of sentence structure or thought.

Do you really think—can you be so naïve as to expect him to come back?

DASHES VS. PARENTHESES AND COMMAS

There's considerable overlap between dashes, parentheses, and commas. In some cases, the writer can choose any of the three.

The team captain—a major bully—entered the locker room.

The team captain, a major bully, entered the locker room.

The team captain (a major bully) entered the locker room.

Commas are used when the writer feels the information should be well integrated into the sentence. Parentheses indicate the information is less integral to the sentence. Dashes can serve as something in between, clearly setting off the text from the main sentence without sending a message that it's less important.

In choosing between parentheses, dashes, and commas to set off parenthetical information, the writer should keep in mind:

- Parentheses have the greatest power to interrupt the flow of a sentence and should therefore be used sparingly.

- Information that does not fit in grammatically with the rest of the sentence must be set off with either parentheses or dashes, not commas.

Em Dashes for Dialogue

❸ In book style, em dashes can be used instead of quotation marks to indicate dialogue.

—I didn't expect to see you here.

—Are you kidding? I wouldn't miss this for the world.

Em Dashes in News Article Datelines

Ⓝ In news articles that begin with datelines, a dash with a space on either side sets off the dateline city.

> *NEW YORK — A transportation workers' strike was averted Wednesday.*

Em Dashes in Lists

Ⓝ In news style, items in vertical lists are often preceded by em dashes.

> *The judge was most heavily influenced by the following factors:*
>
> *—The defendant had shown no remorse.*
>
> *—Witnesses for the defense were unable to corroborate the alibi.*
>
> *—The defendant was a repeat offender.*

✦ A majority of the Punctuation Panel said they would not insert a space after the dash in the above examples.

Spacing of Em Dashes

Ⓑ Ⓢ Ⓐ Do not use a space on either side of the em dash

> *This way she talks—like she's giving a lecture—it's insufferable.*

Ⓝ Place one space on either side of the em dash.

> *This way she talks — like she's giving a lecture — it's insufferable.*

En Dash

The en dash, which is shorter than an em dash but longer than a hyphen, applies solely to book style. It does not exist in news, science, or academic style.

En Dash to Mean *To*, *Through*, or *Until*

An en dash usually means *to*, *through*, or *until* and can replace those words in contexts in which the writer feels that a flow of words is not critical.

The 1999–2000 season was seminal for Jackson.

The Patriots won 21–7.

Happy hour is 3–7.

The Chicago–Dallas flight is departing.

Dick Clark (1929–2012) hosted American Bandstand.

Ryan Seacrest (1974–) hosts American Idol.

En Dash in Unwieldy Compound Adjectives

In compound adjectives made up of other multiword compounds, including hyphenated terms and two-word terms, an en dash can serve as the connector.

a semi-private–semi-public entity

the pre–Civil War years

a Black Dahlia–motivated crime

a Barack Obama–like speaking style

Parenthesis

Parentheses are used to insert information into text and to group or set off numbers and letters.

Inserting Information

Parentheses are used to insert information into text.

EXAMPLES

Parentheses can contain examples relevant to the sentence.

> *Scurvy was a problem for sailors because it was difficult to carry citrus fruits (oranges, grapefruit, lemons) on long voyages.*

ADDITIONAL INFORMATION

Parentheses can contain additional information, explanation, instruction, or translation.

> *The new sedan is fast (it goes from zero to sixty in just six seconds).*

> *The boss (who had walked in just in time to see the accident) was furious.*

The bird should be trussed before it's put in the oven (see page 288).

She strolled the third arrondissement (district).

The Kilgore (Texas) News-Herald covers local government.

REFERENCE INFORMATION

Parentheses can contain reference information.

The study participants showed no improvement in cholesterol levels (McLellan and Frost, 2002).

Grouping and Setting Off
Numbers and Letters

Parentheses are used to indicate how numbers are to be grouped. Parentheses can also enclose numbers and letters used to enumerate items in lists and outlines.

TELEPHONE AREA CODES

Some editing styles use parentheses for area codes. See "Telephone Numbers," page 146, for details.

(626) 555-1212

MATHEMATICAL GROUPINGS

Parentheses are used for certain mathematical groupings.

(12 x 4) + 11

SETTING OFF NUMBERS AND LETTERS

In some publications, parentheses are also used to set off letters or numbers in lists and outlines.

New employees should (a) select an insurance company, (b) select deductibles, and (c) indicate their selections on the online form.

Parentheses vs. Dashes and Commas

There's considerable overlap between parentheses' job and those of commas and dashes. In some cases, the writer can choose any of the three.

The team captain (a major bully) entered the locker room.

The team captain, a major bully, entered the locker room.

The team captain—a major bully—entered the locker room.

In general, parentheses indicate that the enclosed information is less integral to the main sentence, carrying a connotation of *by the way*. Commas are used when the writer feels the information should be well integrated into the sentence. Dashes can serve as something in between, clearly setting off the text from the main sentence without sending a message that it's less important.

In choosing between parentheses, dashes, and commas to set off parenthetical information, the writer should keep this in mind:

- Parentheses have the greatest power to interrupt the flow of a sentence and should therefore be used sparingly.

- Information that does not fit in grammatically to the rest of the sentence must be set off with either parentheses or dashes, not commas.

Placement of Parentheses Relative to Other Punctuation

PERIOD

A period comes before a closing parenthesis if the parentheses contain a complete sentence intended as distinct from surrounding sentences.

Lisa was angrier than usual that day. (For one thing, some jerk had just keyed her car.)

A period comes after a closing parenthesis if the parenthetical insertion is incorporated into the surrounding sentence, regardless of whether the parenthetical is an independent clause.

> *The sunset was obscured by the clouds (which had cast a pall over the afternoon as well).*

> *The sunset was obscured by the clouds (they had cast a pall over the afternoon as well).*

In many cases, the choice of whether to make a parenthetical independent clause its own separate sentence is based solely on the writer's desired emphasis.

> Right: *Dave left work. (His shift ended at nine.)*

> Right: *Dave left work (his shift ended at nine).*

QUESTION MARK OR EXCLAMATION POINT

A question mark or exclamation point can come before or after a closing parenthesis, depending on whether it modifies the whole sentence or the parenthetical alone.

> *Did you know they canceled the parade (due to the weather forecast)?*

> *They canceled the parade (can you believe it?).*

> *They canceled the parade (darn rain!).*

> *They canceled the darn parade (due to rain)!*

COMMA

In running text, an open parenthesis precludes the need for a comma.

> Right: *On Tuesday (when I last saw him) he was wearing blue.*

> Wrong: *On Tuesday, (when I last saw him) he was wearing blue.*

Only when the parentheses contain a letter or number used to list items can it be preceded by a comma.

> *You can bring (a) silverware, (b) ice, or (c) napkins.*

It is common, however, for a comma to follow a closing parenthesis.

Pick up some envelopes (letter size), stamps (a whole roll, please), and pens.

Note that, in this construction, the parenthetical insertion belongs to the item preceding it, so the comma comes after the parenthesis.

SEMICOLON

A semicolon can follow a closing parenthesis when appropriate. But a semicolon does not precede an opening parenthesis unless the parentheses enclose a letter or number indicating a listed item.

The company has offices in (a) Trenton, New Jersey; (b) Newark, New Jersey; and (c) Carpinteria, California.

COLON

A colon can follow a closing parenthesis or, less commonly, it can precede an open parenthesis.

King, DuBois, and Tubman (along with others who had risked their lives for justice): these were her heroes.

A colon never appears immediately before a closing parenthesis or after an open parenthesis.

DASH

In rare cases a writer might want to use a dash next to a parenthesis. The major styles do not have rules for whether and how to do so.

✚ The Punctuation Panel felt that dashes can be used next to parentheses.

He ordered the steak rare (very rare)—his favorite meal on a night like this.

HYPHEN

✚ In the rare cases when a hyphen might immediately follow a parenthesis, the Punctuation Panel split on whether to allow it, supporting the use by a slim majority.

He was a red (maroon, really)-clad man.

QUOTATION MARK

A closing quotation mark can appear after, but not before, a closing parenthesis.

"I can't believe you had the nerve to show your face here (unbelievable)."

In rare situations, an opening quotation mark can appear before, but not after, an opening parenthesis.

PARENTHESES WITHIN PARENTHESES

Parenthetical insertions within parenthetical insertions are usually set off with brackets, not parentheses. See chapter 15.

See Jorgenson's most recent article ("Trauma at sea" [2014]).   ▪

More Than One Sentence in Parentheses

Parenthetical insertions within a sentence are usually either a sentence fragment or a single complete sentence. Parenthetical insertions of two or more sentences usually are not inserted into another sentence. When it is necessary to put more than one sentence in the same set of parentheses, they are usually inserted between complete sentences in the running text.

✚ If necessary to enclose two or more complete sentences parenthetically in the middle of another sentence, Punctuation Panel split on how to punctuate the sentences in parentheses. A majority of the panel preferred just one period in the parentheses.

He wanted to smoke his pipe (Good tobacco was scarce. He had the war to thank for that) with a glass of brandy in his hand.

A minority preferred two periods in the parentheses.

He wanted to smoke his pipe (Good tobacco was scarce. He had the war to thank for that.) with a glass of brandy in his hand.

Note, however, that the panel unanimously preferred a semicolon or em dash within the parentheses.

He wanted to smoke his pipe (good tobacco was scarce; he had the war to thank for that) with a glass of brandy in his hand.

INITIALS AND ACRONYMS

Initials and acronyms are sometimes inserted after a first reference to an organization that will be referred to in the shorter form later in the text.

Mothers Against Drunk Driving (MADD) launched a letter-writing campaign.

However, it is a common mistake to assume that any organization's initials must routinely be inserted after the full name on first reference. News style prohibits this practice and other styles discourage it as it interrupts flow of reading.

Not recommended: *The Organization for North Atlantic States (ONAS), the Association of Oil Producing Nations (AOPN), and the International Brotherhood of Steel Workers (IBSW) all had representatives at the conference.*

Better: *The Organization for North Atlantic States, the Association of Oil Producing Nations, and the International Brotherhood of Steel Workers all had representatives at the conference.*

The inserted initials are necessary only when they will be so crucial to the following text that it's worth the reader's time to stop midsentence and memorize the initialisms. This usually occurs only in longer documents in which (1) the organization must, for lack of a more familiar term, be called by its initials numerous times throughout and (2) the reader needs help in associating the initials with the full name.

An organization such as MADD, for example, can be used on second reference without ever having been introduced parenthetically if the reader would easily make the connection.

15

Bracket

Brackets are most commonly used to insert a parenthetical within another parenthetical.

> *The concerts take place on Saturdays (call [310] 555-1212 for scheduled artists).*

However, different editing styles have additional uses for brackets.

Ⓑ Book style uses brackets in scholarly writing to indicate that an insertion was made by someone other than the original writer. They are also used to insert translations and phonetic spellings.

> *The Parisian-themed store specializes in* fromage *[cheese].*

Ⓝ News style, which is rooted in a tradition of wire reporting, officially eschews brackets because historically they could not be transmitted by wire. However, independent news organizations sometimes use brackets in quotations to indicate that the insertion was the writer's and not the speaker's.

> *"I read about it in the* [New York] *Times."*

S Science style uses brackets to indicate that parenthetical text in a quotation is the writer's and not the source's. Brackets in this style are also used in confidence intervals in statistics. In mathematical contexts, science writers should reverse the normal order of parentheses and brackets. That is, whereas written text would put its main parenthetical in parentheses and a subparenthetical in brackets, science style puts the main grouping of mathematical material in brackets and subgroupings into parentheses within the brackets.

He discovered the equation [b = (y + 1)/4] only after repeated failures.

A Academic style uses brackets to indicate missing, unverified, or inserted information in source documentation.

Twain, Mark [Samuel Clemens], Huckleberry Finn.

]

16

Slash and Backslash

The slash is considered informal, and the major editing styles discourage it in running text.

Slash to Mean *Or, And, Through,* or *Per*

In informal uses, a slash can stand in for *or, and, through,* or *per*.

> *Sparkling and/or still water will be at each server station.*

> *If the student wants to enroll in lab, he/she should do so as soon as possible.*

> *Marcus/Grandpa/Mr. Storyteller is always fun to listen to.*

> *The job pays $800/week.*

> *Light moves at about 186,000 mi/sec.*

In the meaning *through*, the slash usually connects only two consecutive time periods (though hyphens are more popular for this use in professional publishing).

> *In 1996/97, the economy improved.*

Slashes in Web Addresses, Dates, and Telephone Numbers

The slash is also used in many web addresses, but the writer should take care to note whether the web address contains a regular forward slash or a backslash, which leans in the opposite direction.

> Forward slash: /
>
> Backslash: \

In certain formatting styles, slashes are used in dates, *10/22/99*, and, very rarely, phone numbers, *626/555-1212*. In publishing, these should only be used under specific instructions of a house style guide.

17

—

Lists

Listed items in text can appear within a paragraph as part of a sentence, outside a paragraph in outline style though grammatically part of the sentence, or as individual paragraphs headed by bullet points, dashes, letters, or numbers. Book, news, and science styles offer specific guidelines for punctuating lists, which academic writers may consider following as well.

List in Running Text

Most lists are integrated into a sentence with the individual items separated by commas or semicolons: *we'll have pepperoni, onions, and mushrooms*. However, when the writer wants to emphasize the listed items or their hierarchical or chronological relationships, the items can be preceded by a numeral or letter as follows.

🅱 Book style allows the writer to choose either letters or numbers, placed in parentheses. When lowercase letters are used, they can be left in roman type or italicized.

> *We will examine, in detail, (a) the weaponry and battle tactics of the Civil War era, (b) the economy of the South and how it affected the war, and (c) Lincoln's most notable public addresses.*

We will examine, in detail, (1) the weaponry and battle tactics of the Civil War era, (2) the economy of the South and how it affected the war, and (3) Lincoln's most notable public addresses.

Ⓑ If the text introducing the list is a complete sentence, it should be followed by a colon. If the listed items are necessary to complete the sentence, do not use a colon. Listed items in running text take commas or semicolons according to the general rules for those punctuation marks.

He has several priorities: (a) to get a job, (b) to lose weight, and (c) to improve his social life.

He wants (a) to get a job, (b) to lose weight, and (c) to improve his social life.

Ⓢ Science style uses letters only (not numerals) in parentheses.

He wants (a) to get a job, (b) to lose weight, and (c) to improve his social life.

List Set Off from Preceding Paragraph

Lists that are formatted separately from the preceding text can be grammatically part of that sentence or not.

LISTS THAT ARE PART OF THE PRECEDING SENTENCE

Ⓑ Lists that are grammatically part of a single sentence can be set in separate paragraphs, formatted like an outline, with a semicolon after each item except the last, which ends with a period. Letters, numbers, dashes, or bullets may be used.

The ideal candidate is characterized by

- *an exemplary employment history, verified by references;*
- *a clear desire to advance within the organization;*
- *superb verbal and written communication skills.*

1
2
3

✤ For simple lists that make up a complete sentence, a majority of the Punctuation Panel preferred to deviate from the style guides and use no punctuation after each bulleted item.

The ideal candidate is characterized by

- *an exemplary employment history*
- *a clear desire to advance within the organization*
- *superb verbal and written communication skills*

LISTS THAT ARE NOT PART OF THE PRECEDING SENTENCE

Lists that are not grammatically part of a preceding sentence, including lists whose items are complete sentences, may take numerals, letters, dashes, or bullet points, depending on style.

Ⓑ In book style the writer can choose numerals, letters, or bullets for items not incorporated into the previous sentence. When the introductory matter is a complete sentence, it is followed by a colon.

We will need a variety of office supplies:

- *pens*
- *paper*
- *staplers*

When the writer chooses to number the items in a vertical list, book style requires the numerals to be followed by periods (and not be placed in parentheses) and the first letter after the numbered item to begin with a capital letter.

We will need three key office supplies:

1. *Pens*

2. *Paper*

3. *Staplers*

When the listed items are complete sentences, each ends with its own terminal punctuation in book style (usually a period, though possibly a question mark or exclamation point).

Researchers reported similar outcomes:

- *Study participants all complained of headaches.*

- *Approximately 50 percent of participants became jaundiced.*

- *All negative side effects abated after treatments stopped.*

Ⓝ In news style, items in vertical lists are preceded by em dashes and are followed with a period.

The judge was most heavily influenced by the following factors:

—The defendant had shown no remorse.

—Witnesses for the defense were unable to corroborate the alibi.

—The defendant was a repeat offender.

+ A majority of the Punctuation Panel said they would not insert a space after the dash in the above examples.

Numbers and Addresses

There's no one right system for writing numbers. Style guide rules for when to spell out numbers or write them as numerals, as well as how to format dates, addresses, phone numbers, and similar information, exist mainly to ensure consistency and readability, not correctness.

Numerals vs. Spelled-Out Numbers

The chart on pages 140–42 highlights some of the major points for choosing numerals or spelled-out numbers in the major editing styles in regular text. Charts, graphs, and other visual elements are not necessarily subject to these rules, often relying more heavily on numerals to save space. Blank fields mean the style does not offer specific guidelines, and therefore the general guidelines prevail.

Dates

The following guidelines for writing dates are based on the recommendations of the major writing and editing styles and are thought to aid readability and sentence flow in running text.

WRITTEN OUT VS. FULLY NUMERIC

B N A In running text, dates are usually written out, with the month as a word, instead of all numerals with slashes or hyphens.

Preferred: *May 14, 1988*

Not recommended: *5/14/88*

Not recommended: *5-14-88*

However, in tables, info boxes, and other space-restricted graphic elements, the writer can choose a fully numeric style.

COMMAS TO SET OFF YEAR

A date written in the order month-day-year sets off the year with commas. It's a common mistake to omit the second comma.

Right: *The meeting scheduled for June 20, 2015, has been canceled.*

Wrong: *The meeting scheduled for June 20, 2015 has been canceled.*

However, the final comma is replaced by a period, a question mark, an exclamation point, or a semicolon when the date comes at the end of a sentence or before a semicolon.

The meeting was scheduled for June 20, 2015.

Can we reschedule for June 27, 2015?

Alternate dates include June 27, 2015; July 7, 2015; and July 11, 2015.

When a day of the week is included with a date, a comma should separate the day from the date. Days of the week are not abbreviated except when space restrictions require it, such as in tables.

The meeting is scheduled for Tuesday, October 20, 2015.

When writing just the month and year, do not set off the year with commas.

The October 2015 meeting has been canceled.

#

Numerals vs. Spelled-Out Numbers

Numbers less than 10: general rule	Spell out: *five visitors.*	(B) (N) (S) (A)
	Spell out numbers of one or two words in nontechnical contexts: *eight teachers, 115 students.* In technical contexts, use numerals for data and measurements: *specimens measuring 8 centimeters or larger.*	(A)
Numbers greater than 10: general rule	Spell out all numbers less than 100: *eighty-seven visitors.* Use numerals for most numbers greater than 100, except round numbers: *They counted 487 men. The building can hold two thousand people.*	(B)
	Use numerals: *11 visitors.*	(N) (S)
	Same as for numbers less than 10: *eleven visitors.*	(A)
Disregard general rule when necessary for consistency?	Yes: *hosts groups of anywhere from 8 to 256.*	(B)
	No: *sleeps eight to 12.*	(N)
	Yes: *sleeps 8 to 12.*	(A)
Millions, billions, trillions	Usually spelled out: *they served two million customers.*	(B)
	Use numeral followed by the word except in casual uses: *They served 2 million customers. I wish I had a million bucks.*	(N)
	(Optional) Combine numeral with word: *4.5 million.*	(A)
At the beginning of a sentence	Spell out any number that begins a sentence: *Nineteen seventy-six was a good year.*	(B) (S) (A)
	Spell out any number that begins a sentence except years: *Eleven visitors came. 1976 was a good year.*	(N)
Ages	Use numerals: *her son is 5.*	(N) (S)
Measurements	General rules apply in nontechnical contexts: *He is five feet, nine inches tall. It weighs eighty pounds.* But use a numeral before an abbreviation or symbol: *5 cm.*	(B)
	Use numerals and spell out units: *5 centimeters. He is 5 feet 9 inches tall.* For weights, always use numerals.	(N)
	Use numerals: *5 centimeters, 5 cm.*	(S)
	Use a numeral before any abbreviation or symbol: *5 cm., 2 ft.* Can be spelled out in running text: *five centimeters, two feet.*	(A)
Miles	Follows general rule: Spelled out for most round numbers and numbers 100 and under: *he drove eighty-five miles.*	(B)
	Use numerals as a measurement of speed or size: *4 miles per hour, a 2-mile-long mountain range.* Spell out under 10 for distances: *he drove two miles.*	(N)

Decimals	Usually numeric: *8.7.*	Ⓑ
	Use numerals: *8.7.*	Ⓝ Ⓐ
Fractions	Spell out and hyphenate simple fractions less than one: *nine-tenths.* Amounts greater than one can be numeric or spelled out: *one and two-thirds, 1²/₃.*	Ⓑ
	Spell out and hyphenate amounts less than one: *nine-tenths.* Use numerals for fractions greater than one: *2⁴/₅ leagues.*	Ⓝ
	Spell out simple fractions (without a hyphen unless it's an adjective): *nine tenths.*	Ⓢ
Percentages	Usually numeric and with the word *percent: the bond pays 5 percent.* Percent sign (%) okay in scientific contexts.	Ⓑ
	Use numerals and the word *percent: 5 percent.*	Ⓝ
	Use numerals and percent sign: *5%.*	Ⓢ
	Usually a numeral with a percent sign: *5%.* Can be spelled out in running text: *five percent.*	Ⓐ
Dates	Use numerals (cardinals only) with spelled-out month: *May 3* (not *May 3rd*).	Ⓑ Ⓝ Ⓢ Ⓐ
Years	Use numerals except at the beginning of a sentence.	Ⓑ Ⓐ
	Use numerals including at the beginning of a sentence.	Ⓝ
Decades	Can be spelled out, *the nineties,* or written numerically, *the '90s, the 1990s.*	Ⓑ
	Use numerals: *the 1990s, the '90s.*	Ⓝ Ⓢ
	Usually spelled out: *the nineties.* Can be numeric: *the '90s, the 1990s.*	Ⓐ
Centuries	Spell out: *twentieth century.*	Ⓑ Ⓐ
	Spell out only below ten: *the first century, the 21st century.*	Ⓝ
Money	Often spelled out for round numbers under 100: *fare was forty-five dollars.* Numerals and dollar or cent signs can be used where appropriate.	Ⓑ
	Use numeral with dollar sign or numeral with the word *cents: $20, 5 cents.* In casual uses, numbers can be spelled out: *a soda costs five bucks!*	Ⓝ
	Use numerals: *$20.*	Ⓢ
	Usually a numeral and a dollar sign: *$20.* Can be spelled out in running text: *twenty dollars.*	Ⓐ

#

Numerals vs. Spelled-Out Numbers, continued		
Times	Usually spelled out in running text: *We left at three o'clock. Dinner is at six thirty.*	Ⓑ
	Use numerals except for *noon* and *midnight*.	Ⓝ
	Use numerals.	Ⓢ Ⓐ
Ratios	Use numerals or spell out: *2:1, a two-to-one ratio.*	Ⓑ Ⓢ
	Use numerals with hyphens: *2-to-1, a 2-1 ratio.*	Ⓝ
Back-to-back numbers	Alternate numbers and words: *five 4-person families.* (But not when one is cardinal and the other ordinal: *the first three guests.*)	Ⓢ
Scores	Use numerals in sports scores.	Ⓝ
	Use numerals: *The team scored 2 points. The student scored 4 on a 5-point scale.*	Ⓢ
Number representing a statistic or a math function	Use numerals: *it was the usual yield times 5.*	Ⓢ

ORDER OF MONTH AND DAY

Professional publishing prefers a month-day-year format for writing dates (*October 20, 2015*).

Ⓑ Ⓐ However, a day-month-year format (*20 October 2015*) is permitted in academic style and in some cases in book style, for example, in tables.

ABBREVIATING VS. SPELLING OUT MONTHS IN DATES

Ⓑ For full dates, book style prefers a system of not abbreviating months in running text. (However, when space is limited, it allows the abbreviations *Jan.*, *Feb.*, *Mar.*, *Apr.*, *Aug.*, *Sept.*, *Oct.*, *Nov.*, and *Dec.*, but no abbreviations for *May*, *June*, or *July*.)

Ⓝ News style uses the abbreviations *Jan.*, *Feb.*, *Aug.*, *Sept.*, *Oct.*, *Nov.*, and *Dec.* as part of dates. But *March*, *April*, *May*, *June*, and *July* are not abbreviated.

Ⓑ Ⓝ Ⓢ Ⓐ When the month and year are written without the specific date, no comma separates the month from the year, and the month is not abbreviated.

> Ⓑ *January 14, 1970*
>
> Ⓝ *Jan. 14, 1970*
>
> Ⓑ Ⓝ Ⓢ Ⓐ *January 1970*

DECADES

Ⓑ Ⓝ Decades take no apostrophe before an s.

> Right: *1980s*
>
> Wrong: *1980's*

However, when numerals are dropped, an apostrophe replaces them.

> *The band was popular in the '70s and '80s.*

ORDINAL NUMBERS NOT PREFERRED

In dates, the major editing styles discourage use of ordinal numbers such as first, third, sixth, 1st, 3rd, 6th, 23rd, and so on, recommending instead regular cardinal numbers.

> Preferred: *He was born on Sept. 3.*
>
> Not recommended: *He was born on Sept. 3rd.*

Time of Day

Ⓑ In book style, times of day on the hour, half hour, and quarter hour are spelled out in running text. Numbers on the hour with *o'clock* are always spelled out.

> *He didn't wake up until eleven thirty.*
>
> *We left the hotel at four fifteen.*
>
> *That show doesn't come on till eight o'clock.*
>
> *Lunch will be served at noon.*

\#

When *a.m.* or *p.m.* is included, book style prefers lowercase but also allows the writer to use uppercase letters, with or without periods.

Recommended: *8 a.m.*

Permitted: *8 AM*

Permitted: *8 A.M.*

Book style permits adding *:00* after the hour whenever precise time is emphasized. Otherwise, it is not necessary.

Ⓝ News style prefers numerals used with lowercase *a.m.* or *p.m.* and discourages use of *:00* after times.

Right: *8 a.m.*

Wrong: *8:00 a.m.*

Wrong: *8:00 AM*

In conversational contexts, times expressed as numbers can only be spelled out. *"I can't believe we have to wait till nine for dinner."*

It's rare to use *o'clock* in news style, but when it's used, it usually follows a numeral.

4 o'clock

Street Addresses

Questions like whether to abbreviate *Street* or *Avenue* and whether to use two-letter postal abbreviations are matters of style, chosen mainly for reasons of aesthetics and consistency within a publication. The style guidelines are as follows.

BUILDING NUMBERS

Building numbers (house numbers) are usually numeric (*1 Main St.*).

Ⓑ Within running text, however, book style allows the reader to spell out terms, including numerals, when doing so aids readability and the flow of words.

ABBREVIATION OF *STREET, AVENUE,* ETC.

Street, Avenue, and *Boulevard* are abbreviated *St., Ave.,* and *Blvd.* when written with a building number. They are spelled out when the street name appears without the building number.

Ⓝ In news style, all other terms that are part of street names, such as *Circle, Lane, Road,* and *Terrace,* are spelled out in all contexts.

Ⓑ Book style, however, also uses the abbreviations *Ct., Dr., Expy., Hwy., Ln., Pkwy., Pl.,* and *Ter.*

NUMERIC STREET NAMES

Numeric street names are written as ordinals: *102nd Street, 125th Avenue.*

Ⓑ In book style, streets lower than 100 can be spelled out: *Ninety-First Street, Sixty-Sixth Avenue.*

Ⓝ In news style, streets lower than ten are spelled out: *First Street, Sixth Avenue.*

COMPASS POINTS

One-letter compass points in street addresses take a period; those with two letters don't: *123 S. Main St.* but *123 SE Main St.* But compass points are spelled out when the street name appears without a building number: *111 E. Elm St.* but *He lives on East Elm Street.* Compass points are always spelled out when they constitute the street name: *she lives on East Boulevard.*

ABBREVIATION OF STATES

Ⓑ Book style prefers two-letter postal abbreviations: *CA, NH, WA, VA, MO.*

#

Ⓝ News style uses state abbreviations (*Calif.*, *N.H.*, *Wash.*, *Va.*, *Mo.*) except for eight states that are always spelled out (*Alaska, Hawaii, Idaho, Iowa, Maine, Ohio, Texas,* and *Utah*).

A comma comes after the city but no comma should be placed between the state and the zip code.

> *122 Third St., Juneau, Alaska 99801*

PO BOX ADDRESSES

Ⓑ *PO Box* takes no periods in book style.

Ⓝ *P.O. Box* takes periods in news style.

Following are some examples of correctly written addresses.

Ⓑ *123 E. Maple Ct., Shreveport, LA 71101*

Ⓝ *123 E. Maple Court, Shreveport, La. 71101*

Ⓑ *Two Thirty-Third St., Juneau, AK 99801*

Ⓑ *2 Thirty-Third St., Juneau, AK 99801*

Ⓝ *2 33rd St. Juneau, Alaska 99801*

Ⓑ Ⓝ *888 123rd Ave.*

Ⓑ *123 Maple Ln. SE, Santa Fe, NM*

Ⓝ *123 Maple Lane SE, Santa Fe, N.M.*

Ⓑ Ⓝ *The office is on East Orange Boulevard.*

Ⓑ Ⓝ *The office is at 123 E. Orange Blvd.*

Telephone Numbers

Many publications have a house style for writing phone numbers, some opting for periods between sets of digits, *310.555.1212*, others opting for a slash and a hyphen, *310/555-1212*. Placing the area code in parentheses is a very popular style: *(310) 555-1212*.

However, book and news style use hyphens, as explained on the next page. Writers and editors are welcome to adopt their own house style, keeping in mind that consistency is critical.

B **N** Book and news styles recommend using hyphens to separate the elements of a phone number. Book style allows a 1 before a toll-free number, news style does not. Book style also allows the area code, with or without a 1, to appear in parentheses.

> **B** **N** *310-555-0123*

> **B** **N** *800-555-1212*

> **B** *1-800-555-1212*

> **B** *(1-800) 555-1212*

> **B** **N** *011-44-20-2222-5555*

E-mail Addresses and URLs

Writing about e-mail and URLs poses several challenges for writers.

HYPHENATION OF *E-MAIL*

B **A** Book and academic styles prefer a hyphen in the term *e-mail*.

N In news style, *email* takes no hyphen.

Individual publications, however, often adopt their own styles on this matter.

LINE BREAKS IN E-MAIL ADDRESSES

In e-mail addresses, to prevent confusion, avoid letting a line of text break in the middle of the address. If it must, do not use a hyphen or other punctuation mark to indicate the line break.

HOW TO WRITE URLS

For URLs, it's up to the writer or editor to decide whether to include *http://*, *https://*, or similar fragments, or even *www*. Whatever the chosen style, it should be used consistently throughout the publication.

\#

LINE BREAKS IN URLS

B **N** **A** Book, news, and academic styles all specify that when a line of text breaks in the middle of a URL, no hyphen should be inserted.

For more information about the study, visit www.nutritionstudy
.glucoselevelsinsmallmammals.edu/februrary4results.

PUNCTUATION AFTER URLS

B **N** **A** In book, news, and academic styles, terminal punctuation, as the period in the above example, can immediately follow a URL.

A In academic style, a period cannot immediately follow a URL. Writers in academic style should recast the sentence so that the URL does not come at the end or place it in parentheses.

PART II

Punctuation
A to Z

The terms in this list represent preferred use primarily in three styles: book style **B**, news style **N**, and, whenever possible, science style **S**, based on the major style guides and especially their designated dictionaries (*Webster's New World College Dictionary* for news style, *Merriam-Webster's Collegiate* for book and science style). Because authorities in academic style do not designate any one dictionary as arbiter of punctuation matters, academic style **A** is often excluded from this section. Academic writers looking for information not included here should check their chosen dictionaries to see if a term is listed. If it is not, they should consider following book style **B**.

In cases where rules are unclear, Punctuation Panel rulings are sometimes included, marked with **✚**.

Entries without symbols indicate that the rule applied is not based on editing style but is either a universally observed punctuation rule or is a proper name or other invariable form.

Writers not bound to a specific style should consider news style for business and casual communications such as websites and blogs, book style for more in-depth or literary writing, and science style for scientific contexts.

Preferred forms in each style are not always the writer's only option. If a preferred form listed here appears awkward or difficult to read and the dictionary allows another, the writer can choose the alternate style, keeping in mind that consistency is important.

Note: Numeric terms like *3-D* and *9/11* are alphabetized as if spelled out, with *3-D* listed under *T*, *9/11* listed under *N*, and so on. Grouped entries are listed in the order of book **B**, news **N**, science **S**, and academic style **A**.

AA Abbrev. for *Alcoholics Anonymous*.		Ⓑ Ⓝ Ⓢ Ⓐ
AAA Abbrev. for *American Automobile Association*.		Ⓑ Ⓝ Ⓢ Ⓐ
ABCs		Ⓑ Ⓝ
A-bomb Abbrev. for *atom bomb*.		Ⓑ Ⓝ Ⓢ
AC, A/C, a/c	Use capital letters and no periods or slash as abbreviation for *air-conditioning*, *alternating current*, *ante Christum* (before Christ), *area code*, or *athletic club*.	Ⓑ Ⓢ
	News style prefers capital letters and no slash or periods in the abbreviation for *air conditioning* or *alternating current*, but also allows it to be written with a slash. *Alternating current* can also be written lowercase with a slash.	Ⓝ
AC/DC	Abbrev. for *alternating current/direct current* or term meaning bisexual.	Ⓑ Ⓝ Ⓢ
	References to the rock band should use a slash and no periods.	Ⓝ
A.C.E., ACE The *American Cinema Editors* use periods in *A.C.E.* after names in film credits, which contradicts editing style rules that call for no periods. Writers should choose whichever form is most appropriate for the context. In running text, set off with commas: *John Doe, ACE, was among the credited editors.*		
-ache	Do not hyphenate as part of a compound: *toothache*, *stomachache*, *headache*.	Ⓑ
	The major dictionaries used in publishing list *ache* as a word but not as a suffix. So for compounds not found in the dictionary, the writer can use either open or hyphenated forms: *an elbow ache*, *an elbow-ache*. (See also "Compound Nouns," page 108.)	Ⓑ Ⓝ Ⓢ Ⓐ
Achilles' heel		Ⓑ Ⓝ Ⓢ
Achilles tendon		Ⓑ Ⓝ Ⓢ
AD		Ⓑ Ⓢ Ⓐ
A.D.		Ⓝ
	Scientific style's potentially contradictory instructions state that Latin abbreviations such as *e.g.* and *i.e.* take periods but that capitalized abbreviations such as *IQ* do not. Thus, in scientific style, *BC* takes no periods but *AD*, which unlike *BC* derives from the Latin, may or may not take periods according to one's interpretation of the rules. The writer in science style may opt to make these consistent by using no periods in either *BC* or *AD*.	Ⓢ
ad-lib, **ad lib** In the sense meaning "to improvise," hyphenate in all forms. The rarer adverb form representing the Latin term for "in accordance with someone's wishes" takes no hyphen.		Ⓑ Ⓝ Ⓢ

adverbs, hyphenation of Adverbs ending in *ly* are not hyphenated as part of compound modifiers: *a happily married couple*. Adverbs not ending in *ly* may or may not be hyphenated, according to style rules and, to an extent, the writer's discretion: *a well-loved story*. (See chapter 11 for more on hyphenating adverbs. See Appendix B for more on adverbs.)

Term	Styles
A-frame	Ⓑ Ⓝ Ⓢ
African American (n., adj.) *A famous African American. An African American community.*	Ⓑ Ⓢ
African-American (n., adj.) *A famous African-American. An African-American community.*	Ⓝ
afterbirth (n.), **after birth** (adv.)	Ⓑ Ⓝ Ⓢ
aftercare	Ⓑ Ⓝ Ⓢ
aftereffect	Ⓑ Ⓝ Ⓢ
afterglow	Ⓑ Ⓝ Ⓢ
after-hours (adj.), **after hours** (adv.)	Ⓑ Ⓝ Ⓢ
afterlife	Ⓑ Ⓝ Ⓢ
after-party (n.)	Ⓑ Ⓝ Ⓢ
aftershave	Ⓑ Ⓢ
after-shave	Ⓝ
aftershock	Ⓑ Ⓝ Ⓢ
aftertaste	Ⓑ Ⓝ Ⓢ
after-tax, after tax (adj.) Hyphenate as an adjective before a noun. Hyphenate after a noun only if hyphen improves readability.	Ⓑ
after-tax Hyphenate as an adjective: *his after-tax earnings.*	Ⓝ Ⓢ
age-group	Ⓑ Ⓢ
age group	Ⓝ
age-old, age old (adj.) Hyphenate as an adjective before a noun. Hyphenate after a noun only if hyphen improves readability.	Ⓑ
age-old (adj.) Hyphenate as an adjective.	Ⓝ Ⓢ
AIDS Acronym for *acquired immunodeficiency syndrome.*	Ⓑ Ⓝ Ⓢ
ain't	Ⓑ Ⓝ Ⓢ Ⓐ
air bag	Ⓑ Ⓝ Ⓢ
airborne	Ⓑ Ⓝ Ⓢ
air-condition (v.), **air-conditioned** (v., adj.) *We should air-condition this room. The meeting was held in an air-conditioned room.*	Ⓑ Ⓝ Ⓢ
air conditioner	Ⓑ Ⓝ Ⓢ
air-conditioning (n.) *The car has air-conditioning.*	Ⓑ Ⓢ
air conditioning (n.) *The car has air conditioning.*	Ⓝ

Term	Styles
airfare	B N S
airhead, **airheaded**	B N S
air strike	B S
airstrike	N
airtight	B N S
a.k.a. Abbrev. of *also known as.*	B
aka	N S
al Join the Arabic definite article to the following word with a hyphen: *al-Qaida, al-Shabab.*	B N
à la carte	B S
a la carte	N
à la mode	B S
a la mode	N
A-line	B N S
A-list	B N S
Al-Jazeera	
all-around (adj.), **all around** (adv.) *He was an all-around good guy. He ordered drinks all around.*	B S
all-around (adj., adv.) *He was an all-around good guy. He ordered drinks all-around.*	N
all get-out	B N S
All Hallows' Eve	B S
all or nothing (n.) *He could have all or nothing.* As an adjective, standard rules for hyphenating compound modifiers apply. In general, hyphenate before a noun: *an all-or-nothing proposition.*	B N S A
all-out (adj.), **all out** (adv.)	B N S
allover (adj.), **all over** (adv.)	B N S
all-powerful	B N S
all-purpose	B N S
all right (adj., adv.) In publishing, this two-word term is normally preferred over *alright.*	B N S
All Saints' Day	B N S
all-star (n., adj.)	B N S
all time (n.), **all-time** (adj.)	B N S
alma mater	B N S
al-Qaeda, **al-Qaida** Book style prefers the spelling *al-Qaeda* but allows *al-Qaida.* In news style spell it *al-Qaida.*	B N

Term	Description	Styles
already	Hyphenate as part of a compound adjective before a noun: *an already-forgotten incident*.	Ⓑ Ⓝ Ⓢ Ⓐ
	Not hyphenated after a noun: *the incident is already forgotten*.	Ⓑ Ⓝ Ⓢ Ⓐ
also, commas with The major styles do not give express instructions on whether commas should set off *also*. The Punctuation Panel split on whether to use commas in *He wrote "Love Story," also./He wrote "Love Story" also*.		✚
also-ran (n.)		Ⓑ Ⓝ Ⓢ
Alzheimer's disease, Alzheimer's		Ⓑ Ⓝ Ⓢ
a.m. Abbrev. for *ante meridiem*, used to indicate morning. All major styles prefer lowercase and periods, though book publishing sometimes uses small capitals, either with or without periods.		Ⓑ Ⓝ Ⓢ Ⓐ
AM Abbrev. for radio broadcasting system known as *amplitude modulation*.		Ⓑ Ⓝ
American Indian		Ⓑ Ⓝ Ⓢ
amuse-bouche		Ⓑ Ⓝ Ⓢ
and, commas with	The question of whether a comma should precede the coordinating conjunction *and* depends on the word's function in the sentence and also on the editing style being followed. (For more, see chapter 2.)	
	When *and* joins two complete clauses, a comma customarily precedes it. The writer can omit the comma if the clauses are short and closely related.	Ⓑ Ⓝ Ⓢ Ⓐ
	In series, such as *red, white, and blue*, a comma (known as the serial or Oxford comma) precedes *and*.	Ⓑ Ⓢ Ⓐ
	In series, such as *red, white and blue*, no comma precedes *and*.	Ⓝ
and so forth, **and the like** *And so forth, and the like,* and similar terms are usually set off with commas (preceded with a comma and, unless at the end of a sentence, followed by a comma): *bedding, linens, and the like, can be purchased upstairs.*		Ⓑ
anti-	Standard rules for hyphenating prefixes apply. In general, not hyphenated, except before a capital letter, *anti-American*, before the letter *i*, *anti-inflation*, with double prefixes, *anti-antihistamine*, or before hyphenated compounds, *anti-money-making*.	Ⓑ Ⓝ Ⓢ Ⓐ
	In news style, also hyphenate *anti-abortion, anti-aircraft, anti-bias, anti-labor, anti-social*, and *anti-war*.	Ⓝ
antiabortion		Ⓑ Ⓢ Ⓐ
anti-abortion		Ⓝ
antiaircraft		Ⓑ Ⓢ Ⓐ
anti-aircraft		Ⓝ

antibias	Ⓑ Ⓢ Ⓐ
anti-bias	Ⓝ
antibiotic	Ⓑ Ⓝ Ⓢ Ⓐ
Antichrist, **anti-Christ** The *Antichrist* is a Biblical figure. The term *anti-Christ* means opposed to Christ.	Ⓑ Ⓝ Ⓢ Ⓐ
anticlimax	Ⓑ Ⓝ Ⓢ Ⓐ
antidepressant	Ⓑ Ⓝ Ⓢ Ⓐ
antifreeze	Ⓑ Ⓝ Ⓢ Ⓐ
antigen	Ⓑ Ⓝ Ⓢ Ⓐ
antihistamine	Ⓑ Ⓝ Ⓢ Ⓐ
anti-inflation	Ⓑ Ⓝ Ⓢ Ⓐ
antilock	Ⓑ Ⓢ Ⓐ
anti-lock	Ⓝ
antimatter	Ⓑ Ⓝ Ⓢ Ⓐ
antioxidant	Ⓑ Ⓝ Ⓢ Ⓐ
antipasto	Ⓑ Ⓝ Ⓢ Ⓐ
antiperspirant	Ⓑ Ⓝ Ⓢ Ⓐ
antipsychotic	Ⓑ Ⓝ Ⓢ Ⓐ
antiseptic	Ⓑ Ⓝ Ⓢ Ⓐ
antisocial	Ⓑ Ⓢ Ⓐ
anti-social	Ⓝ
antitrust	Ⓑ Ⓝ Ⓢ Ⓐ
anyone else's Possessive. Never *anyone's else* or *anyone elses'*.	Ⓑ Ⓝ Ⓢ Ⓐ
A-OK	Ⓑ Ⓝ Ⓢ
A&P Grocery company name, previously abbrev. of *The Great Atlantic & Pacific Tea Company*.	
appearance' sake	Ⓝ
appearance's sake	Ⓑ
appositive Any word or phrase that restates another is set off with commas: *the executive, a great leader, will speak.* (For more, see chapter 2.)	
April Fools' Day	Ⓝ Ⓑ Ⓢ Ⓐ
area, hyphenation of No hyphen in compound nouns: *they live in the Chicago area.* Usually hyphenated as part of a compound adjective: *two D.C.–area couples.*	Ⓑ Ⓝ Ⓢ Ⓐ
arm-in-arm (adj.) *An arm-in-arm stroll.*	Ⓝ Ⓑ Ⓢ Ⓐ
arm in arm (adv.) *They walked arm in arm.*	✚

article titles	Place in quotation marks titles of articles that appear in periodicals or as individual pages within larger websites: *"Ten Ways to Save for College."*	Ⓑ Ⓝ Ⓐ
	Science style does not have guidelines for formatting titles in running text because such citations are customarily included in a reference list at the end of a document and indicated in the text with only the name of the author and the date of the work: *Dyslexia exists in a significant portion of the population (Doe, 2004).*	Ⓢ
As Plural form of the capital letter, including letter grades.		Ⓑ
A's Plural form of the capital letter, including letter grades.		Ⓝ Ⓐ
a's Plural form of the lowercase letter.		Ⓑ Ⓝ Ⓢ Ⓐ
ASAP		Ⓑ Ⓝ Ⓢ Ⓐ
Asian American (n., adj.) Do not hyphenate noun or adjective forms: *A famous Asian American. An Asian American community.*		Ⓑ Ⓢ
Asian-American (n., adj.) Hyphenate noun and adjective forms: *A famous Asian-American. An Asian-American community.*		Ⓝ
as-is (adj.), **as is** (adv.)		Ⓑ Ⓝ Ⓢ Ⓐ
ASL Abbrev. for *American Sign Language.*		Ⓑ
Asperger's syndrome, Asperger's		Ⓑ Ⓝ Ⓢ
asshole		Ⓑ Ⓝ Ⓢ
as well, commas with Punctuation Panel members split on whether *as well* should be set off with commas: *He spoke to the vice president as well./ He spoke to the vice president, as well.* In general, the shorter and clearer the sentence, the less likely commas are needed to set off *as well.*		✚
as well as, commas with Punctuation Panel members split on whether *as well as* should be set off with commas. A majority preferred no comma in shorter sentences where clarity was not at stake: *He spoke to the vice president as well as the president.* Some indicated, however, that commas can be used when extra emphasis conveyed by a pause is desired: *He spoke to the vice president, as well as the president.*		✚
AT&T Company name, previously abbrev. of *American Telephone & Telegraph.*		
athlete's foot		Ⓑ Ⓝ Ⓢ
at-large, at large (adj., adv.) Hyphenate as adjective before a noun or anytime it means representing an entire geographic area and not just a portion of it: *She will serve as mayor at-large. They held an at-large election.* Do not hyphenate as an adverb meaning "unrestrained": *The convict is still at large. He is a critic at large.*		Ⓑ Ⓝ Ⓢ
autoworker		Ⓑ Ⓝ Ⓢ
autumn *See* seasons		

averse, hyphenation of	Before a noun, standard rules of hyphenation apply. Hyphenate whenever hyphen improves readability: *a risk-averse manager.*	**B** **N** **S** **A**
	A majority of the Punctuation Panel preferred hyphenating compound adjectives with *averse* after the noun. *He is risk-averse.* (majority preference) *She seems people-averse.* (unanimous preference)	✚
awards, hyphenation of	The proper names of awards follow the basic rules of hyphenation: *An Oscar-winning actor. An Emmy-winning episode.*	**B** **N** **A**
	When the award's proper name contains two or more words, do not place a hyphen within the proper noun, but use an en dash to attach it to any other parts of the compound: *The Grammy Award–winning singer. The Tony Award–nominated performer.*	**B**
	When the award's proper name contains two or more words, do not place a hyphen within the proper noun, but hyphenate any other parts of the compound: *The Grammy Award-winning singer. The Tony Award-nominated performer.*	**N** **A**
award winner (n.), **award-winning** (adj.)		**B** **N** **S**
awestruck		**B** **S**
awe-struck		**N**
AWOL Acronym for *absent without leave.*		**B** **N** **S** **A**
BA, **BS** Abbrev. for *bachelor of arts* and *bachelor of science: Carrie Altman, BA, gave a presentation.*		**B** **S** **A**
B.A., **B.S.** Abbrev. for *bachelor of arts* and *bachelor of science: this is Carrie Altman, B.A.*		**N**
baby's breath		**B** **N** **S**
babysit, babysat, babysitting, babysitter		**B** **S**
baby-sit, baby-sat, baby-sitting, baby sitter		**N**
bachelor's degree, bachelor's See also B.A.		**N**
back-to-back (adj.) *We have back-to-back meetings. They sat on the beach back-to-back.*		**B** **N** **S**
back-to-back (adv.) *We have back-to-back meetings.*		**B** **S**
backup (n.), **back up** (v.)		**B** **N** **S**
backup (adj.)		✚
Baha'i		**B** **N** **S**
ballpark		**B** **N** **S**

ballplayer		Ⓑ	Ⓝ	Ⓢ	
baker's dozen		Ⓑ	Ⓝ	Ⓢ	
baker's yeast		Ⓑ	Ⓝ	Ⓢ	
Band-Aid Trade name for adhesive bandage used in both the literal and metaphorical senses.		Ⓑ	Ⓝ	Ⓢ	
B and B, **B and Bs,** **B and B's**		Ⓑ		Ⓢ	
	Punctuation Panel book style experts split on use of apostrophe in the plural: *B and Bs. B and B's.*	✚			
B&B, B&Bs Use this abbreviation only after a first reference to *bed-and-breakfast.*			Ⓝ		
barely there (adj., adv.) *A barely there bikini.*		Ⓑ	Ⓝ	Ⓢ	Ⓐ
Barneys New York department store.					
Batman					
BB, BB gun		Ⓑ	Ⓝ	Ⓢ	
BBs (plural)		Ⓑ		Ⓢ	
BB's (plural)			Ⓝ		
BC		Ⓑ		Ⓢ	Ⓐ
B.C.			Ⓝ		
	Scientific style's potentially conflicting instructions state that Latin abbreviations such as *e.g.* and *i.e.* take periods but that capitalized abbreviations such as IQ do not. Thus, in scientific style, BC takes no periods but AD, which unlike BC derives from the Latin, may or may not take periods according to one's interpretation of the rules. The writer may opt to make these consistent by using no periods in either BC or AD.			Ⓢ	
beachgoer		Ⓑ		Ⓢ	
beach goer			Ⓝ		
bed-and-breakfast, bed-and-breakfasts (pl.)		Ⓑ	Ⓝ	Ⓢ	
best seller (n.), **best-selling** (adj.)		Ⓑ			Ⓐ
best-seller (n.), **best-selling** (adj.)			Ⓝ		
betting odds News style uses hyphens in betting odds: *they're giving him 50-1 odds in Vegas.*			Ⓝ		
between . . . and . . . , dashes in Though a dash can sometimes show a range, *Patients 18–44,* when the word *between* introduces the numbers, the word *and,* and not a dash or hyphen, must go between them: *patients between 18 and 44.*					
biannual		Ⓑ	Ⓝ	Ⓢ	
biennial		Ⓑ	Ⓝ	Ⓢ	

bifocal	Ⓑ Ⓝ Ⓢ
bilateral	Ⓑ Ⓝ Ⓢ
bilingual	Ⓑ Ⓝ Ⓢ
bimonthly	Ⓑ Ⓝ Ⓢ
biofuel	Ⓑ Ⓝ Ⓢ
bioterrorism	Ⓑ Ⓝ Ⓢ
bird's-eye view	Ⓑ Ⓝ Ⓢ
bird-watch, bird-watching, bird-watcher	Ⓑ Ⓢ
News style experts on the Punctuation Panel preferred no hyphen in *bird watching* and *bird watcher*.	✚
biweekly	Ⓑ Ⓝ Ⓢ
black and white (n.), **black-and-white** (adj.) *The movie was shown in black and white. A black-and-white situation.*	Ⓑ Ⓝ Ⓢ
black-and-white (n.) Police car: *a black-and-white was parked out front.*	Ⓑ
black and white (n.) Police car: *a black and white was parked out front.*	Ⓝ
B'nai B'rith	
bobblehead	Ⓑ Ⓝ Ⓢ
bona fide (adj.) *A bona fide expert.*	Ⓑ Ⓝ Ⓢ
bonbon	Ⓑ Ⓝ Ⓢ
boo-boo, **boo-boos**	Ⓑ Ⓝ Ⓢ
-borne Hyphenate in all compounds that don't appear in the dictionary: *A food-borne illness. A truck-borne load.*	Ⓑ Ⓝ
Bosnia-Herzegovina	Ⓝ
box office (n.) *The movie did well at the box office.*	Ⓑ Ⓝ Ⓢ Ⓐ
box-office (adj.) *The box-office sales were disappointing.*	Ⓝ
brand-new	Ⓑ Ⓝ Ⓢ
breakdown (n.), **break down** (v.)	Ⓑ Ⓝ Ⓢ
breakdown (adj.)	✚
break-in (n., adj.), **break in** (v.)	Ⓑ Ⓝ Ⓢ
breakout (n.), **break out** (v.)	Ⓑ Ⓝ Ⓢ
breakup (n.), **break up** (v.)	Ⓑ
bright plus color as adjective Punctuation Panel book style experts split on whether to hyphenate compounds with *bright* before a noun: *A bright blue sky. A bright-blue sky.*	✚

Bs Plural form of capital letter.	(B)
B's The plural form of the capital letter, including when discussing student grades, takes an apostrophe in news and academic styles.	(N) (A)
b's Plural form of the lowercase letter.	(B) (N) (S) (A)
BS, **bs** Abbrevs. for *bullshit*.	(B) (N) (S)
bull's-eye, **bull's-eyes** (pl.)	(B) (N) (S)
but, commas with When *but* joins two complete clauses, a comma customarily precedes it. However, the writer can omit the comma if the clauses are short and closely related.	(B) (N) (S) (A)
bypass (n., v.)	(B) (N) (S)
by-product	(B) (S)
byproduct	(N)
Caesars Palace	
Campbell's Soup Trade name. In some contexts the company uses the nonpossessive *Campbell* as an adjective, for example, *the Campbell brands*.	
cap-and-trade (adj.), **cap and trade** (v.)	(B) (N) (S) (A)
cap and trade (n.) A majority of the Punctuation Panel would not hyphenate the noun form: *the trend seems to be toward cap and trade*.	+
capitals, forming plurals in all-capital contexts of A sign announcing *DVDs for Sale* does not take an apostrophe to form the plural. But this practice can create confusion in all-capital contexts, such as storefront signs. *DVDS FOR SALE* without an apostrophe could be construed as something pronounced dee-vee-dee-ess. For this reason, in the rare cases in which the plural of a letter or multiple letters appears in an all-capital context, an apostrophe to form the plural is appropriate.	(B) (N) (S)
carat, hyphenation of The Punctuation Panel unanimously preferred a hyphen in a *4-carat diamond*.	+
cardholder, **credit card holder** One word, no hyphen when standing alone. Two words, no hyphen in the common term *credit card holder*.	(B) (N) (S)
carefree	(B) (N) (S)
caregiver, **caregiving**	(B) (N) (S)
carry-on (n.) Meaning luggage. *Please stow your carry-on.*	(B) (S)
	Punctuation Panel news style experts split on whether to hyphenate the noun: *Please stow your carry on. Please stow your carry-on.*	+
carry on (v.) *He will carry on this bag. Why must these kids always carry on?*	(B) (N) (S)
carry-on (adj.) *Place carry-on bags below the seat in front of you.*	(B) (N) (S)
carryout (n.), **carry out** (v.)	(B) (N) (S)

Term	Description	Styles
carryover (n.)		(B) (S)
carry-over (n.)		(N)
carry over (v.)		(B) (N) (S)
case in point		(B) (N) (S)
Catch-22, catch-22	Hyphenate and lowercase in all senses except the title of the Joseph Heller book: *we found ourselves in a real catch-22*. Hyphenate and capitalize first letter of book title.	(B) (S)
	Hyphenate and capitalize first letter in all senses: *we found ourselves in a real Catch-22*.	(N)
cat-o'-nine-tails		(B) (N) (S)
cat's-paw Use apostrophe and hyphen for noun form meaning a person used by another as a tool. The appendage of a feline is a *cat's paw*.		(B) (N) (S)
'cause	Contracted form of because.	
	Takes an apostrophe in book and science styles: *he left home 'cause he wanted to see the world*.	(B) (S)
	Punctuation Panel was unanimous in the view that, in the meaning *because*, *'cause* written with an apostrophe is preferable to *cause* without an apostrophe or to the spelling *cuz*.	+
CD, CDs (pl.)		(B) (N) (S)
CD-ROM		(N)
CDT Abbrev. for *Central Daylight Time*.		(B) (N) (S) (A)
cease-fire (n., adj.), **cease fire** (v.) *They called for a cease-fire. They demand that you cease fire.*		(B) (N) (S)
cell phone		(B)
cellphone		(N) (S)
CEO		(B) (N) (S) (A)
charge-off (n.) *They considered it a charge-off.*		(B) (S) +
charge off (n.) *They considered it a charge off.*		(N)
charge off (v.) *The bank charged off the delinquent debt so they could get a tax exemption.*		(B) (N) (S) (A) +
checkout (n.), **check out** (v.)		(B) (N) (S)
checkout (adj.)		+
checkup (n.), **check up** (v.)		(B) (N) (S)
checkup (adj.)		+
cherry picker (n.), **cherry-pick** (v.), **cherry-picking** (n., v., adj.)		(B) (N) (S)

child care (n.) *They put their son in child care.*	Ⓑ Ⓝ Ⓢ Ⓐ
child-care (adj.) *They put their son in a child-care center.*	Ⓑ Ⓢ
child care (adj.) *They put their son in a child care center.*	Ⓝ Ⓐ
child rearing (n.) *Child rearing took up much of her life.*	Ⓑ ✚
child-rearing (adj.) *Her child-rearing years are over.*	Ⓑ
children's In the plural possessive, the apostrophe always comes before the *s*. Thus, *children's program* is the correct form and *childrens' program* is an error. Note how that differs from *kids' program*, because *kid*, unlike *child*, forms its plural by adding an *s*.	
Chili's The chain restaurant has an apostrophe in its name. To make the plural or the singular or plural possessive, the Punctuation Panel unanimously favored using the singular name with no modifications.	✚
chip-maker	Ⓝ
chip maker	✚
churchgoer	Ⓑ Ⓝ Ⓢ
Church of Jesus Christ of Latter-day Saints	
CIA	Ⓑ Ⓝ Ⓢ Ⓐ
citywide	Ⓑ Ⓝ Ⓢ
click-through (n., v.)	Ⓝ ✚
CliffsNotes	
cloak-and-dagger	Ⓑ Ⓝ Ⓢ
clockwise	Ⓑ Ⓝ Ⓢ
closed-captioned (adj.)	Ⓑ Ⓝ Ⓢ
closed-captioning	Ⓑ Ⓢ
closed circuit (n.), **closed-circuit** (adj.) *The camera system operates on a closed circuit. The actions were captured on closed-circuit television.*	Ⓑ Ⓝ Ⓢ
close-knit	Ⓑ Ⓝ Ⓢ
close-up (n., adj., adv.) The photography/film term is hyphenated in all forms: *The director uses a lot of close-ups. The director uses a lot of close-up shots. The director shot the scene close-up.*	Ⓑ Ⓝ Ⓢ
close up (v.) The verb *close up* means to seal something: *the surgeon must close up the wound.*	Ⓑ Ⓝ Ⓢ
cm Abbrev. for *centimeter.*	Ⓢ
co., cos. (pl.) Abbrev. for *company* or *companies.* Note the plural puts the period after the *s*.	Ⓑ Ⓝ Ⓢ Ⓐ

co-	Do not hyphenate a temporary compound with *co-* unless it comes before a proper noun, it comes before a word that begins with *o*, or the hyphen aids readability: *coauthor, coworker, co-opt*.	Ⓑ Ⓢ Ⓐ
	Hyphenate terms not listed in the dictionary when *co-* indicates occupation or position: *co-author, co-worker, co-chairman, co-defendant*. Otherwise no hyphen: *coequal, coeducational*.	Ⓝ
coauthor		Ⓑ Ⓢ Ⓐ
co-author		Ⓝ
Coca-Cola		
co-chairman		Ⓝ ✚
c.o.d. Abbrev. of *cash on demand*.		Ⓝ
co-defendant		Ⓝ ✚
coed, coeducational		Ⓑ Ⓝ Ⓢ Ⓐ
coequal		Ⓑ Ⓝ Ⓢ Ⓐ
Coeur d'Alene Idaho city name.		
coexist, coexistence		Ⓑ Ⓝ Ⓢ Ⓐ
coffeemaker		Ⓑ Ⓢ
coffee maker		Ⓝ
cohost		Ⓑ Ⓢ Ⓐ
co-host		Ⓝ
collector's item		Ⓑ Ⓢ
collectors' item		Ⓝ
color-blind		Ⓑ Ⓢ
colorblind		Ⓝ
color blindness		Ⓑ Ⓝ Ⓢ
commander in chief No hyphens. All lowercase unless used as a title immediately before a name: *Commander in Chief John Arthur*.		Ⓑ Ⓝ Ⓢ
comparatives, hyphenation of	Comparatives are forms of adjectives that usually end in *er: slower, faster, longer*.	
	Science style specifies that comparatives are not hyphenated as part of compound modifiers: *a slower burning fuel*.	Ⓢ
	In other styles, standard rules for hyphenating compound modifiers apply. In general, hyphenate whenever doing so aids clarity or readability.	Ⓑ Ⓝ Ⓐ

C

compound adjective A compound adjective is any term of two or more words, usually connected with hyphens, used to modify a noun: *A good-looking man. An ill-intentioned woman. A well-known fact.* Permanent compound adjectives are listed in dictionaries, which show whether or not the compound is hyphenated. Compound adjectives not listed in the dictionary, sometimes called temporary compounds, are hyphenated according to the guidelines in chapter 11. In general, compound adjectives before a noun or after a form of *be* are usually hyphenated unless they contain an *ly* adverb: *A snow-covered roof. A nicely dressed man. The man is ill-intentioned.* (For more information and exceptions, see chapter 11.)

compound adverb A compound adverb is any term of two or more words, often connected with hyphens, that are used to modify a verb, adjective, or adverb. Some compounds are listed in dictionaries, which indicate whether they contain a hyphen. For compound adverbs not listed in the dictionary, the major styles don't offer standardized rules on whether to hyphenate. In general, writers can use their own judgment to determine whether a hyphen in a compound adverb aids readability. (But see also Punctuation Panel rulings on page 107.)

compound modifier Any compound adjective or adverb.

confectioners' sugar	Ⓑ Ⓝ Ⓢ Ⓐ
conscience' sake	Ⓝ
conscience's sake	Ⓑ
convenience' sake	Ⓝ
convenience's sake	Ⓑ
cookie cutter (n.), **cookie-cutter** (adj.)	Ⓑ Ⓝ Ⓢ
co-op	Ⓑ Ⓝ Ⓢ
cooperate	Ⓑ Ⓝ Ⓢ Ⓐ
co-opt	Ⓑ Ⓝ Ⓢ
coordinate	Ⓑ Ⓝ Ⓢ

coordinate adjective Coordinate adjectives modify a noun independently and are separated by commas: *he wants to meet a kind, gentle, sweet girl.* Noncoordinate adjectives, which have different relationships to the noun, often take no commas between them. For example, in *He wore bright red wingtip shoes, wingtip* is more integral to the noun than the other adjectives and *bright* modifies not the noun *shoes* but the adjective that immediately follows it, *red.* So the adjectives in *bright red wingtip shoes* are not coordinate and not separated by commas. (For more, see "Exception: Noncoordinate Adjectives Before a Noun," page 26.)

coordinating conjunction The primary coordinating conjunctions are *and, but,* and *or,* though *for, nor, yet,* and *so* are often included in the category. Coordinating conjunctions link units of equal status in a sentence: *Marcy has cats and dogs. Joe wants to go skiing, and Beth wants to go to the beach.* In a list of three or more items, a comma is placed before a coordinating conjunction in book, science, and academic styles: *she has cats, dogs, and birds.* This is called the serial comma. In news style, the serial comma is not used.

A comma often precedes a coordinating conjunction that joins two independent clauses: *I'm going to make liver for dinner, and I don't want to hear any complaints.* Though short, closely related clauses connected with a coordinating conjunction can often omit the comma at the writer's or editor's discretion: *I'm making liver and I don't want any complaints.* (For more, see chapter 2.)

co-owner	Ⓑ Ⓝ Ⓢ Ⓐ
copilot	Ⓑ Ⓢ Ⓐ
co-pilot	Ⓝ
copter Short for *helicopter*.	Ⓑ Ⓝ Ⓢ
copular verbs, hyphenation of compound modifiers after *See* linking verbs	
copyedit (v.)	Ⓑ Ⓢ
copy-edit (v.)	Ⓝ
copy editor	Ⓑ Ⓝ Ⓢ
cosigner	Ⓑ Ⓢ Ⓐ
co-signer	Ⓝ
cosponsor	Ⓑ Ⓢ Ⓐ
co-sponsor	Ⓝ
costar	Ⓑ Ⓢ Ⓐ
co-star	Ⓝ
cost of living (n.), **cost-of-living** (adj.) *The cost of living in New York is too high. The employees got a cost-of-living raise.*	Ⓑ Ⓝ Ⓢ
could've Contraction of *could have*. This should never be written *could of*.	
countdown (n.), **count down** (v.)	Ⓑ Ⓝ Ⓢ
countdown (adj.)	✛
counter- Standard rules for hyphenating prefixes apply. When forming compounds not found in the dictionary, do not hyphenate except before a proper noun or to avoid awkward compounds.	Ⓑ Ⓝ Ⓢ Ⓐ
counterclockwise	Ⓑ Ⓝ Ⓢ
coup d'état	Ⓑ Ⓝ Ⓢ Ⓐ
couples, couple's, couples' Style guides and dictionaries leave unclear whether popular terms like *couple's massage* and *couples' retreat* are to be construed as plural possessive, singular possessive, or adjectival. Punctuation Panel members, who recommend considering these terms on a case-by-case basis, preferred the singular possessive in *They got a couple's massage* and the plural possessive in *They went on a couples' retreat.*	✛
court-martial, court-martialed, courts-martial Hyphenate in all contexts.	Ⓑ Ⓝ Ⓢ
cover-up (n.), **cover up** (v.) Hyphenate as noun: *prosecutors alleged a cover-up.* No hyphen as verb: *they tried to cover up the scandal.*	Ⓑ Ⓝ Ⓢ
coworker	Ⓑ Ⓢ Ⓐ
co-worker	Ⓝ
crime-fighter	Ⓝ
crime fighter	✛

crime fighting	Ⓑ ✚
crisscross	Ⓑ Ⓝ Ⓢ
Crock-Pot	
Crohn's disease	
cross-check (n., v., adj.)	Ⓑ Ⓢ
crosscheck (n., v., adj.)	Ⓝ
crosscut	Ⓑ Ⓝ Ⓢ
cross-examination (n.), **cross-examine** (v.)	Ⓑ Ⓝ Ⓢ
crossover (n., adj.), **cross over** (v.) *She drives a crossover. She drives a crossover vehicle. They will cross over to the other side.*	Ⓑ Ⓝ Ⓢ
cross-reference (n., v.)	Ⓑ Ⓝ Ⓢ
cross section (n.)	Ⓑ Ⓝ Ⓢ
cross-section (v.) *Researchers normally cross-section the sample so they can examine the tissue.*	Ⓑ Ⓝ Ⓢ
crosswise	Ⓑ Ⓝ Ⓢ
crowd-pleaser	Ⓑ Ⓢ
crowdsourcing (n.) The major dictionaries and style guides do not discuss the verb form. The writer can make two words or hyphenate: *crowd source, crowd-source.*	Ⓑ Ⓝ Ⓢ
Cs Plural form of capital letter, including letter grades.	Ⓑ
C's Plural form of the capital letter, including when discussing a student's grades.	Ⓝ Ⓐ
c's Plural form of the lowercase letter.	Ⓑ Ⓝ Ⓢ Ⓐ
CST Abbrev. for *Central Standard Time.*	Ⓑ Ⓝ Ⓢ Ⓐ
cum, phrases containing, hyphenation of Compounds formed with the Latin *cum,* meaning "with" or "along with being," take hyphens: *actor-cum-dancer, politics-cum-theater, kitchen-cum-dining room.*	Ⓑ Ⓝ Ⓢ
cum laude	Ⓑ Ⓝ Ⓢ
cure-all (n.)	Ⓑ Ⓝ Ⓢ Ⓐ
cut-and-dried, cut and dried Hyphenate as an adjective before a noun: *a cut-and-dried debate.* Do not hyphenate after a noun: *the issue is cut and dried.*	Ⓑ Ⓝ Ⓢ
cutback (n.), **cut back** (v.) *There will be severe cutbacks. Try to cut back on sugary snacks.*	Ⓑ Ⓝ Ⓢ
cutback (adj.) Do not hyphenate as an adjective: *the cutback procedures have become too severe.*	Ⓝ ✚
cutoff (n., adj.), **cut off** (v.) *The applicant missed the cutoff. The applicant missed the cutoff date. Be careful not to cut off other drivers.*	Ⓑ Ⓝ Ⓢ

cutout (n.), **cut out** (v.)		🅑 🅝 🅢
cutting edge (n.) They operate on the cutting edge.		🅑 🅝 🅢 🅐
cutting-edge, cutting edge (adj.)	Hyphenate as adjective before a noun in book and science styles: the factory uses cutting-edge techniques.	🅑 🅢
	Hyphenate as an adjective before a noun and after forms of to be in news style when hyphen aids comprehension: I like cutting-edge art. They were cutting-edge artists.	🅝
	Do not hyphenate as an adjective before a noun in academic style: the factory uses cutting edge techniques.	🅐
	Do not hyphenate as an adjective after the noun: the techniques the factory uses are cutting edge.	🅑 🅢 🅐
CV Abbrev. for curriculum vitae.		🅑 🅝 🅢
'd Contraction of had or would. If I'd known is a contracted form of If I had known. I'd love to is a contracted form of I would love to.		🅑 🅝 🅢 🅐
data processing (n.)		🅑 🅝 🅢
date rape (n.)		🅑 🅝 🅢
date-rape (v.)		🅑 🅢
date rape (v.)		🅝
date-rape (adj.)		✛
daybed		🅑 🅝 🅢
day care (n.) They put their son in day care.		🅑 🅝 🅢 🅐
day-care (adj.) They put their son in a day-care center.		🅑 🅢
day care (adj.) They put their son in a day care center.		🅝 🅐
daylight saving time		🅑 🅝 🅢
day's, days' Expressions such as a hard day's work and two days' time, are normally construed as possessive. Use apostrophes accordingly, taking care to distinguish between the singular possessive one day's and the plural possessive two days'. (See "Quasi Possessives," page 15.)		🅑 🅝 🅢
daytime (n., adj.)		🅑 🅝 🅢
day-to-day (adj.) Hyphenate adjective form before a noun: a day-to-day occurrence.		🅑 🅝 🅢 🅐
day to day (adv.) As an adverb after a verb, leave open unless hyphen is necessary to aid readability: he survives day to day.		🅑 🅝 🅢 🅐 ✛
day trip, day-tripper		🅑 🅝 🅢
D.C., DC See Washington, D.C.		
D-Day Hyphenated with two capital D's.		🅝
D-day Hyphenated with the first D capitalized.		🅑 🅢

de- Standard rules for hyphenating prefixes apply. In general, no hyphen except before a proper noun or to avoid awkward compounds.	B N S A
deal breaker	B N S A +
dean's list	B N S
decades No apostrophe to form the plural: *1980s*. But replace any dropped numerals with an apostrophe: *'80s*.	B N S A
degree Compounds with *degree* that come before a noun are usually hyphenated: *a 90-degree angle, a 10-degree rise in temperature*.	B N S A +
deep-fry, **deep-fried** Both verb and adjective forms take hyphens.	B N S
defining clauses *See* restrictive	
Denny's To make the plural, possessive, or plural possessive, the Punctuation Panel unanimously favored using the singular name with no modifications: *Our town has three Denny's. Denny's location is convenient. All three Denny's locations are convenient.*	+
-designate Hyphenate: *chairman-designate*.	N
devil's advocate	B N S
devil's food cake	B S
devil's-food cake	N
die-hard (adj.) Usually hyphenated: *a die-hard supporter*.	B N S A +
die hard (v.) *Old habits die hard.*	B N S A
die-off (n.) *The ice age brought a massive die-off.*	B S +
die off (v.) *The mammoths died off.*	B N S A
dimensions, hyphenation of Dimensions are subject to standard hyphenation rules. In general, dimensions used as a compound adjective before a noun are hyphenated: *an 11-by-9-inch pan*. But they are not hyphenated in other contexts: *the pan is 11 by 9 inches*. (See also "Compound adjective containing a number," page 104, and "Numerals vs. Spelled-Out Numbers," page 140.)	B N S A
dis- Standard rules for hyphenating prefixes apply. In general, no hyphen except to avoid awkward compounds.	N
dis The slang term meaning "show disrespect for": *you shouldn't dis your boss*.	B N S
dismember	B N S A
disservice	B N S A
District of Columbia *See* Washington, D.C.	
DNA Abbrev. for *deoxyribonucleic acid*.	B N S A
DNS Abbrev. for *domain name system*.	B N S A

dollar amounts as modifiers, hyphens in Punctuation Panel members split on how to hyphenate complex dollar terms used as adjectives, opting equally for *a $25 million losing proposition, a $25 million-losing proposition,* and *a $25-million-losing proposition.*	✚
dollar's worth This quasi possessive takes an apostrophe: *you get your dollar's worth.*	Ⓑ Ⓝ
-door *See* two-door; four-door	
dos and don'ts	Ⓑ
do's and don'ts	Ⓝ
dot-com	Ⓑ Ⓝ Ⓢ Ⓐ
double-blind	Ⓑ Ⓝ Ⓢ
double-breasted	Ⓑ Ⓝ Ⓢ
double check (n.)	Ⓑ Ⓢ
double-check (n.)	Ⓝ
double-check (v.)	Ⓑ Ⓝ Ⓢ
double-click	Ⓝ
double cross (n.)	Ⓑ Ⓝ Ⓢ
double-cross (v.)	Ⓑ Ⓝ Ⓢ
double date (n.)	Ⓑ Ⓝ Ⓢ
double-date (v.)	Ⓑ Ⓝ Ⓢ
double-edged	Ⓑ Ⓝ Ⓢ
double entendre	Ⓑ Ⓢ
double-entendre	Ⓝ
double jeopardy	Ⓑ Ⓝ Ⓢ
double-jointed	Ⓑ Ⓝ Ⓢ
double-park (v.)	Ⓑ Ⓝ Ⓢ
double play	Ⓑ Ⓝ Ⓢ
double prefixes Hyphenate: *sub-subgroup, pre-prewar, anti-antimatter.*	Ⓑ Ⓝ
double-space (v.)	Ⓑ Ⓝ Ⓢ
double standard	Ⓑ Ⓝ Ⓢ
-down Most nouns that end with *down* are listed in the dictionary without hyphens: *breakdown, countdown, lockdown, rundown, shutdown.* Exception: *sit-down.* Most phrasal verbs that end with *down* are written as two words with no hyphen: *break down, count down, lock down, run down, shut down, sit down.*	Ⓑ Ⓝ Ⓢ
downsize	Ⓑ Ⓝ Ⓢ

D

Down syndrome	Ⓑ Ⓝ Ⓢ
Dr. Abbrev. of *doctor*.	Ⓑ Ⓝ Ⓢ Ⓐ
drive-by (n., adj.)	Ⓑ Ⓝ Ⓢ
drive-in (n., adj.)	Ⓑ Ⓝ Ⓢ
driver's license, driver's licenses (pl.)	Ⓑ Ⓝ Ⓢ Ⓐ
driver's-side	+
drive-through (n., adj.)	Ⓑ Ⓢ
drive-thru (n., adj.)	Ⓝ
dropout (n.), **drop out** (v.)	Ⓑ Ⓝ Ⓢ
dropout (adj.)	+
drugmaker	Ⓑ Ⓝ Ⓢ
Ds Plural form of capital letter, including letter grades.	Ⓑ
D's Plural form of the capital letter, including letter grades.	Ⓝ Ⓐ
d's Plural form of the lowercase letter.	Ⓑ Ⓝ Ⓢ Ⓐ
DSL Abbrev. of *digital subscriber line*.	Ⓑ Ⓝ Ⓢ Ⓐ
DVD, DVDs (pl.)	Ⓑ Ⓝ Ⓢ
DVR, DVRs (pl.)	Ⓑ Ⓝ Ⓢ
e- (prefix) — Hyphenate in book style.	Ⓑ
News style does not specify whether to hyphenate *e-* in temporary compounds but shows a preference for hyphenating many specific terms including *e-commerce*, *e-tickets*, *e-banking*, and *e-book*. Exception: *email*.	Ⓝ
each other's Singular possessive, the apostrophe comes before the *s*.	Ⓑ Ⓝ Ⓢ Ⓐ
eagle-eyed	Ⓑ Ⓝ Ⓢ
early, hyphenation of Though often hyphenated in compound adjectives (*an early-winter snowfall*), do not hyphenate a noun or adverb. *It was early winter. They will visit in early September.*	+
eBay	
e-book	Ⓑ Ⓝ Ⓢ
eco-, hyphenation of Editing styles have no specific guidelines for when to hyphenate *eco-* in terms not found in the dictionary. The rules of prefixes and dictionary entries for the combining form *eco-* would suggest a preference for no hyphen after *eco-*, including in awkward constructions like *ecohero* and *ecocatastrophe*. However, the Punctuation Panel showed a strong preference for hyphenating *eco-* in most adjectives (*eco-smart*) and nouns (*eco-smarts*).	
eco-conscious	Ⓑ Ⓢ +
eco-friendly	Ⓑ Ⓢ +

E. coli	Ⓑ Ⓝ Ⓢ
e-commerce	Ⓑ Ⓝ Ⓢ
ecosystem	Ⓑ Ⓝ Ⓢ
ecotour, ecotourist, ecotourism	Ⓑ Ⓝ Ⓢ
ed. Abbrev. of *edition*.	Ⓢ
Ed., Eds. Abbrev. of *editor, editors,* distinguished from that of *edition* by use of capital *E*.	Ⓢ
EDT Abbrev. for *Eastern Daylight Time*.	Ⓑ Ⓝ Ⓢ Ⓐ
e.g., periods with Abbrev. of the Latin *exempli gratia,* meaning *for example*, takes a period after each letter.	Ⓑ Ⓝ Ⓢ Ⓐ
e.g., commas with Always followed by a comma.	Ⓑ Ⓝ
egghead	Ⓑ Ⓝ Ⓢ
egg roll	Ⓑ Ⓝ Ⓢ
eggshell (n., adj.)	Ⓑ Ⓝ Ⓢ
either, commas with The major styles do not give express instructions on whether commas should set off *either*. The Punctuation Panel split on whether to use a comma in the following: *I didn't see that movie, either./ I didn't see that movie either*.	✚
-elect Noun and adjective forms are hyphenated: *Consult the councilwoman-elect. Mayor-elect John Ramsey.*	Ⓑ Ⓝ Ⓢ
'em Contracted form of *them*. Note the direction in which the apostrophe curves and make sure it isn't erroneously changed into an open single quotation mark. (See "Direction of the Apostrophe," page 20.)	Ⓑ Ⓝ Ⓢ Ⓐ
e-mail	Ⓑ Ⓢ Ⓐ
email	Ⓝ
emcee, emceed, emceeing News style prefers this shortened term for *master of ceremonies* spelled as a word instead of written as initials *M.C.*	Ⓝ
Emmys Note no apostrophe in the plural of the award from the Academy of Television Arts & Sciences. *See also* awards	
empty handed (adj., adv.) Usually open after a noun or as an adverb but may be hyphenated if hyphen aids comprehension or readability.	Ⓑ
empty handed (adj.) Can be hyphenated before a noun if hyphen aids comprehension or readability.	Ⓑ
empty-handed (adj.) Hyphenated before a noun.	Ⓑ Ⓝ Ⓢ
empty-handed (adj., adv.)	Ⓝ Ⓢ
endgame	Ⓑ Ⓝ Ⓢ
end user	Ⓑ Ⓢ
end-user	Ⓝ

E

energy efficient, energy efficiency *See* fuel efficient	
entitled, commas after *See* titled	
ER Abbrev. of *emergency room.*	Ⓑ Ⓝ Ⓢ
'er Contracted form of *her* used in colloquial dialogue. Note the direction the apostrophe curves and make sure it isn't erroneously changed into an open single quotation mark. (See "Direction of the Apostrophe," page 20.)	Ⓑ Ⓝ Ⓢ Ⓐ
e-reader	Ⓑ Ⓢ **+**
Esq Abbrev. for esquire.	Ⓑ Ⓝ Ⓢ
-esque A majority of the Punctuation Panel advocated hyphenating *-esque* whenever it would reduce awkwardness or improve readability: *modelesque, Youngmanesque.*	**+**
essential clauses *See* restrictive	
EST Abbrev. for *Eastern Standard Time.*	Ⓑ Ⓝ Ⓢ Ⓐ
et al. Abbreviation for the Latin term *et alia* (*and others*) takes a period after the *l*. The term is normally set off with commas.	Ⓑ
etc. Abbreviation of *et cetera* takes a period, is preceded by a comma and, unless it appears at the end of a sentence, is followed by a comma.	Ⓑ
E-Trade Use hyphen in place of asterisk in name.	Ⓝ
EU Abbrev. for *European Union.*	Ⓑ Ⓝ Ⓢ
Euro- In the meaning *European*, often hyphenated in noun, adjective, and adverb forms not found in dictionary: *Euro-styled, Euro-mess*. The *e* is normally capitalized.	Ⓑ Ⓝ Ⓢ
Euro-American	Ⓝ
Eurotrash	Ⓑ Ⓢ
every day (n., adv.), **everyday** (adj.) *Every day is a new adventure. We visit every day. The store offers everyday values.*	Ⓑ Ⓝ Ⓢ
ex- Hyphenate compounds formed with this prefix unless indicated otherwise in the dictionary: *ex-friend, ex-lover*.	Ⓑ Ⓝ
Exception: in book style, use an en dash to connect *ex* to generic terms or proper names of two or more words: *ex–Vice President Dick Cheney*.	Ⓑ
ex-boyfriend	Ⓑ Ⓝ
excommunicate, excommunication	Ⓑ Ⓝ Ⓢ
ex-convict, ex-con	Ⓑ Ⓝ Ⓢ
ex-girlfriend	Ⓑ Ⓝ
expedience' sake	Ⓝ
expedience's sake	Ⓑ
expropriate, expropriation	Ⓑ Ⓝ Ⓢ

extra, hyphenation of	In general, book style opts for closed forms with *extra* whenever possible: *extramural, extrafine,* but *extra-articulate.*	Ⓑ
	In news style, hyphenate *extra* in the meaning "beyond the usual size, extent, or degree," *an extra-large room, an extra-dry martini, extra-spicy sauce.* When *extra* means "outside of," the standard rules of hyphenating prefixes apply: *extramarital, extrasensory, extracurricular.*	Ⓝ
	For terms not listed in the dictionary, the writer in science or academic style can choose open *(an extra dry martini)*, hyphenated *(an extra-dry martini)*, or closed *(an extradry martini)* forms.	Ⓢ Ⓐ
	Punctuation Panel book style experts preferred hyphenating compounds with *extra* before a noun but not after: *He ordered an extra-dry martini. Be extra nice.*	✚
extracurricular		Ⓑ Ⓝ Ⓢ Ⓐ
extramarital		Ⓑ Ⓝ Ⓢ Ⓐ
extrasensory		Ⓑ Ⓝ Ⓢ Ⓐ
extraterrestrial		Ⓑ Ⓝ Ⓢ Ⓐ
extra-virgin		Ⓑ Ⓝ Ⓢ
face-lift		Ⓑ Ⓝ Ⓢ
face-off (n.)		Ⓑ Ⓝ Ⓢ
face off (v.)		Ⓑ Ⓝ Ⓢ
face-to-face (adj., adv.) *A face-to-face meeting. Let's meet face-to-face.*		Ⓑ Ⓢ
face to face (adj., adv.) *A face to face meeting. Let's meet face to face.*		Ⓝ
fact-check (v.)		Ⓑ Ⓝ Ⓢ
fact-checker		Ⓑ Ⓢ
fact checking, fact-checking (n.) Preferred form as a gerund is with no hyphen, though the hyphen is permitted: *fact checking is important.*		Ⓑ ✚
fact-finding		Ⓑ Ⓝ Ⓢ
fall *See* seasons		
family Do not make the common mistake of confusing *family* with an *ly* adverb for hyphenation purposes. Adverbs ending in *ly* are not hyphenated as part of compound modifiers: *a happily married couple.* But *family*, a noun, is: *a family-friendly excursion.*		
family-owned and -operated *See also* suspensive hyphenation		Ⓝ
FAQ, FAQs (pl.) No apostrophe in the plural except in all-capital contexts where an apostrophe is necessary to prevent confusion.		Ⓑ Ⓝ Ⓢ Ⓐ
faraway (adj.) *A faraway place.*		Ⓑ Ⓝ Ⓢ
far-flung		Ⓑ Ⓝ Ⓢ

E

farmers' market *They went to the weekly farmers' market.*	Ⓑ
farmers market News style experts on the Punctuation Panel preferred no apostrophe. *They went to the weekly farmers market.* (See also "Possessive vs. Adjective Forms," page 16.)	✚
far-off (adj.)	Ⓑ Ⓝ Ⓢ
far-ranging	Ⓝ
farsighted	Ⓑ Ⓝ Ⓢ
Father's Day	Ⓑ Ⓝ Ⓢ Ⓐ
FBI Abbrev. for *Federal Bureau of Investigation.*	Ⓑ Ⓝ Ⓢ Ⓐ
F-bomb The Punctuation Panel preferred a hyphen.	✚
FDR Initials for *Franklin Delano Roosevelt.*	Ⓑ Ⓝ Ⓢ Ⓐ
FedEx	
figure skate (v.), **figure skating** (v., n.), **figure skater**	Ⓑ Ⓝ Ⓢ
filmgoer	Ⓑ Ⓝ Ⓢ
filmmaker, filmmaking	Ⓑ Ⓝ Ⓢ
firefight (n.) An exchange of gunfire.	Ⓑ Ⓝ Ⓢ
firefighter, firefighting	Ⓑ Ⓝ Ⓢ
first class (n.) *They are seated in first class.*	Ⓑ Ⓝ Ⓢ
first-class (adj.) Hyphenated before or after a noun: *they have first-class seats.*	Ⓝ Ⓢ
first-class (adj.) Usually hyphenated before a noun: *they have first class seats.* Hyphenate after the noun only if doing so aids readability or comprehension.	Ⓑ
first class, first-class (adv.) Punctuation Panel split on whether to hyphenate as an adverb after the verb: *He flies first-class. He flies first class.*	✚
firsthand	Ⓑ Ⓝ Ⓢ
501(c)(3), 501(c)(3)s (pl.) This section of the Internal Revenue Code dealing with certain tax-exempt entities is written with parentheses and no spaces.	
No apostrophe in the plural.	✚
fixer-upper	Ⓑ Ⓝ Ⓢ
flare-up (n.), **flare up** (v.)	Ⓑ Ⓝ Ⓢ
flashback	Ⓑ Ⓝ Ⓢ
flashbulb	Ⓑ Ⓝ Ⓢ
flash card	Ⓑ Ⓢ
flashcard	Ⓝ
flash flood	Ⓑ Ⓝ Ⓢ
flash-forward (n.), **flash forward** (v.)	Ⓑ Ⓝ Ⓢ

flash in the pan (n.)	Ⓑ	Ⓢ			
flash mob	Ⓑ	Ⓢ	✚		
flatbed (n., adj.)	Ⓑ	Ⓝ	Ⓢ		
flatbread	Ⓝ	✚			
flatfoot Slang for *police officer.*	Ⓑ	Ⓝ	Ⓢ		
flatfoot A foot that, due to a low arch, is flat: *he had a flatfoot.*	Ⓑ	Ⓢ			
flat foot *He had a flat foot.*	Ⓝ				
flat-footed, flat-footedness	Ⓑ	Ⓝ	Ⓢ		
flatland	Ⓑ	Ⓝ	Ⓢ		
flat-out (adj.), **flat out** (adv.)	Ⓑ	Ⓝ	Ⓢ		
flat-panel (adj.)	Ⓑ	Ⓝ	Ⓢ		
flat-panel (n.)	Ⓝ				
flat screen (n.)	Ⓑ	Ⓝ	Ⓢ		
flip-flop (n., v.)	Ⓝ				
flyaway	Ⓑ	Ⓝ	Ⓢ		
flyby	Ⓑ	Ⓝ	Ⓢ		
fly-by-night (n., adj.)	Ⓑ	Ⓝ	Ⓢ		
fly-fishing	Ⓑ	Ⓝ	Ⓢ		
flyweight	Ⓑ	Ⓝ	Ⓢ		
FM Abbrev. for radio broadcasting system known as *frequency modulation.*	Ⓑ	Ⓝ			
-fold (suffix) Do not hyphenate unless it follows a numeral (*125-fold*) or it follows another hyphenated term (*twenty-eight-fold*).	Ⓑ	Ⓝ			
follow-up (n.), **follow up** (v.)	Ⓑ	Ⓝ	Ⓢ		
fool's errand	Ⓑ	Ⓝ	Ⓢ	Ⓐ	
fool's gold	Ⓑ	Ⓝ	Ⓢ	Ⓐ	
for, phrases beginning with, commas around When the word *for* heads up an introductory phrase like "for example" or "for more information," the phrase is often but not necessarily set off with commas: *For more information, visit our website. For more information visit our website.*	Ⓑ	Ⓝ	Ⓢ	Ⓐ	
forefather	Ⓑ	Ⓝ	Ⓢ		
foregoing	Ⓑ	Ⓝ	Ⓢ		
four-door (n.) Hyphenate as a noun if hyphen aids readability or comprehension: *her car is a four-door.*	Ⓑ	Ⓝ	Ⓢ	Ⓐ	
four-door (adj.) Usually hyphenated before a noun: *a four-door sedan.*	Ⓑ	Ⓝ	Ⓢ	Ⓐ	
401(k)	Ⓝ				
401(k)s (pl.)	✚				

F

forward-looking (adj.)	Hyphenate before a noun: *a forward-looking statement.*	(B) (N) (S)
	Do not hyphenate after a noun: *this statement is forward looking.*	(B)
	Hyphenate after a form of *be*: *this statement is forward-looking.*	(N)
fractions, hyphens in	Hyphenate fractions as adjectives: *a two-thirds majority.*	(B) (N) (S) (A)
	Hyphenate fractions as nouns in book and news styles: *he took one-third and left us the remaining two-thirds.*	(B) (N)
	Do not hyphenate fractions as nouns in science style: *he took one third and left us the remaining two thirds.*	(S)

fragment The term *sentence fragment* refers to any word or group of words that is punctuated as a complete sentence even though it does not meet the minimum criteria for a sentence. The minimum criteria for a sentence are at least a subject and a verb: *Joe left.* Note that imperative verb forms carry the implied subject *you*, making imperatives (commands) the only complete sentences that may contain just one word: *Leave! Stop! Eat.* Sentence fragments are used frequently in published writing, especially creative writing. Thus, in any context that allows fragments, it is possible to punctuate a unit that does not make up a complete sentence as if it were one, assuming that the fragment is clearly understood by the reader: *Jerry! Baked beans. Coffee?*

frame-up (n.)	(B) (N) (S)
frame up (v.)	(N)
-free For terms not listed in the dictionary, hyphenate a compound adjective that ends with *-free* before or after a noun: *a tax-free donation.*	(B) (N) (S) (A)
free-associate (v.)	(N)
free association (n.)	(B) (N) (S)
free-for-all (n., adj.)	(B) (N) (S)
free-form (adj.)	(B) (N) (S)
freehand	(B) (N) (S)
freelance (n.) An independent worker.	(N)
free lance (n.) As an independent worker, usually two words, though the one-word form is allowed.	(B) (S)
free lance (n.) Medieval-era soldier who sold his services.	(B) (N) (S)
freelance (v., adj., adv.) *She prefers to freelance. She has been freelancing. She got a freelance assignment. She works freelance.*	(B) (N) (S)
freelancer	(B) (S)
free-lancer	(N)
freeload, freeloader, freeloading	(B) (N) (S)
free market (n.)	(B) (N) (S)
Freemason	(B) (N) (S)

free-range	Hyphenated before or after a noun.	Ⓝ Ⓢ
	Hyphenated before a noun, can be hyphenated after a noun if hyphen aids readability.	Ⓑ
freestanding		Ⓑ Ⓝ Ⓢ
freethinker (n.), **freethinking** (adj.)		Ⓑ Ⓝ Ⓢ
free throw		Ⓑ Ⓝ Ⓢ
free verse		Ⓑ Ⓝ Ⓢ
freewheeling		Ⓑ Ⓝ Ⓢ
freeze-dry, freeze-dried, freeze-drying		Ⓑ Ⓝ Ⓢ
freeze-frame (n.)		Ⓑ Ⓢ
freeze frame (n.)		Ⓝ
freeze-frame (v.)		Ⓑ Ⓝ Ⓢ
French Canadian (n., adj.)		Ⓑ Ⓝ Ⓢ
freshwater (n.) *They live in freshwater.*		Ⓑ Ⓢ
fresh water (n.) *They live in fresh water.*		Ⓝ
freshwater (adj.) *They are a freshwater species.*		Ⓑ Ⓝ Ⓢ
-friendly	When combined with a noun to form a compound adjective, hyphenate before a noun: *they use ocean-friendly solvents.*	Ⓑ Ⓝ Ⓢ Ⓐ
	Do not hyphenate after a noun unless hyphen aids comprehension.	Ⓑ Ⓢ Ⓐ
	Hyphenate after a form of *be*: *their practices are ocean-friendly.*	Ⓝ
	After an *ly* adverb, do not hyphenate: *environmentally friendly practices.*	Ⓑ Ⓝ Ⓢ Ⓐ
from . . . to . . . constructions, commas with Punctuation Panel unanimously preferred no commas in *from soup to nuts* and the majority preferred no commas to separate *to* items in longer constructions like: *They serve everything you can imagine, from the famous homemade potato bisque soup to the pan-seared ahi crusted with macadamia nuts to the fresh fruit sorbet with real mango and pineapple served in a carved-out half pineapple.* A minority of the panel indicated that very long and convoluted *from . . . to . . .* constructions can sometimes be improved by adding a comma before each *to*.		✦
from . . . to . . . constructions, dash in place of *to*, *through*, or *until* Though in some contexts it's appropriate to use an en dash to show a range, *Open 8–midnight*, any such construction using *from* must use *to*, *through*, or *until* instead of a dash: *they're open from 8 to midnight.*		Ⓑ
front and center (adv.) *The issue was front and center.*		Ⓑ Ⓝ Ⓢ Ⓐ
front man		Ⓑ Ⓢ
frontman		Ⓝ

front-runner		(B) (N) (S)
fruitcake		(B) (N) (S)
Fs Plural form of capital letter, including letter grades		(B)
F's Plural form of the capital letter, including when discussing a student's grades		(N) (A)
f's Plural form of the lowercase letter		(B) (N) (S) (A)
FTP Abbrev. for *File Transfer Protocol.*		(B) (N) (S) (A)
fuckup (n.), **fuck up** (v.) *That guy is a total fuckup. He's afraid he'll fuck up.*		(B) (N) (S)
fucked-up (adj.) *The whole evening was fucked-up.*		(B) (S)
fuel-efficiency		(N)
fuel efficiency The Punctuation Panel preferred no hyphen in this noun phrase.		✛
fuel-efficient, fuel efficient	Hyphenate before a noun.	(B) (N) (S) (A)
	Not usually hyphenated after a noun.	(B) (S) (A)
	Hyphenate after a noun.	(N)
full-time (adj.), **full time** (adv.) *She has a full-time job. She works full time.*		(B) (N)
fund-raising, fund-raiser		(B) (S)
fundraising, fundraiser		(N)
	For verb forms, Punctuation Panel preferred one word: *volunteers fundraise frequently.*	✛
F-word		(N) ✛
FYI Abbrev. for *for your information.*		(B) (N) (S) (A)
G-8 Abbrev. for *Group of Eight.*		(N)
G-20 Abbrev. for *Group of Twenty.*		(N)
GED Abbrev. for *General Educational Development,* the high school equivalence test and certificate.		(B) (N) (S) (A)
gerund, hyphenation with noun	Book style specifies that, when combining a gerund (an *ing* verb form functioning as a noun) with another noun to create a term not found in the dictionary, do not hyphenate in noun form: *Hat making is a lost art. Dog walking is a good way to earn extra money.* The Punctuation Panel also preferred no hyphens in these forms.	(B) ✛
	As an adjective, standard rules for hyphenating compound modifiers apply. In general, hyphenate before a noun whenever doing so aids readability: *Hat-making skills are hard to find these days. His dog-walking business is booming.*	(B) (N) (S) (A)
getaway (n.)		(B) (N) (S)
get-go (n.) *He was in trouble from the get-go.*		(B) (N) (S)

get-out (n.) *It's hot as all get-out.*	Ⓑ Ⓝ Ⓢ Ⓐ
getting In compound nouns, a majority of the Punctuation Panel preferred hyphens: *He's only interested in vote-getting. She's all about attention-getting.*	✚
get-together (n.), **get together** (v.)	Ⓑ Ⓝ Ⓢ
get up (v.)	Ⓑ Ⓝ Ⓢ
getup (n.) *That's quite a getup you're wearing.*	Ⓑ Ⓢ
get-up (n.) *That's quite a get-up you're wearing.*	Ⓝ
GI, GIs (pl.)	Ⓑ Ⓝ Ⓢ Ⓐ
gift giving (n.) *It's the time for gift giving.*	Ⓑ ✚
girls' night out The Punctuation Panel favored treating *girls* as plural possessive. (See also "Possessive vs. Adjective Forms," page 16.)	✚
giveaway (n.), **give away** (v.)	Ⓑ Ⓝ Ⓢ
GMT Abbrev. for *Greenwich Mean Time.*	Ⓑ Ⓝ Ⓢ Ⓐ
go-between (n.)	Ⓑ Ⓝ Ⓢ
goer Compound nouns with *goer* not appearing in the dictionary are two words, no hyphen: *park goer, show goer, mall goer,* but *operagoer, moviegoer, filmgoer.*	Ⓑ Ⓝ Ⓢ
go-go (n., adj.)	Ⓑ Ⓝ Ⓢ
good-bye (n.) *It was a long and mournful good-bye.*	Ⓑ Ⓢ
goodbye (n., interj.) *It was a long and mournful goodbye. John yelled, "Goodbye!"*	Ⓝ
good-looking	Ⓑ Ⓝ Ⓢ
goodness' sake	Ⓑ Ⓝ
GOP Abbrev. for *Grand Old Party.*	Ⓑ Ⓝ Ⓢ Ⓐ
go-to (adj.) *She's my go-to person for these jobs.*	Ⓑ Ⓢ
Gov. Abbrev. for *governor* when used as a title before a name.	Ⓑ Ⓝ Ⓢ Ⓐ
GPA Abbrev. for *grade point average.*	Ⓑ Ⓝ Ⓢ Ⓐ
GPS Abbrev. for *global positioning system.*	Ⓑ Ⓝ Ⓢ Ⓐ
grader *A fifth grader.*	Ⓑ Ⓢ
-grader *A fifth-grader.*	Ⓝ
grades See entries under individual letters.	
Grammys (pl.)	
great- Hyphenated when used to indicate family relationships: *great-grandfather, great-aunt.*	Ⓑ Ⓝ
gridiron	Ⓑ Ⓝ Ⓢ
gridlock	Ⓑ Ⓝ Ⓢ

G

Groundhog Day	Ⓑ Ⓝ Ⓢ
grown-up (n., adj.)	Ⓑ Ⓝ Ⓢ
guess what, periods or question marks after A majority of the Punctuation Panel favored a period after *Guess what*. A minority preferred a question mark: *Guess what?*	✛
gung ho	Ⓑ Ⓢ
gung-ho	Ⓝ
G-string	Ⓑ Ⓝ Ⓢ
hairdo, **hairdos** (pl.)	Ⓑ Ⓝ Ⓢ
hair-raising (adj.) Usually hyphenated.	Ⓑ Ⓝ Ⓢ Ⓐ
hairsplitting (n., adj.)	Ⓑ Ⓝ Ⓢ
half Hyphenate all temporary compounds: *A half-eaten breakfast. The report was half-finished.*	Ⓑ Ⓝ
halfback	Ⓑ Ⓝ Ⓢ
half-baked	Ⓑ Ⓝ Ⓢ
half blood (n.)	Ⓑ Ⓢ
half-blood (n.)	Ⓝ
half-blood (adj.)	Ⓑ Ⓝ Ⓢ
half brother	Ⓑ Ⓝ Ⓢ
half-cocked	Ⓑ Ⓝ Ⓢ
half day (n.), **half-day** (adj.)	Ⓑ Ⓝ
half dollar	Ⓑ Ⓝ
half-dollar	Ⓢ
halfhearted, halfheartedly	Ⓑ Ⓝ Ⓢ
half hour (n.)	Ⓑ
half-hour (n.)	Ⓝ
half-hour (adj.)	Ⓑ Ⓝ Ⓢ Ⓐ
half-life	Ⓑ Ⓝ Ⓢ
half-moon	Ⓑ Ⓝ Ⓢ
half note	Ⓑ Ⓝ Ⓢ
half sister	Ⓑ Ⓝ Ⓢ
half size	Ⓑ Ⓝ
half tide	Ⓑ Ⓝ
halftime	Ⓑ Ⓝ Ⓢ
halftone	Ⓑ Ⓝ Ⓢ

Term	Description	Styles
half-truth		Ⓑ Ⓝ Ⓢ
halfway		Ⓑ Ⓝ Ⓢ
half-wit		Ⓑ Ⓝ Ⓢ
handcraft (n., v.), **handcrafted** (adj.)		Ⓑ Ⓝ Ⓢ
handheld, hand-held	One word, no hyphen as noun or adjective.	Ⓑ Ⓢ
	Hyphenated as an adjective.	Ⓝ
	Punctuation Panel book style experts preferred one word for the noun form: *he used his handheld.* News style experts preferred to hyphenate the noun: *he used his hand-held.*	✛
hand in glove (adv.) *They worked hand in glove.*		Ⓑ Ⓝ Ⓢ Ⓐ
hand in hand (adv.) *They walked hand in hand.*		Ⓑ Ⓢ ✛
handmade		Ⓑ Ⓝ Ⓢ
hands-on		Ⓑ Ⓝ Ⓢ
hands-off		Ⓑ Ⓝ Ⓢ
hand washing (n.)		Ⓑ ✛
hand-washing (n.)		Ⓝ
hand-wringing		Ⓑ Ⓝ Ⓢ
Hansen's disease		Ⓑ Ⓝ Ⓢ
hard-and-fast	Hyphenate before a noun: *a hard-and-fast rule.*	Ⓑ Ⓝ Ⓢ Ⓐ
	Hyphenate after a noun if hyphens aid readability.	Ⓑ Ⓝ Ⓢ Ⓐ
	Hyphenate after a form of *be.*	Ⓝ
hard-boil (v.), **hard-boiled** (adj.)		Ⓑ Ⓝ Ⓢ
hard-core (adj.)		Ⓑ Ⓝ Ⓢ
hardcover (n., adj.)		Ⓑ Ⓝ Ⓢ
Hawaii		Ⓑ Ⓝ Ⓢ
H-bomb Abbrev. for *hydrogen bomb.*		Ⓑ Ⓝ Ⓢ
headache		Ⓑ Ⓝ Ⓢ
head-on (adj., adv.) *A head-on collision. They collided head-on.*		Ⓑ Ⓝ Ⓢ
heads-up (n.) *Joe gave us a heads-up that he is on his way.*		Ⓑ Ⓝ Ⓢ
heads up (interj.) *Heads up, everyone!*		Ⓑ Ⓢ
health care (n.) *They have good health care.*		Ⓑ Ⓝ Ⓢ
health care (adj.) *She has a good health care plan.*		Ⓝ
health-care (adj.) Book style experts on the Punctuation Panel favored hyphenating the adjective form: *she has a good health-care plan.*		✛

H

Heaven's sake Punctuation Panel unanimously favored the singular possessive form, with an apostrophe before the *s*.	✚
he'd Contraction of *he had* or *he would*.	(B)(N)(S)(A)
hello, commas after When followed by a name or other direct address, a comma usually follows *hello*: *Hello, Dan!*	
hers Never contains an apostrophe.	(B)(N)(S)(A)
he's Contraction of *he is* or *he has*.	(B)(N)(S)(A)
hey, commas after When followed by a name or other direct address, a comma usually follows *hey*: *Hey, Brenda!*	
hi, commas after When followed by a name or other direct address, a comma usually follows *hi*: *Hi, Brenda!*	
hi-fi	(B)(N)(S)
high-chair (n.)	(B)(S)
highchair (n.)	(N)
highfalutin	(B)(N)(S)
high five (n.)	(B)(S)
high-five (n., v.)	(B)(N)(S)
high jinks Preferred form in book, news, and scientific style is two words, no hyphen (though both *hijinks* and *hi-jinks* are also acceptable).	(B)(N)(S)
high-rise (n., adj.)	(B)(N)(S)
high school (n.)	(B)(N)(S)(A)
high school (adj.)	(A)
high tech (n.), **high-tech** (adj.)	(B)(N)(S)
hip-hop (n., adj.)	(B)(N)(S)
his Never contains an apostrophe.	(B)(N)(S)(A)
hit-and-run (n., adj.) *He was arrested for hit-and-run. It was a hit-and-run accident.*	(B)(N)(S)
hit and run (v.) *He's not the kind of driver who would hit and run.*	(N)
HIV Abbrev. for *human immunodeficiency virus*.	(B)(N)(S)
HMO, HMOs (pl.)	(B)(N)(S)(A)
ho-hum	(B)(N)(S)
holdover (n.)	(B)(N)(S)
holdup (n.), **hold up** (v.)	(B)(N)(S)
homegrown	(B)(N)(S)
homemade	(B)(N)(S)
homeowner's, **homeowners'**, **homeowners** See "Possessive vs. Adjective Forms," page 16.	

homeschooler, homeschooling (n.), **homeschool** (v.), **homeschooled** (adj.)	Ⓑ Ⓢ
home-schooler (n.), **home-school** (v.), **home-schooled** (adj.)	Ⓝ
home schooling (n.)	Ⓝ
home-style (adj.) A majority of the Punctuation Panel preferred to hyphenate: *they specialize in home-style cooking.*	✚
homespun	Ⓑ Ⓝ Ⓢ
hometown	Ⓑ Ⓝ Ⓢ
-hood The suffix is usually not hyphenated, except when absence of a hyphen could create awkwardness or confusion: *victimhood.*	Ⓑ Ⓝ Ⓢ Ⓐ
hors d'oeuvre An apostrophe comes after the *d.*	Ⓑ Ⓝ Ⓢ
hot dog (n.) The noun referring to a food item is two words, no hyphen.	Ⓑ Ⓝ Ⓢ
hotdog (v.) The verb meaning to show off is one word in book and science styles: *The surfer likes to hotdog. The surfer was hotdogging.*	Ⓑ Ⓢ
hot-dog (v.) The verb meaning to show off is hyphenated in news style: *The surfer likes to hot-dog. The surfer was hot-dogging.*	Ⓝ
hot plate The electric cooking appliance.	Ⓑ Ⓝ Ⓢ
hour's, hours' Expressions such as *an hour's drive* and *two hours' worth,* are normally construed as possessive. Use apostrophes accordingly, taking care to distinguish between the singular possessive *hour's* and the plural possessive *hours'*. (See "Quasi Possessives," page 15.)	
however, commas with When *however* serves as an adverb, it may or may not be set off with commas, depending on whether the writer judges it to be a parenthetical insertion or well integrated into the sentence: *Jane, however, won't attend.* If integral to the structure of the sentence or if no pause is intended, no commas are needed: *Jane however won't attend.* When *however* serves as a conjunction, a comma never follows: *however you look at it, we have a problem.*	Ⓑ Ⓝ Ⓢ Ⓐ
Hula-Hoop	Ⓑ Ⓝ Ⓢ
hula hoop News style allows generic use, with lowercase letters and no hyphen.	Ⓝ
hush-hush	Ⓑ Ⓝ Ⓢ
i's plural form of the lowercase letter. Takes an apostrophe: *dot your i's and cross your t's.*	Ⓑ Ⓝ Ⓢ Ⓐ
icebreaker	Ⓑ Ⓝ Ⓢ
ice maker	Ⓑ Ⓢ
ice-maker	Ⓝ
ice pick	Ⓑ Ⓝ Ⓢ
I'd Contraction of *I would* or *I had.*	Ⓑ Ⓝ Ⓢ Ⓐ
ID Abbrev. for *identification.*	Ⓑ Ⓝ Ⓢ Ⓐ

H

I'd've Contraction of *I would have*.	(B)(N)(S)(A)
i.e., periods with Abbrev. of the Latin *id est*, meaning *that is*, takes a period after each letter.	(B)(N)(S)(A)
i.e., comma with Always followed by a comma.	(B)(N)
ifs, ands, or buts	(B)(S)(A)
ifs, ands or buts	(N)
IM abbreviation for instant message. Inflected forms are *IMed* and *IMing*.	(B)(N)(S)(A)
I'm Contraction of *I am*.	(B)(N)(S)(A)
'im Contracted form of *him* used in colloquial dialogue. Note the direction the apostrophe curves and make sure it isn't erroneously changed into an open single quotation mark. (See "The Direction of the Apostrophe," page 20.)	(B)(N)(S)(A)
"in" When used to mean that something is fashionable or popular, place in quotation marks when followed by a noun: *he hangs with the "in" crowd*. But do not use quotation marks otherwise: *that color palette is very in right now*.	(N)
in' Shortened form of *ing* used to indicate a regional accent or casual speech, as in *walkin', talkin', thinkin'*, etc.	(B)(N)(S)(A)
in- (prefix) Be careful not to confuse the prefix *in-*, which means "not," with the preposition *in*. Most terms that use the negative prefix *in-* are listed in the dictionary and are customarily not hyphenated: *insufferable, inaccurate, indecision, indecisive, intolerable, indiscreet, indiscretion, indirect, infallible*. Compounds formed with the word *in* follow the rules for forming compound modifiers: *an in-depth study, an in-house recruitment effort*.	(B)(N)(S)(A)
inbound	(B)(N)(S)
Inc. In book style, commas around *Inc., Ltd.,* etc. are not required: *he has worked for ABC Inc. for three years*. But if the writer chooses to put a comma before *Inc.,* a comma is required after it as well. Right: *he has worked for ABC, Inc., for three years*. Wrong: *he has worked for ABC, Inc. for three years*.	(B)
In news style, *Inc., Ltd.,* and similar terms are never set off with commas: *he has worked for ABC Inc. for three years*.	(N)
including, colon after Do not use a colon after *including* to introduce a list: *they have many toppings available including garlic, pepperoni, and onions*.	(B)(N)
including, comma with A comma often precedes *including*, but no comma should come after: *America has many great cities, including New York, Chicago, and San Francisco. America has many great cities including New York, Chicago, and San Francisco.*	(B)(N)(S)(A)

in-depth, in depth	Hyphenate as an adjective. *The in-depth study has been completed.*	Ⓑ Ⓝ Ⓢ Ⓐ
	In news style, hyphenate as an adverb. *The partners discussed the matter in-depth.*	Ⓝ
	Book style experts on the Punctuation Panel preferred no hyphen when used as an adverb: *the partners discussed the matter in depth.*	✚
infield		Ⓑ Ⓝ Ⓢ
infighting		Ⓑ Ⓝ Ⓢ
in-house	Hyphenate as an adjective: *the in-house study has been completed.*	Ⓑ Ⓝ Ⓢ Ⓐ
	In news style, hyphenate as an adverb: *the partners discussed the matter in-house.*	Ⓝ
initials for people's names, period and spaces in	Initials representing parts of names are followed by both a period and a space: *H. L. Mencken, W. E. B. DuBois.* Initials representing full names, such as *JFK* and *FDR* take no periods or spaces.	Ⓑ Ⓢ Ⓐ
	Use periods but no spaces for initials standing in for a portion of a person's name: *H.L. Mencken, W.E.B. DuBois.*	Ⓝ
initials for people's names, other punctuation with	The final period in an initialism may serve as terminal punctuation in a sentence: *Though students called him professor, friends just called him W. B.* For sentences or phrases ending with a question mark, exclamation point, semicolon, or colon, the terminal punctuation comes after and in addition to the final period in the initials: *Do his friends call him W. B.?*	Ⓑ Ⓝ Ⓢ Ⓐ
in-law's Form the possessive of *in-law* according to standard rules of possessives. Apply an apostrophe and *s* at the end of *law* for both the singular and plural possessives (the plural is shown in the first part of the term): *My father-in-law's house. All three of my sisters-in-law's husbands.* (See also "Possessives of Compound Terms," page 15.)		Ⓑ Ⓝ Ⓢ Ⓐ
in-line (adj.)		Ⓑ Ⓝ Ⓢ
in-line (adv.)		Ⓑ Ⓢ
inpatient		Ⓑ Ⓝ Ⓢ
inside out (adj., adv.)	*His shirt was inside out.*	Ⓑ Ⓝ Ⓢ
	For a compound adjective before a noun, a majority of the Punctuation Panel preferred to hyphenate: *he wore an inside-out shirt.*	✚
insufferable		Ⓑ Ⓝ Ⓢ Ⓐ
inter- Standard rules for hyphenating prefixes apply. In general, no hyphen except before a proper noun or to avoid awkward compounds.		Ⓑ Ⓝ Ⓢ Ⓐ

interminable		Ⓑ Ⓝ Ⓢ Ⓐ
in-the-know	Hyphenate before a noun whenever doing so aids readability or comprehension. After a noun, hyphens are not required.	Ⓑ Ⓝ Ⓢ Ⓐ
in utero	(adj., adv.) *an in utero procedure.*	Ⓑ
in vitro	(adj., adv.) *in vitro fertilization.*	Ⓑ
in vivo	(adj., adv.) *in vivo response.*	Ⓑ
IOU, IOUs	(pl.) No apostrophe in the plural except in all-capital contexts where an apostrophe is necessary to prevent confusion.	Ⓑ Ⓝ Ⓢ Ⓐ
iPad, iPod		
IQ, IQs	(pl.) Abbreviation of *intelligence quotient*. No apostrophe in the plural except in all-capital contexts where an apostrophe is necessary to prevent confusion.	Ⓑ Ⓝ Ⓢ Ⓐ
IRS	Abbrev. of *Internal Revenue Service*.	Ⓑ Ⓝ Ⓢ Ⓐ
is is, commas with	When a subject ends with *is* and is followed by a verb phrase that begins with *is*, style guides indicate that a comma should intervene whenever it aids comprehension, leaving it up to the writer's judgment.	Ⓑ Ⓝ Ⓢ Ⓐ
	The majority of the Punctuation Panel favored no comma in *What it is is a good idea.*	✛
-ism, hyphenation of	Standard rules of suffixes apply. In general, do not hyphenate unless absence of a hyphen could cause confusion or awkwardness.	Ⓑ Ⓝ Ⓢ Ⓐ
isn't	Contraction of *is not*.	Ⓑ Ⓝ Ⓢ Ⓐ
IT	Abbrev. for *information technology*.	Ⓑ Ⓝ Ⓢ Ⓐ
Italian American	(n., adj.) *A famous Italian American. An Italian American community.*	Ⓑ Ⓢ
Italian-American	(n., adj.) *A famous Italian-American. An Italian-American community.*	Ⓝ
it'd	Contraction of *it would* or *it had*.	Ⓑ Ⓝ Ⓢ Ⓐ
it's	Contraction of *it is* or *it has. It's raining. It's been quite a week.* Not to be confused with possessive *its* (below).	Ⓑ Ⓝ Ⓢ Ⓐ
its	Possessive of *it: the dog wagged its tail.* The possessive form never takes an apostrophe. (*See* it's *above for the contraction.*)	Ⓑ Ⓝ Ⓢ Ⓐ
IUD, IUDs	(pl.) Abbrev. for *intrauterine device*.	Ⓑ Ⓝ Ⓢ Ⓐ
I've	Contraction of *I have*.	Ⓑ Ⓝ Ⓢ Ⓐ
Jack Daniel's	Short for the brand name *Jack Daniel's Tennessee Whiskey*. Same in singular and plural forms: *He ordered a Jack Daniel's. He ordered two Jack Daniel's.*	
jack-o'-lantern		Ⓑ Ⓝ Ⓢ
J.C. Penney		
Jell-O		

Entry		Styles
Jesus's In book, science, and academic styles, possessives usually take an apostrophe and s regardless of whether they end with s: *Jesus's teachings.*		Ⓑ Ⓢ Ⓐ
Jesus' Possessive. In news style, singular proper nouns ending in s form the plural with just an apostrophe: *Jesus' teachings.*		Ⓝ
JFK Initials for *John F. Kennedy.*		Ⓑ
JPEG, JPEGs (pl.)		Ⓑ Ⓝ Ⓢ
Jr.		Ⓑ Ⓝ Ⓢ Ⓐ
Jr., commas with	Do not set off from a proper name with commas: *Dr. Martin Luther King Jr. was commemorated that day.*	Ⓑ Ⓝ Ⓢ
	Set off with commas: *Dr. Martin Luther King, Jr., was commemorated.*	Ⓐ
K2		Ⓑ Ⓢ
K-9		Ⓑ Ⓝ Ⓢ
karat, hyphenation of *See* carat		
kick ass (v.), **kick-ass** (adj.)		Ⓑ Ⓝ Ⓢ
kilowatt-hour		Ⓑ Ⓝ Ⓢ
the King's English		Ⓑ Ⓢ
the king's English		Ⓝ
King of (country name)'s Possessive: *King of Jordan's visit,* not *King's of Jordan visit. See also* of forms as possessives		Ⓑ Ⓝ Ⓢ
Kmart		
knockdown (adj.)		Ⓑ Ⓝ Ⓢ
knock-down-drag-out (n.), **knock-down, drag-out** (adj.)		Ⓑ Ⓢ
knockoff (n.), **knock off** (v.)		Ⓑ Ⓝ Ⓢ
knockout (n.), **knock out** (v.)		Ⓑ Ⓝ Ⓢ
know-it-all (n., adj.)		Ⓑ Ⓝ Ⓢ
know-nothing (n.)		Ⓑ Ⓝ Ⓢ
known, hyphenation of Standard hyphenation rules for compound adjectives apply. Hyphenate when doing so aids comprehension: *a lesser-known man.* Do not hyphenate after an *ly* adverb: *a nationally known actor.*		Ⓑ Ⓝ Ⓢ Ⓐ
Kool-Aid		
LA Abbrev. for *Los Angeles.*		Ⓑ Ⓢ Ⓐ
L.A. Abbrev. for *Los Angeles.*		Ⓝ
laid-back (adj.)		Ⓑ Ⓝ Ⓢ Ⓐ
landline		Ⓑ Ⓝ Ⓢ
Lands' End Trade name of a clothing manufacturer.		
laptop		Ⓑ Ⓝ Ⓢ

Entry	Styles
late, hyphenation of Though often hyphenated in compound adjectives (*a late-winter snowfall*), do not hyphenate as part of a noun phrase: *It was late winter. They will visit in late September.*	✚
late night (n.) *He does his best work in the late night.*	B N S A
late-night (adj.) Usually hyphenated before a noun: *he hosts a late-night program.*	B N S A
Latin American (n., adj.)	N
layoff (n.), **lay off** (v.) *They had a lot of layoffs this year. I hope they don't lay off any employees.*	B N S
layout (n.), **lay out** (v.) *I like the layout of this apartment. Lay out your clothes for tomorrow.*	B N S
layover (n.), **lay over** (v.) *He has a nine-hour layover in Chicago. The flight will lay over for nine hours in Chicago.*	B N S
lb. Book style recommends spelling out *pound* instead of using *lb.* but allows the abbreviation when appropriate (e.g., in tables). Normally, *lb.* includes a period. In highly technical contexts, the period can be omitted. In this style, note that the form does not change in the plural: *1 lb., 5 lb., 100 lb.*	B
News style does not abbreviate *pound*.	N
Science and academic styles allow abbreviated form, with period, in contexts where the writer deems it appropriate.	S A
left-click (n., v.) *Only a left-click will pull up the submenu. You must left-click in the document body.*	✚
left hand, left-hander (n.), **left-handed** (adj.)	B N S
left wing, left-winger (n.), **left-wing** (adj.) *She represents the left wing of the party. He is a left-winger. They say he has a left-wing agenda.*	B N S
lengthwise, lengthways	B N S
-less Standard rules for hyphenating suffixes apply. In general, no hyphen except before a proper noun or to avoid awkward compounds.	B N S A
let's A contraction of *let us*, often used for invitations and suggestions: *let's go to the movies.* Not to be confused with *lets*, which is a conjugated form of the verb *to let*.	
lets The third-person singular conjugation of the verb *let*: *he lets the cat out at night.* Never takes an apostrophe.	
letter grades *See entries for individual letters*	
letters, lowercase The plural of a lowercase letter takes an apostrophe before the *s*: *the name Mississippi has multiple i's, s's, and p's.*	B N S A
Levi's Singular and plural of the brand name for the jeans company: *He wore his Levi's. They wore their Levi's.*	
lifeblood One word, not possessive.	B N S

lifesaver, Life Savers The generic term is one word: *this loan is a real lifesaver.* The candy is two words: *I love to eat Life Savers.*	Ⓑ Ⓝ Ⓢ
lifestyle	Ⓑ Ⓝ Ⓢ
liftoff (n.), **lift off** (v.)	Ⓑ Ⓝ Ⓢ
-like Hyphenate terms not found in the dictionary: *A secretary-like position. A dog-like devotion.* When *-like* is combined with a term of two or more words that isn't usually hyphenated, the entire compound is hyphenated: *it's a wine-cellar-like space.*	Ⓑ Ⓝ Ⓢ

likely Often an adjective: *likely voters.* Do not make the mistake of confusing *likely* with an *ly* adverb for hyphenation purposes. Adverbs ending in *ly* are not hyphenated as part of compound modifiers: *a happily married couple.* But *likely*, an adjective, is. Correct: *likely-voter response.*

lineup (n.) *We have a great lineup this year.*	Ⓑ Ⓝ Ⓢ
line up (v.), **lineup** (adj.)	*Line up at the door.*	Ⓑ Ⓝ Ⓢ Ⓐ
	As an adjective, a majority of the Punctuation Panel would use one unhyphenated word: *your lineup procedure won't work.*	✦

LinkedIn Proper name of social and professional networking website.

linking verbs, hyphenation of compound adjectives after Also called copular verbs, linking verbs express being or the senses: *become, seem, appear, smell,* and *act* are examples. News style, which specifies that compound adjectives be hyphenated after the verb *be*, does not specify whether the rule applies to such other verbs of being. A majority of the Punctuation Panel opted to treat linking verbs the same way as *to be: Their service eventually became family-style. This dessert seems guilt-free.*	✦

Lions Club, Lions Clubs International

lion's den Singular possessive in book style.	Ⓑ
lion's share An apostrophe comes before the *s*.	Ⓑ Ⓝ Ⓢ
lockdown (n.), **lock down** (v.)	Ⓑ Ⓝ Ⓢ
lockdown (adj.)	✦
log-in (n.)	Ⓑ Ⓢ
login (n.)	Ⓝ
log in (v.)	Ⓑ Ⓝ Ⓢ Ⓐ
log off (v.)	Ⓑ Ⓝ Ⓢ Ⓐ
logoff (n.)	Ⓝ
log-on (n.)	Ⓑ Ⓢ
logon (n.)	Ⓝ
log on (v.)	Ⓑ Ⓝ Ⓢ Ⓐ
LOL Abbrev. for *laughing out loud.*	Ⓑ Ⓝ Ⓢ Ⓐ ✦

long-standing Hyphenate: *they have a long-standing commitment.*	Ⓑ Ⓝ Ⓢ Ⓐ ✚
long term (n.), **long-term** (adj.) *We will see growth in the long term. Long-term growth projections are encouraging.*	Ⓑ Ⓝ Ⓢ
long time (n.), **longtime** (adj.) *They haven't visited in a long time. The longtime friends had their first argument.*	Ⓑ Ⓝ Ⓢ
Lord's Prayer	Ⓑ Ⓝ Ⓢ
Lou Gehrig's disease	Ⓑ Ⓝ Ⓢ
lover Do not hyphenate in most noun phrases where the first word is the thing loved: *movie lover, chocolate lover.*	Ⓑ Ⓐ ✚
lover's, lovers', lovers A majority of the Punctuation Panel favored the singular possessive in *chocolate lover's special* but the plural possessive in *fashion lovers' paradise,* suggesting the choice should be based on whether the unit emphasizes a single lover or multiple. (See also "Possessive vs. Adjective Forms," page 16.)	✚
lowercase (n., v.), **lowercased, lowercasing**	Ⓑ Ⓝ Ⓢ
LLC Do not set off with commas.	Ⓑ
LLP Do not set off with commas.	Ⓑ
Ltd. (See Inc. *for use of commas with*)	Ⓑ Ⓝ
M1, M16 *An M16 military rifle.*	Ⓝ
MA, MS Abbrev. for *master of arts* and *master of science: Carrie Altman, MS, gave a presentation.*	Ⓑ Ⓢ Ⓐ
M.A., M.S. Abbrev. for *master of arts* and *master of science: this is Carrie Altman, M.S.*	Ⓝ
Ms. Courtesy title. *Ms. Jones will see you now.*	Ⓑ Ⓝ Ⓢ Ⓐ
ma'am Informal term for *madam.*	Ⓑ Ⓝ Ⓢ
machine gun (n.), **machine-gun** (v., adj.)	Ⓑ Ⓝ Ⓢ
Macy's Despite the corporate logo that uses a star in place of the apostrophe, use an apostrophe. This is consistent with company's press materials.	✚
To make the plural and the singular or plural possessive, the Punctuation Panel unanimously favored using the singular name with no modifications: *Our town has three Macy's. Macy's location is perfect. All three Macy's locations are perfect.*	
magna cum laude (adj., adv.)	Ⓑ Ⓝ Ⓢ
maitre d', accent mark with Book and science styles prefer an accent mark over the *i (î), maître d',* but allow it with no accent mark.	Ⓑ Ⓢ
News style uses no accent mark.	Ⓝ
maitre d', plural of Book and sciences styles and a majority of the Punctuation Panel form the plural as *maitre d's.* A minority of the panel preferred *maîtres d'.*	Ⓑ Ⓝ Ⓢ ✚

make-believe (n., adj.)		Ⓑ Ⓝ Ⓢ
makeover (n.)		Ⓑ Ⓝ Ⓢ
maker	Hyphenate a compound noun containing *maker* that is not listed in the dictionary: *pie-maker, chart-maker.* Exceptions: *coffee maker, drugmaker, policymaker.*	Ⓝ
	Do not hyphenate compound nouns: *pie maker, chart maker.*	✚
makeup (n., adj.) *She applied her makeup. Kindness is in his makeup. Take the makeup exam.*		Ⓑ Ⓝ Ⓢ
make up (v.)		Ⓑ Ⓝ Ⓢ
making, -making	To create nouns (gerunds) not found in the dictionary, do not hyphenate: *he enjoys guitar making.*	Ⓑ ✚
	In news style, noun form can be hyphenated if the writer feels the hyphen aids readability: *he enjoys guitar-making.*	Ⓝ
	For adjective forms, standard rules for hyphenating compound modifiers apply. In general, hyphenate whenever doing so aids readability: *he saw his guitar-making career come to an end.*	Ⓑ Ⓝ Ⓢ Ⓐ
Martha's Vineyard		Ⓑ Ⓝ Ⓢ Ⓐ
Martin Luther King Jr. Day		Ⓑ Ⓝ
mash-up (n.)		Ⓑ Ⓢ
mashup (n.)		Ⓝ
mass market (v.), **mass-market** (adj.), **mass-marketed** (adj.) *They will mass market their new product line. The publisher focuses on mass-market paperbacks. Consumers favor mass-marketed products.*		Ⓑ Ⓝ Ⓢ
mass-produce (v.)		Ⓑ Ⓢ
mass produce (v.)		Ⓝ
mass-produced (adj.)		Ⓑ Ⓝ Ⓢ Ⓐ
master's degree, master's Can also be written *master of arts* or *master of science.*		Ⓑ Ⓝ Ⓢ Ⓐ
matter of fact (n.) *That's a matter of fact.*		Ⓑ Ⓝ Ⓢ Ⓐ
matter-of-fact (adj.)	Hyphenate as an adjective before a noun: *he had a matter-of-fact tone.*	Ⓑ Ⓝ Ⓢ Ⓐ
	Hyphenate after a form of *be: his tone was matter-of-fact.*	Ⓝ
matter-of-factly (adv.) *He said it matter-of-factly.*		Ⓑ Ⓝ Ⓢ ✚
MBA		Ⓑ Ⓝ Ⓢ Ⓐ
M.C., MC *See* emcee		

M

McDonald's To make the plural or singular or plural possessive, the Punctuation Panel unanimously favored using the singular name with no modifications: *Our town has three McDonald's. McDonald's location is perfect. All three McDonald's locations are perfect.*		✚
MD, MDs Abbrev. for *doctor of medicine*: *Carlos Iglesia, MD, gave a presentation.*		Ⓑ Ⓢ Ⓐ
M.D., M.D.s Abbrev. for *doctor of medicine*: *This is Carlos Iglesia, M.D.*		Ⓝ
MDT Abbrev. for *Mountain Daylight Time.*		Ⓑ Ⓝ Ⓢ Ⓐ
measurements, hyphenation of Measurements used as adjectives can be hyphenated to aid clarity: *A 300-acre farm. A 40-mile drive. A 25-inch waist.* Otherwise, measurements are usually not hyphenated: *300 acres. 40 miles. 25 inches.*		Ⓑ Ⓝ Ⓢ Ⓐ
Megan's Law		Ⓑ Ⓝ Ⓢ Ⓐ
meltdown (n.), **melt down** (v.) *The power plant had a meltdown. They will melt down the gold.*		Ⓑ Ⓝ Ⓢ
men's The plural possessive of *man*. Though some trade names may exclude the apostrophe, doing so is widely considered an error.		Ⓑ Ⓝ Ⓢ Ⓐ
Mercedes-Benz		
merry-go-round		Ⓑ Ⓝ Ⓢ
Mexican American (n., adj.)		Ⓑ Ⓢ
Mexican-American (n., adj.)		Ⓝ
mg Abbrev. of *milligram*		Ⓑ Ⓢ
MIA Abbrev. for *missing in action*		Ⓑ Ⓝ Ⓢ Ⓐ
mid, hyphenation of	Do not hyphenate unless before a proper noun or a numeral, or when necessary to prevent an awkward or confusing compound: *midforties, midsentence,* but *mid-September, mid-1840s.*	Ⓑ Ⓝ Ⓢ Ⓐ
	Punctuation Panel unanimously supported hyphenating *mid* before a season: *we will visit in mid-spring.*	✚
	In book style, use just one hyphen in compound nouns form with *mid* plus an open compound: *He lived in the mid-thirteenth century. We will visit mid-next year.* (Though as an adjective, the entire compound would be hyphenated: *A mid-thirteenth-century cathedral. A mid-next-year plan.*)	Ⓑ
	Before an open compound like *next year*, the Punctuation Panel split. The majority opted for no hyphens in the noun phrase *mid next year*. Others opted for one hyphen, *mid-next year*, or two hyphens, *mid-next-year.*	✚
mid- to late- In expressions such *as mid- to late-1980s, mid-* takes a hyphen. (See also "Suspensive Hyphenation," page 105.)		Ⓑ Ⓝ Ⓢ

middle class, middle-class	Noun form takes no hyphen: *they are members of the middle class.*	Ⓑ Ⓝ Ⓢ Ⓐ
	Adjective form is hyphenated before a noun: *they have middle-class sensibilities.*	Ⓑ Ⓝ Ⓢ Ⓐ
	Adjective form is hyphenated after a form of *be: that family is middle-class.*	Ⓝ
Middle Eastern		Ⓑ Ⓝ Ⓢ
military titles When abbreviated, military titles take periods: *Gen., Lt. Col., Maj., Cpl.* To form the plural, place the *s* before the period: *Gens., Majs., Cpls.,* etc.		Ⓑ Ⓝ Ⓢ Ⓐ
mind-set		Ⓑ Ⓝ Ⓢ
mind's eye		Ⓑ Ⓝ Ⓢ
mini General rules of prefixes apply. In general, no hyphen unless needed for clarity: *miniseries, minivan, miniskirt, minicourse, minibus.*		Ⓑ Ⓝ Ⓢ Ⓐ
mixed bag		Ⓑ Ⓝ Ⓢ
mixed-up (adj.) *The police were all mixed-up.*		Ⓑ Ⓝ Ⓢ
mix-up (n.), **mix up** (v.) *There has been a terrible mix-up. I mix up their names all the time.*		Ⓑ Ⓝ Ⓢ
mL Abbrev. of *milliliter.*		Ⓑ
ml		Ⓢ
MLB Abbrev. for *Major League Baseball.*		
mm Abbrev. of *millimeter.*		Ⓑ Ⓢ
M&M'S		Ⓑ Ⓢ
M&M's		Ⓝ
mock-up (n.)		Ⓑ Ⓝ Ⓢ
moneymaker, moneymaking		Ⓑ Ⓝ Ⓢ
monthlong		Ⓑ Ⓝ Ⓢ
month's, months', as in *one month's vacation, three months' time,* etc. Treat as possessive, taking care to distinguish the singular possessive *one month's* from the plural possessive *two months'.* (See "Quasi Possessives," page 15.)		Ⓑ Ⓝ Ⓢ Ⓐ
moonlight, moonlighting, moonlit One word, no hyphen in all uses.		Ⓑ Ⓝ Ⓢ
moped (n.)		Ⓑ Ⓢ
mo-ped (n.)		Ⓝ
motherboard		Ⓑ Ⓝ Ⓢ
motherfucker (n.), **motherfucking** (adj.)		Ⓑ Ⓝ Ⓢ
mother-in-law, mothers-in-law (pl.)		Ⓑ Ⓝ Ⓢ

M

mother lode		Ⓑ Ⓝ Ⓢ
Mother's Day		Ⓑ Ⓝ Ⓢ
mother tongue		Ⓑ Ⓝ Ⓢ
moviegoer		Ⓑ Ⓝ Ⓢ
movie titles, quotation marks vs. italics	Book, science, and academic style use italics. (For more, see "Quotation Marks vs. Italics for Titles of Works," pages 74–75.)	Ⓑ Ⓢ Ⓐ
	News style puts quotation marks around movie titles.	Ⓝ
MP3, MP3s (pl.)		Ⓑ Ⓝ
mpg Abbrev. of *miles per gallon.*		Ⓑ Ⓝ
mph Abbrev. of *miles per hour.*		Ⓑ Ⓝ Ⓢ
Mr., Mrs., Ms.		Ⓑ Ⓝ Ⓢ Ⓐ
MST Abbrev. for *Mountain Standard Time.*		Ⓑ Ⓝ Ⓢ Ⓐ
much, hyphenation of	Hyphenate before but not after the noun: *A much-needed rest. Rest that was much needed.*	Ⓑ
	Do not hyphenate: *A much needed rest. Rest that was much needed.*	Ⓐ
	For news and science styles, standard rules of hyphenation apply. Hyphenate whenever hyphen can aid comprehension or readability.	Ⓝ Ⓢ
multi- Standard rules for hyphenating prefixes apply. In general, no hyphen except before a proper noun or to avoid awkward compounds.		Ⓑ Ⓝ Ⓢ Ⓐ
multimillion, multimillionaire		Ⓑ Ⓝ Ⓢ Ⓐ
multimillion-dollar (adj.), **multibillion-dollar** (adj.) *A multimillion-dollar home. A multibillion-dollar deal.*		Ⓑ Ⓝ Ⓢ Ⓐ
nationwide		Ⓑ Ⓝ Ⓢ
Native American No hyphen as noun or adjective.		Ⓑ Ⓝ Ⓢ
NATO Acronym for *North Atlantic Treaty Organization.*		Ⓑ Ⓝ Ⓢ Ⓐ
NBA Abbrev. for *National Basketball Association.*		
NBC Abbrev. for *National Broadcasting Corporation* .		
NC-17		Ⓝ
nearsighted, nearsightedness		Ⓑ Ⓝ Ⓢ
never-ending (adj.)	Usually hyphenated before a noun.	Ⓑ Ⓝ Ⓢ Ⓐ
	Hyphenate after a form of *be: this problem is never-ending.*	Ⓝ

nevertheless, commas with Sentence adverbs like *nevertheless* may or may not be set off with commas, depending on whether the writer judges it a parenthetical insertion or well integrated into the sentence.	Ⓑ Ⓝ Ⓢ Ⓐ		
Right: *The parking garage, nevertheless, was almost empty.*			
Right: *The parking garage nevertheless was almost empty.*			
New Year's, New Year's Day, New Year's Eve	Ⓑ Ⓝ Ⓢ		
NFL Abbrev. for *National Football League.*			
NHL Abbrev. for *National Hockey League.*			
night-blind	Ⓑ Ⓢ ✛		
night blindness	Ⓑ Ⓝ Ⓢ		
nightcap	Ⓑ Ⓝ Ⓢ		
nightclub	Ⓑ Ⓝ Ⓢ		
nightfall	Ⓑ Ⓝ Ⓢ		
nightgown	Ⓑ Ⓝ Ⓢ		
nightlife	Ⓑ Ⓢ		
night life	Ⓝ		
night-light (n.)	Ⓑ Ⓢ		
night light (n.)	Ⓝ		
night owl	Ⓑ Ⓝ Ⓢ		
night school (n.)	Ⓑ Ⓝ Ⓢ		
night-school, night school (adj.)	Hyphenate in book and science styles: *he received his night-school diploma.*	Ⓑ Ⓢ	
	Hyphenate in news style when it comes before the noun it modifies or after *be* only if the hyphen aids comprehension.	Ⓝ	
	Do not hyphenate in academic style: *he received his night school diploma.*	Ⓐ	
nightstand	Ⓑ Ⓝ Ⓢ		
night table	Ⓑ Ⓝ Ⓢ		
nighttime (n.)	Ⓑ Ⓝ Ⓢ		
night vision (n.) Two words, no hyphen as a noun: *cats have excellent night vision.*	Ⓑ Ⓝ Ⓢ		
night-vision (adj.) *They use night-vision goggles.*	Ⓑ		
9/11 Can be written numerically as a nickname for the events of September 11, 2001, but especially in book style, consider spelling out.	Ⓑ Ⓝ		
911 call	Ⓝ		
nitty-gritty	Ⓑ Ⓝ Ⓢ		

N

Entry	Styles
no, commas with *No* is often, but not necessarily, set off with commas. The writer can choose to omit commas if they do not aid readability or rhythm: *No, coyotes don't come this far south. No you don't.*	Ⓑ
no, plural of The plural of *no* takes an *e* and no apostrophe: *among the votes, there were only three noes.* (*Nos* is also acceptable.)	Ⓑ Ⓝ Ⓢ
No. Capitalize the *N* and use a period when abbreviating *number*: *the group had the No. 1 hit single.*	Ⓝ
no-go (adj.)	Ⓑ Ⓝ Ⓢ
For the noun form, Punctuation Panel unanimously supports hyphenating: *the plan was a no-go.*	✚
no-hitter	Ⓑ Ⓝ Ⓢ
no-holds-barred Hyphenated as an adjective: *a no-holds-barred competition.* Otherwise, no hyphen: *they fought with no holds barred.*	Ⓑ Ⓝ Ⓢ
non- In general don't hyphenate. Exceptions below.	
In book style, hyphenate *non* only when necessary to avoid an awkward compound (*non-wine-drinking*). Hyphenate with one-word proper nouns (*non-English*). But for proper nouns and other compounds of two or more words, use an en dash (*non–French Canadian, non–high school*).	Ⓑ
In news style, hyphenate *non* only when necessary to avoid an awkward compound (*non-nuclear, non-wine-drinking, non-French Canadian, non-high school*) or when used with a proper noun (*non-English*).	Ⓝ
noncoordinate adjective *See* coordinate adjective	
nondefining clause. *See* nonrestrictive	
nonessential clause *See* nonrestrictive	
nonetheless, commas with Sentence adverbs like *nonetheless* may or may not be set off with commas, depending on whether the writer judges it a parenthetical insertion or well integrated into the sentence. Right: *The parking garage, nonetheless, was almost empty.* Right: *The parking garage nonetheless was almost empty.*	Ⓑ Ⓝ Ⓢ Ⓐ
no-no Hyphenate singular noun form: *looking at another student's paper is a major no-no.*	Ⓑ Ⓝ Ⓢ
no-no's Use an apostrophe to form the plural in book and science styles: *talking and chewing gum are both major no-no's.*	Ⓑ Ⓢ
no-nos Do not use an apostrophe to form the plural in news style: *talking and chewing gum are both major no-nos.*	Ⓝ
no-nonsense (adj.)	Ⓑ Ⓝ Ⓢ
nonprofit (n., adj.)	Ⓑ Ⓝ Ⓢ Ⓐ

nonrestrictive A nonrestrictive clause or phrase is one that does not specify or narrow down the noun it modifies: *the workers, who respect the boss, do well.* The commas indicate that all the workers do well, and their respect for the boss is universal. In this example, the clause *who respect the boss* does not narrow down the number of workers referred to. This is nonrestrictive. (For more, see "Comma to Set Off a Nonrestrictive or Parenthetical Word, Phrase, or Clause," page 32.)

nonstick	Ⓑ Ⓝ Ⓢ Ⓐ
nor'easter	Ⓑ Ⓝ Ⓢ
not, commas with Noun phrases that begin with *not*, when inserted into a sentence for contrast, are set off with commas: *The student with the best grades, not the most popular student, will be appointed. It was Rick, not Alan, who cleaned the microwave.*	Ⓑ Ⓝ Ⓢ Ⓐ
not only ... but ... , commas with No comma is generally needed before the *but* in phrases following this structure: *not only children on vacation from school but also adults on vacation from work flocked to the theater.*	Ⓑ Ⓝ Ⓢ Ⓐ
NRA Abbrev. for *National Rifle Association.*	Ⓑ Ⓝ Ⓢ Ⓐ
n't Contraction of *not*, used in *isn't, aren't, wasn't, weren't, can't, couldn't, doesn't, didn't, hasn't, hadn't, won't, wouldn't, shouldn't,* etc.	Ⓑ Ⓝ Ⓢ Ⓐ
numbers, spelled out, hyphens in When spelled out, the numbers *twenty-one* through *ninety-nine* are hyphenated.	
N-word	Ⓝ
NYC	Ⓑ Ⓝ Ⓢ Ⓐ
o'clock	Ⓑ Ⓝ Ⓢ

odd	Hyphenate a compound adjective beginning with *odd*: *Odd-number days.*	Ⓑ Ⓝ
	Hyphenate a compound adjective ending with *odd*: *I've told you a thousand-odd times.*	Ⓑ

odds, hyphenation of *See* betting odds	
of forms as possessives In compound constructions with *of* that represent a singular noun, such as *Queen of England* or *chairman of the board*, form the possessive by adding the apostrophe and *s* to the word that comes immediately before the modified word: *the Queen of England's crown*, not *the Queen's of England crown; chairman of the board's leadership*, not *chairman's of the board leadership.*	Ⓑ Ⓝ Ⓢ Ⓐ
-off, meaning discounted, as part of compound modifier	✚
A majority of the Punctuation Panel preferred to hyphenate compound modifiers like *a $10-off coupon.*	
off-and-on (adj.) Usually hyphenated. *They have an off-and-on relationship.*	Ⓑ Ⓝ Ⓢ Ⓐ
off and on (adv.) *They see each other off and on.*	Ⓑ Ⓝ Ⓢ Ⓐ

off-Broadway, off-off-Broadway (adj.), **off Broadway** (adv.) *He starred in an off-Broadway play.* Used adverbially to indicate location, no hyphen: *the show is playing off Broadway.*	Ⓑ Ⓝ Ⓢ
off-line	Ⓑ Ⓢ
offline	Ⓝ
off-putting	Ⓑ Ⓝ Ⓢ
offset (n., v., adj., adv.) *They calculated their offsets. The deposits offset our losses. They use offset printing processes.*	Ⓑ Ⓝ Ⓢ
off-site (adv.) *They filmed off-site.*	Ⓑ
off-site (adj., adv.) *They filmed off-site. It was an off-site shoot.*	Ⓝ
offstage One word, no hyphen in all uses: *An offstage spat. The incident happened offstage.*	Ⓑ Ⓝ Ⓢ
oh, commas with *Oh* is often, but not necessarily, set off with commas. The writer can choose to omit commas if they do not aid readability or rhythm: *Oh, I see what you're up to. Oh you.*	Ⓑ
okay When using the spelled-out *okay* as a verb, which is an option in book style, no apostrophe is used: *okays, okayed, okaying.*	Ⓑ
OK'd As a verb, *OK* forms its past tense with an apostrophe. (Note that news style uses no periods. Book style does not specify whether to include periods, though *The Chicago Manual of Style* indicates in its own usage a preference for omitting the periods as well.)	Ⓑ Ⓝ
OK'ing The progressive form of the verb *OK* takes an apostrophe. (Note that news style uses no periods. Book style does not specify whether to include periods, though *The Chicago Manual of Style* indicates in its own usage a preference for omitting the periods as well.)	Ⓑ Ⓝ
OKs When *OK* is used as a verb in the third-person singular present tense, no apostrophe: *I hope the boss OKs my raise.*	Ⓝ
-old Combined with a number and *year* to form a noun, hyphenate: *the school began admitting five-year-olds.* Also hyphenate adjective forms used before nouns: *Carrie works on a five-year-old computer.* But no hyphen in contexts like *He is five years old.* (For when to use numerals or spelled-out numbers, see "Numerals vs. Spelled-Out Numbers," pages 140–42)	Ⓑ Ⓝ
old-fashioned	Ⓑ Ⓝ Ⓢ

old-school, **old school**	Hyphenate as an adjective before a noun: *he has an old-school style.*	Ⓑ Ⓢ
	Hyphenation after a noun is optional: *that look is old school.*	Ⓑ
	Hyphenate as an adjective after a form of *be*: *that look is old-school.*	Ⓝ
	For adverb forms, the Punctuation Panel split on whether to hyphenate, with half opting for *He dances old school* and half preferring *He dances old-school.*	**✛**

old-timer (n.), **old-time** (adj.)		Ⓑ Ⓝ Ⓢ
Old World (proper noun), **old-world** (adj.) Use two words, no hyphen, and capitals when using as a proper name to refer to the geographic area: *back in the Old World, our ancestors kept things simple.* Hyphenate as a generic adjective: *their children picked up their old-world mannerisms and attitudes.*		Ⓑ Ⓝ Ⓢ Ⓐ
on-again, off-again (adj.)		Ⓑ Ⓢ
on-air (adj., adv.)		Ⓑ Ⓝ Ⓢ
onboard (adj.) *An onboard computer.*		Ⓑ Ⓝ Ⓢ
on board (adv.) *Hurry up and get on board.*		Ⓑ Ⓢ
onboard (adv.) *Hurry up and get onboard.*		Ⓝ
onetime, one-time	The one-word form usually means "former": *a onetime child star.* But it can also be an adjective meaning "occurring only once": *hurry to take advantage of this onetime deal.*	Ⓑ Ⓢ
	The one-word form means "former": *a onetime child star.* The adjective meaning "occurring only once" is hyphenated: *hurry to take advantage of this one-time deal.*	Ⓝ
online		Ⓑ Ⓝ Ⓢ
on-site (adj., adv.) *An on-site restaurant. Products manufactured on-site.*		Ⓑ Ⓝ Ⓢ
onstage (adj., adv.) *An onstage incident. The incident happened onstage.*		Ⓑ Ⓝ Ⓢ
on-time (adj.), **on time** (adv.) *On-time delivery. It must arrive on time.*		Ⓑ Ⓝ Ⓢ
operagoer		Ⓑ Ⓝ Ⓢ
or, commas with	Between independent clauses, a comma usually does not precede *or* unless the clauses are very short and closely related: *he will be on the flight first thing in the morning, or perhaps he will change his mind last minute as he often does.*	Ⓑ Ⓝ Ⓢ Ⓐ
	In a series of two or more items, *or* is preceded by a comma in book, science, and academic styles: *a cherry, apple, or peach pie.*	Ⓑ Ⓢ Ⓐ
	In news style, the comma before *or* in a series is omitted: *a cherry, apple or peach pie.*	Ⓝ
	See also serial comma	
ours Never contains an apostrophe.		Ⓑ Ⓝ Ⓢ Ⓐ

out-	Do not hyphenate *out-* in the meaning "to do better" or "exceed" unless lack of a hyphen would cause an awkward or confusing construction: *outjump, outmambo, outcalculate.*	**B** **S** **A**
	Hyphenate prefix *out-* in the meaning "to do better" or "exceed" in any term not listed in *Webster's New World College Dictionary*: *out-jump, out-mambo, out-calculate.* Terms listed in the dictionary customarily take no hyphen: *outbid, outdance, outdrink, outeat, outfox, outflank, outgrow, outgun, outlast, outperform, outscore, outspend, outstrip, outtalk, outthink.*	**N**

-out Hyphenate all nouns and adjectives ending in *out* that do not appear in the dictionary: *cop-out, fade-out.* For verbs, keep as two words and do not hyphenate: *fade out, hide out, pull out, walk out, wash out.*	**N**
outbid	**B** **N** **S** **A**
outbound	**B** **N** **S**
outbreak	**B** **N** **S**
outdance	**B** **N** **S** **A**
outdated	**B** **N** **S**
outdo	**B** **N** **S** **A**
outdrink	**B** **N** **S** **A**
outeat	**B** **N** **S** **A**
outer space Two words, no hyphen as a noun.	**B** **N** **S**
outfield	**B** **N** **S** **A**
outfox	**B** **N** **S** **A**
outgrow	**B** **N** **S** **A**
outgun, outgunned	**B** **N** **S** **A**
outlast	**B** **N** **S** **A**
out-of-towner	**B** **N** **S**
outpatient	**B** **N** **S**
outperform	**B** **N** **S** **A**
output	**B** **N** **S**
outrun	**B** **N** **S** **A**
outscore	**B** **N** **S** **A**
outsource, outsourcing	**B** **N** **S**
outspend	**B** **N** **S** **A**
outstrip	**B** **N** **S** **A**

outtalk	Ⓑ Ⓝ Ⓢ Ⓐ
outthink	Ⓑ Ⓝ Ⓢ Ⓐ

over- Do not hyphenate compounds that begin with *over-* unless necessary to prevent awkwardness or to aid comprehension: *overeager, overnourish, overstaff.*   Ⓑ Ⓝ Ⓢ Ⓐ

overall, over all, overalls No hyphen for the adjective (*An overall success*) or the adverb (*Overall, we succeeded*). Two words as a prepositional phrase *(The victors will reign over all)*. The garment is termed *overalls.*   Ⓑ Ⓝ Ⓢ

over-the-counter (adj.)   Ⓑ Ⓝ Ⓢ

over the counter, over-the-counter (adv.) Punctuation Panel split on whether to hyphenate as an adverb: *They sell it over the counter. They sell it over-the-counter.*   ✚

overweight   Ⓑ Ⓝ Ⓢ

owner's manual The Punctuation Panel preferred the singular possessive *owner's* in this phrase. (See also "Possessive vs. Adjective Forms," page 16.)   ✚

Oxford comma *See* serial comma

pallbearer   Ⓑ Ⓝ Ⓢ

pan- Hyphenate and capitalize before a proper noun. *Pan-African, Pan-American, Pan-Asiatic.* Otherwise, standard rules of hyphenation apply. Hyphenate whenever doing so aids readability. Otherwise, no hyphen: *panspectral, panchromatic.*   Ⓝ

Hyphenate but keep lowercase before a proper noun: *pan-African.* Standard rules of hyphenation apply. Hyphenate whenever doing so aids readability. Otherwise, no hyphen: *panspectral, panchromatic.*   Ⓑ Ⓢ Ⓐ

pari-mutuel   Ⓑ Ⓝ Ⓢ

Parkinson's disease, Parkinson's   Ⓑ Ⓝ Ⓢ

participial phrase A single participle or group of words headed by a participle: *Seething, Joe waited. Seething with hatred, Joe waited. Discussed at length, the proposal eventually passed.* Participial phrases are subject to standard comma rules: they are often set off with commas unless they are short and pose no danger of confusion without a comma. (See also chapter 2.)

part-time (adj.), **part time** (adv.) *She has a part-time job. She works part time.*   Ⓑ Ⓝ

passenger-side For the compound adjective, the Punctuation Panel preferred the nonpossessive form and a hyphen: *passenger-side window, passenger-side air bag.*   ✚

passer-by, passers-by (pl.)   Ⓝ

passerby, passersby (pl.)   Ⓑ Ⓢ

Term	Description	Styles
pat down (n.) Not hyphenated as noun in book or science style: *police gave him the requisite pat down.*		Ⓑ Ⓢ
pat-down (n.) Hyphenated as a noun in news style: *police gave him the requisite pat-down.*		Ⓝ
pat down (v.) *The officer must pat down the suspect.*		Ⓑ Ⓢ Ⓝ
pat-down (adj.) *They followed standard pat-down procedure.*		Ⓝ
PDF Abbrev. for *Portable Document Format.*		Ⓑ Ⓝ Ⓢ Ⓐ
PDT Abbrev. for *Pacific Daylight Time.*		Ⓑ Ⓝ Ⓢ Ⓐ
peacekeeping, peacemaker, peacemaking		Ⓑ Ⓝ Ⓢ
peacetime (n., adj.)		Ⓑ Ⓝ Ⓢ
penny-wise		Ⓑ Ⓝ Ⓢ
people watching, people-watching	Usually not hyphenated: *he enjoys people watching.*	Ⓑ ✚
	Noun form can be hyphenated if the writer feels the hyphen aids readability: *he enjoys people-watching.*	Ⓝ
percent (n., adj) No hyphen: *The difference was just 2 percent. He got a 2 percent raise.*		Ⓑ Ⓝ
periodical titles	In book and academic style, italicize periodical titles but do not place in quotation marks.	Ⓑ Ⓐ
	In news style, do not place titles of newspapers, magazines, or similar periodicals in quotation marks and do not italicize.	Ⓝ
	Science style does not customarily deal with periodicals in running text but instead lists them italicized bibliography-style at the end of a document with only an author-and-year reference in the text.	Ⓢ
Pete's sake		Ⓑ Ⓝ Ⓢ Ⓐ
PG, PG-13		Ⓝ
PGA Abbrev. for *Professional Golfers' Association.*		
PhD, PhDs Abbrev. for *doctor of philosophy*: *Jason Wellsley, PhD, gave a presentation.*		Ⓑ Ⓢ Ⓐ
Ph.D., Ph.D.s Abbrev. for *doctor of philosophy*: *this is Jason Wellsley, Ph.D.*		Ⓝ
pick-me-up (n.)		Ⓑ Ⓝ Ⓢ
pickup (n., adj.) Use the one-word form for a noun meaning a truck, a person or thing picked up, or the act of picking something up: *We drove my pickup. The kids joined in a pickup game. I need to schedule a pickup.*		Ⓑ Ⓝ Ⓢ
pick-up truck		Ⓑ Ⓢ
pickup truck		Ⓝ
piecemeal		Ⓑ Ⓝ Ⓢ

Term	Styles
pigskin	Ⓑ Ⓝ Ⓢ
Pikes Peak	Ⓑ Ⓝ Ⓢ
ping-pong	Ⓑ Ⓢ
pingpong	Ⓝ
pipeline	Ⓑ Ⓝ Ⓢ
placekick (n., v.), **placekicker**	Ⓑ Ⓢ
place kick (n., v.), **place-kicker**	Ⓝ
play off (v.), **playoff** (n.)	Ⓑ Ⓝ Ⓢ
please, commas with Editing styles do not have express rules on when to set off *please* with commas. A majority of the Punctuation Panel preferred a comma in: *May I have your attention, please?*	✚
PLO Abbrev. for *Palestine Liberation Organization*.	Ⓑ Ⓝ Ⓢ Ⓐ
plug and play (n.)	Ⓑ Ⓢ
plug-and-play (adj.)	Ⓑ Ⓝ Ⓢ
plug-in (n., adj.), **plug in** (v.)	Ⓑ Ⓝ Ⓢ
p.m. Abbrev. for *post meridiem*. All major styles prefer lowercase and periods, though book publishing sometimes uses small capitals, either with or without periods.	Ⓑ Ⓝ Ⓢ Ⓐ
PO Box Use a capital B in addresses, though in generic contexts the b is lowercase: *she stopped to check her PO box.*	Ⓑ
P.O. Box Use a capital B in addresses, but not in generic references: *she stopped to check her P.O. box.*	Ⓝ
po'boy	Ⓑ Ⓝ Ⓢ
point-blank (adj., adv.)	Ⓑ Ⓝ Ⓢ
pom-pom In the meaning of tufts used by cheerleaders or as embellishments of clothing or furniture, hyphenate: *the cheerleaders waved their pom-poms.*	Ⓑ Ⓢ
pompom One word, no hyphen: *the cheerleaders waved their pompoms.*	Ⓝ
pooh-pooh, pooh-poohing (v.) Meaning to show disdain for: *must you pooh-pooh everything I suggest?*	Ⓑ Ⓝ Ⓢ
possessive as part of compound Standard hyphenation rules apply to compounds that contain internal possessives, such as *crow's-nest view* and *quail's-egg omelet.*	Ⓑ Ⓝ Ⓢ Ⓐ
post-	Standard rules for hyphenating prefixes apply. In general, no hyphen except to prevent awkward combinations.	Ⓑ Ⓢ Ⓐ
	Hyphenate terms that don't appear in the dictionary: *post-mortem, post-convention, post-picnic, post-breakup.* Two exceptions: *postelection, postgame.*	Ⓝ

	B	N	S	A
postdate	B	N	S	A
postdoctoral	B	N	S	A
postelection	B	N	S	A
postgame	B	N	S	A
postgraduate	B	N	S	A
Post-it Proper name for adhesive notes contains a hyphen and a lowercase *i*.				
postmortem (n., adj., adv.)	B		S	
post-mortem (n., adj., adv.)		N		
postoperative	B	N	S	A
postscript	B	N	S	A
post-traumatic stress disorder Hyphen after *post*.	B	N	S	A
postwar	B	N	S	
potluck	B	N	S	
potpie	B	N	S	
pot sticker	B	N	S	
pound, abbreviation of *See* lb.				
ppm Abbrev. of *parts per million* or *pages per minute*.	B		S	
PPO Abbrev. for *preferred provider organization*.	B	N	S	
pre- Hyphenate if the word that follows begins with an *e*, regardless of whether the compound appears unhyphenated in the dictionary: *pre-election, pre-eminent, pre-empt, pre-establish, pre-exist*.		N		
Standard rules for hyphenating prefixes apply. In general, do not hyphenate unless necessary for clarity.	B		S	A
preapprove	B	N	S	A
prearrange	B	N	S	A
precondition	B	N	S	A
preconvention	B		S	A
pre-convention		N		
precook	B	N	S	A
predate	B	N	S	A
predecease	B	N	S	A
predispose	B	N	S	A
pre-election		N		
preeminent, preeminence	B		S	
pre-eminent		N		

preempt, preemptive	B S
pre-empt, pre-emptive	N
pre-establish	B N S A
preexist, preexisting	B S
pre-exist, pre-existing	N
prefixes Major editing styles agree that prefixes should not be hyphenated unless they precede a proper noun or a number (*pre-1960s, post-Edwardian*), end with an *a* or *i* and precede a word beginning with the same vowel that begins the following word (*anti-icing*), or would create a term that can be confused for another term (*recreate* vs. *re-create*). (For exceptions to this basic guideline, see "Prefixes," pages 111–15.)	B N S A
preflight	B N S A
pregame	B N S A
preheat	B N S A
prehistoric	B N S A
prejudge	B N S A
premarital	B N S A
prenatal	B N S A
prenoon	B S A
pre-noon	N
prenuptial Usually not hyphenated.	B N S A
pretax Usually not hyphenated.	B N S A
prewar Usually not hyphenated.	B N S A

preposition, prepositional phrase Preposition is a word category whose members usually pair with nouns or pronouns to modify other parts of a sentence. The group includes *about, above, across, after, against, along, among, around, at, before, behind, below, beneath, beside, between, beyond, by, concerning, despite, down, during, except, for, from, in, inside, into, like, near, of, off, on, onto, out, outside, over, past, regarding, since, through, throughout, till, to, toward, under, underneath, until, up, upon, with, within,* and *without*. However, because words can function as different parts of speech, no definitive list of prepositions can be made.

preposition, prepositional phrase, commas with Prepositional phrases, which include a preposition and its object, are often but not necessarily set off with commas: *With great care, he opened the door. On Tuesday, will we visit our grandparents.* (For more, see chapter 2.)

Presidents Day	N
Presidents' Day	B S

P

Term	Rule	Styles
prima facie, prima-facie (adj., adv.)	No hyphen as an adjective: *a prima facie solution.*	Ⓑ Ⓢ
	Hyphenate as an adjective: *a prima-facie solution.*	Ⓝ
	No hyphen as an adverb: *he reached his conclusion prima facie.*	Ⓑ Ⓝ Ⓢ
prime time (n.), **prime-time** (adj.) Do not capitalize.		Ⓝ
Prince/Princess of (country name), forming possessive of *Prince of England's visit, not Prince's of England visit. See also* of forms as possessives		Ⓑ Ⓝ Ⓢ Ⓐ
pro, hyphenation of	When using *pro* to form a compound adjective not found in the dictionary, the writer in book, science, and academic styles can choose open, hyphenated, or closed forms: *He is pro labor. He is pro-labor. He is prolabor.*	Ⓑ Ⓢ Ⓐ
	A majority of the Punctuation Panel preferred hyphenated forms: *She is pro-labor. He is pro-peace.* A minority preferred open forms: *She is pro labor. He is pro peace.* None opted for closed forms. (See also "pro-," page 114.)	✛
	In news style, hyphenate *pro* whenever it's used in a coinage meaning "in favor of something": *pro-labor, pro-chocolate.*	Ⓝ
proactive		Ⓑ Ⓝ Ⓢ Ⓐ
pro-business		Ⓝ
profit sharing (n.)		Ⓑ Ⓢ
profit-sharing (n.)		Ⓝ
profit-sharing (adj.)		Ⓑ Ⓝ Ⓢ
profit-taking (n.)		Ⓝ
pro forma (adj., adv.)		Ⓑ Ⓝ
pro-labor		Ⓝ
pro-peace		Ⓝ
pro-war		Ⓝ
psi Abbrev. for *pounds per square inch.*		Ⓢ
PST Abbrev. for *Pacific Standard Time.*		Ⓑ Ⓝ Ⓢ Ⓐ
PTA Abbrev. for *Parent-Teacher Association.*		Ⓑ Ⓝ Ⓢ Ⓐ
PT boat		Ⓑ Ⓝ Ⓢ Ⓐ
pullback (n.), **pull back** (v.)		Ⓑ Ⓝ Ⓢ
pullout (n.), **pull out** (v.)		Ⓑ Ⓝ Ⓢ

push button (n.)		Ⓑ Ⓢ
push-button (n., adj.)		Ⓝ
put-on (n., adj.), **put on** (v.)		Ⓑ Ⓝ Ⓢ
put-together, hyphenation of, in longer modifiers A majority of the Punctuation Panel preferred two hyphens in *a well-put-together woman* but only one hyphen in a *nicely put-together woman*.		✚
Q-and-A format Abbrev. of *question-and-answer format*.		Ⓝ
quasi Usually hyphenated as part of a compound adjective, *a quasi-successful venture*, but not as part of a noun, *a quasi possessive*.		Ⓑ
quasi possessive Quasi possessive is a term used to describe expressions like *two weeks' notice, a half-hour's pay, a year's supply, a day's drive*. These terms customarily are treated as possessives and take apostrophes.		
Queen Anne's lace		Ⓑ Ⓝ Ⓢ
Queen of (country name) as possessive Add apostrophe and s after the last word. *Queen of England's visit*, not *Queen's of England visit*. *See also* of forms as possessives		Ⓑ Ⓝ Ⓢ Ⓐ
quotation marks, forming plurals of terms in Various styles require quotation marks around certain titles. For example, news style puts quotation marks around movie titles like "Casablanca" and words as words, such as "if." To make into a plural, place the s inside the quotation marks: *How many "Casablancas" can Hollywood churn out? We will hear no "ifs," "ands," or "buts."*		Ⓑ Ⓝ Ⓢ
quotation marks, forming possessives of terms in The possessive apostrophe and, when appropriate, the s go inside the quotation marks. "Casablanca's" cinematography.		Ⓑ Ⓝ Ⓢ
Quran No apostrophe in this variant spelling of *Koran*.		Ⓑ Ⓝ Ⓢ
radio station call letters Use all capitals and no periods. Insert hyphen only when adding type of station to main call letters: *WMNF. WMNF-FM. KROQ.*		Ⓑ Ⓝ Ⓢ Ⓐ
rainmaker		Ⓑ Ⓝ Ⓢ
ranges	In running text, ranges of numerically valued things like ages, money, and time are usually written out with the word *to, through,* or *until. The job pays $50,000 to $55,000 a year. The park is open 5 to 7. Children ages 11 through 15 can enroll.* In casual contexts, they can be punctuated as follows.	
	In book style, use an en dash: *The job pays $50,000–$55,000 a year. The park is open 5–7. Children 11–15 can enroll.*	Ⓑ
	In news, science, or academic style, use a hyphen: *The job pays $50,000-$55,000 a year. The park is open 5-7. Children 11-15 can enroll.*	Ⓝ Ⓢ Ⓐ
rank and file (n.), **rank-and-file** (adj.)		Ⓑ Ⓝ Ⓢ Ⓐ

P

ratios	In book and science styles, a ratio expressed numeri-cally takes a colon and no spaces. *2:1.* In running text, however, the writer can choose to write out the words: *pigeons in the area exceed gulls by a two-to-one ratio.*	ⒷⓈ
	In news style, ratios are expressed with numerals and hyphens. After words such as *ratio* or *majority*, use the word *to: a ratio of 2-to-1.* Before words such as *ratio* or *majority*, do not use the word *to: a 2-1 ratio.*	Ⓝ
R & B (n., adj.) Short for *rhythm and blues.*		ⒷⓈ
R&B (n., adj.)		Ⓝ
re, period after The preposition *re*, meaning *regarding*, is not followed by a period (unless at the end of a sentence).		ⒷⓃⓈ
re, colon with The standard rules of colons apply. In theory, the preposi-tion *re* carries no greater need for a colon than the word *regarding.* However, because sentences and phrases containing *re* are often used for emphasis or introduction, colons are commonly used with *re.* The colon can go after the whole *re* phrase: *Re your recent correspondence: we will discuss payroll further next week.* Or, especially at the top of business cor-respondence, *re* can be followed immediately by a colon: *Re: Your letter.*		ⒷⓃⓈ
re- Standard rules for hyphenating prefixes apply. In general, do not hyphenate unless doing so aids readability or prevents confusion. For example, *re-create* vs. *recreate.*		ⒷⓃⓈⒶ
re-cover, recover In the meaning "to cover again," use a hyphen to distinguish from *recover*, meaning "to become well."		ⒷⓃⓈⒶ
re-create, recreate In the meaning "to create again," use a hyphen to distinguish from *recreate*, meaning "to play" or "to enjoy leisure time."		ⒷⓃⓈⒶ
recur		ⒷⓃⓈ
redhead, redheaded		ⒷⓃⓈ
red-hot Hyphenated. The candies are *Red Hots*, no hyphen.		ⒷⓃⓈⒶ
redneck		ⒷⓃⓈ
redo, redid, redone, redoing		ⒷⓃⓈ
reelect, reelection		ⒷⓈ
re-elect, re-election		Ⓝ
reemerge, reemergence		ⒷⓈ
re-emerge, re-emergence		Ⓝ
reemploy, reemployment		ⒷⓈ
re-employ, re-employment		Ⓝ
reenact, reenactment		ⒷⓈ
re-enact, re-enactment		Ⓝ

reenlist	Ⓑ Ⓢ
re-enlist	Ⓝ
reenter, reentry	Ⓑ Ⓢ
re-enter, re-entry	Ⓝ
reestablish	Ⓑ Ⓢ
re-establish	Ⓝ
reexamine, reexamination	Ⓑ Ⓢ
re-examine, re-examination	Ⓝ
refi, re-fi Punctuation Panel split on whether to hyphenate.	✛
refinance	Ⓑ Ⓝ Ⓢ Ⓐ

relative clause, relative pronoun A relative clause is a clause that is introduced by one of four relative pronouns: *that*, *which*, *who*, or *whom*. Its job is to modify a noun that precedes it. Relative clauses are set off with commas when they are nonrestrictive (*The interview, which I had marked on my calendar, was rapidly approaching*) but take no commas when they are restrictive (*The dress that I want to buy is on sale*). (For more, see "Comma to Set Off a Nonrestrictive or Parenthetical Word, Phrase, or Clause," page 32.)

relay, re-lay Relay means "to convey." He tried to *relay the information to his subordinates*. *Re-lay* means "to lay again." *You'll have to re-lay that tile.*	Ⓑ Ⓝ Ⓢ Ⓐ
release, re-lease *Release* means "to let go of." *Re-lease* means "to lease again."	Ⓑ Ⓝ Ⓢ Ⓐ
reread	Ⓑ Ⓝ Ⓢ Ⓐ
re-sign In the meaning "to sign again," the hyphen is required to distinguish it from *resign*, meaning "to quit."	Ⓑ Ⓝ Ⓢ Ⓐ
respectively, commas with The Punctuation Panel unanimously favored setting off *respectively* with commas.	✛

restrictive A restrictive clause or phrase is one that specifies or narrows down the noun it modifies: *the workers who respect the boss do well*. In this example, the clause *who respect their boss* is restrictive because it narrows down the noun phrase *the workers* to specify only those who respect the boss. Commas are often key to understanding whether a term is restrictive.

The workers, who respect the boss, do well. In this second example, the commas indicate that all the workers do well and their affection for the boss is universal. In this nonrestrictive example, the clause *who respect the boss* does not narrow down the number of workers referred to. (For more, see "Comma to Set Off a Nonrestrictive or Parenthetical Word, Phrase, or Clause," page 32.)

Rhodes scholar	
rib eye (n.)	Ⓑ Ⓢ
rib-eye (n., adj.)	Ⓝ
right-click The Punctuation Panel preferred a hyphen in the verb and noun forms: *You must right-click in the document body. Only a right-click will pull up the submenu.*	✛

R

righteousness' sake	Ⓑ Ⓝ
right hand (n.), **right-hander** (n.), **right-handed** (adj.)	Ⓑ Ⓝ Ⓢ
right-of-way	Ⓑ Ⓢ
right of way	Ⓝ
right wing (n.), **right-winger** (n.), **right-wing** (adj.)	Ⓑ Ⓝ Ⓢ
rip-off (n.), **rip off** (v.)	Ⓑ Ⓝ Ⓢ
RN In book style, this abbreviation for *registered nurse*, takes no periods and when it comes after a proper name, is set off with commas: *John Doe, RN.* As a noun, the plural would be formed without an apostrophe: *two RNs were on duty.*	Ⓑ
R.N. In news style, the use of credentials after a name is discouraged. However, when necessary to use after a name, in news style, *R.N.* would take periods and be set off with commas: *John Doe, R.N.* As a noun, the plural would be formed without an apostrophe: *two R.N.s were on duty.*	Ⓝ
rock 'n' roll Contraction of *rock and roll.*	Ⓑ Ⓝ Ⓢ Ⓐ
roll call (n.)	Ⓑ Ⓝ Ⓢ
rollover (n.), **roll over** (v.)	Ⓑ Ⓝ Ⓢ
Rolls-Royce	
roundup (n.), **round up** (v.)	Ⓑ Ⓝ Ⓢ
rpm Abbrev. of *revolutions per minute.* Preferred plural is *rpms.*	Ⓑ Ⓢ Ⓐ
RSS Abbrev. for *Really Simple Syndication.*	Ⓑ Ⓝ Ⓢ Ⓐ
RSVP	Ⓑ Ⓝ Ⓢ Ⓐ
rubber stamp (n.), **rubber-stamp** (v.)	Ⓑ Ⓝ Ⓢ
rundown (n.), **run down** (v.)	Ⓑ Ⓝ Ⓢ
run-in (n.), **run in** (v.)	Ⓑ Ⓝ Ⓢ
runner-up Plural is *runners-up.*	Ⓑ Ⓝ Ⓢ
run-on sentence	Ⓑ Ⓝ Ⓢ
's Can either show possession or be a contracted form of *is* or *has.* In *My husband's sister's visiting, husband's* shows possession but *sister's* is a contraction of *sister is.* In *Jane's been here for three weeks, Jane's* is the contracted form of *Jane has.*	Ⓑ Ⓝ Ⓢ Ⓐ
said, quotation attribution, comma with When used to attribute a quotation to a person, *said* is customarily set off with a comma: *Bill said, "That's nice." "That's nice," Bill said.*	Ⓑ Ⓝ Ⓢ Ⓐ
saltwater	Ⓑ Ⓝ Ⓢ

scores	Sentences with scores can use the word *to*: *the Patriots beat the Dolphins 21 to 7*. Or *to* can be replaced by punctuation, per below.	
	Use an en dash in book style: *the Patriots beat the Dolphins 21–7*.	Ⓑ
	Use a hyphen in news, science, and academic styles: *the Patriots beat the Dolphins 21-7*.	Ⓝ Ⓢ Ⓐ
scot-free		Ⓑ Ⓝ Ⓢ
screwup (n.)		Ⓑ Ⓢ
screw-up (n.)		Ⓝ
screw up (v.)		Ⓑ Ⓝ Ⓢ
SEAL, SEALs (pl.) Acronym for the Navy's sea-air-land special forces.		Ⓑ Ⓝ Ⓢ Ⓐ
seasons Do not use commas to separate a season from a year: *he graduated in spring 2012*. Do not capitalize.		Ⓝ
season's greetings None of the major style guides or their dictionaries indicate whether this term takes an apostrophe. The writer can choose to interpret *season's* as a quasi-possessive: *season's greetings*. The less common interpretation puts *seasons* as an adjective with no apostrophe: *seasons greetings*.		
II, III, etc. Not set off from a proper name with commas. *Robert Ableman II attended*.		Ⓑ Ⓝ Ⓢ
secondhand (adj., adv.)		Ⓑ Ⓝ Ⓢ
self- (prefix)	Terms formed with this prefix are customarily hyphenated in news and science styles.	Ⓝ Ⓢ
	Book style also hyphenates compounds formed with self, except when *self* attaches to a suffix (*selfless*) or when the compound is preceded by another prefix (*unselfconscious*).	Ⓑ
self-conscious, self-consciousness		Ⓑ Ⓝ Ⓢ
self-discipline		Ⓑ Ⓝ Ⓢ
self-esteem		Ⓑ Ⓝ Ⓢ
self-restraint		Ⓑ Ⓝ Ⓢ
sell-off (n., adj.), **sell off** (v.)		Ⓑ Ⓝ Ⓢ
sellout (n.), **sell out** (v.)		Ⓑ Ⓝ Ⓢ
semi- Standard rules for hyphenating prefixes apply. In general, no hyphen except before a proper noun or to prevent an awkward compound: *semiannual, semi-American, semi-imminent*.		Ⓑ Ⓝ Ⓢ Ⓐ
semiautomatic		Ⓑ Ⓢ
semi-automatic		Ⓝ
send-off (n.), **send off** (v.)		Ⓑ Ⓝ Ⓢ

S

Term	Styles
send-up (n.) *The show was a hilarious send-up of modern mores.*	Ⓑ Ⓢ
sendup (n.) *The show was a hilarious sendup of modern mores.*	Ⓝ
send up (v.)	Ⓑ Ⓝ Ⓢ
Senior *See* Sr.	
sentence fragment *See* fragment	
sergeant at arms	Ⓑ Ⓢ
sergeant-at-arms	Ⓝ
serial comma — Also sometimes called the Oxford comma, serial comma refers to a comma before a coordinating conjunction such as *and* or *or* in a list of three or more words, phrases, or clauses: *The flag is red, white, and blue. Barry bought his ticket, entered the theater, and took his seat.*	
Use the serial comma in book, scientific, and academic styles: *The flag is red, white, and blue. Barry bought his ticket, entered the theater, and took his seat.*	Ⓑ Ⓢ Ⓐ
Omit the serial comma in news style: *The flag is red, white and blue. Barry bought his ticket, entered the theater and took his seat.*	Ⓝ
set-aside (n.), **set aside** (v.)	Ⓑ Ⓝ Ⓢ
7UP	
shakedown (n.), **shake down** (v.)	Ⓑ Ⓝ Ⓢ
shake-up (n.), **shake up** (v.)	Ⓑ Ⓝ Ⓢ
she'd Contraction of *she had* or *she would.*	Ⓑ Ⓝ Ⓢ Ⓐ
she's Contraction of *she is* or *she has.*	Ⓑ Ⓝ Ⓢ Ⓐ
shithead, shit head, shit-head A majority of the Punctuation Panel favored the one-word form, but some preferred two words without a hyphen or the hyphenated form.	✦
shoestring	Ⓑ Ⓝ Ⓢ
shopworn	Ⓑ Ⓝ Ⓢ
short circuit (n.), **short-circuit** (v.)	Ⓑ Ⓢ
short circuit (n., v.)	Ⓝ
shortcut	Ⓑ Ⓝ Ⓢ
short sale (n.)	Ⓑ Ⓝ Ⓢ
shouldn't Contraction of *should not.*	Ⓑ Ⓝ Ⓢ Ⓐ
should've Contraction of *should have.* This should never be written *should of.*	Ⓑ Ⓝ Ⓢ Ⓐ
show-off (n.)	Ⓑ Ⓢ
showoff (n.)	Ⓝ
show off (v.)	Ⓑ Ⓝ Ⓢ

shutdown (n.) **shut down** (v.)		Ⓑ Ⓝ Ⓢ
shut-in (n.)		Ⓑ Ⓝ Ⓢ
shut in (v.)		Ⓑ Ⓢ ✚
shutoff (n.)		Ⓑ Ⓢ
shut-off (n.)		Ⓝ
shut off (v.)		Ⓑ Ⓝ Ⓢ
shutout (n.), **shut out** (v.)		Ⓑ Ⓝ Ⓢ
-shy, -shyness, hyphenation of	Compounds with *-shy* are usually compound adjectives, subject to the standard rules of hyphenation: *A girl-shy young man. She is people-shy.*	Ⓑ Ⓝ Ⓢ Ⓐ
	For noun compounds with *shyness*, Punctuation Panel split on whether to hyphenate: *He suffers from girl-shyness/girl shyness. She suffers from people-shyness/people shyness.*	✚
-side Standard rules for hyphenating suffixes apply. In general, no hyphen unless necessary for clarity or readability.		Ⓑ Ⓝ Ⓢ Ⓐ
side by side (adv.) *They walked side by side.* Usually hyphenated as an adjective: *a side-by-side comparison.*		Ⓑ Ⓝ Ⓢ
sidesplitting		Ⓑ Ⓝ Ⓢ
sidestep (v.)		Ⓑ Ⓝ Ⓢ
sidetrack (v.)		Ⓑ Ⓝ Ⓢ
sidewalk		Ⓑ Ⓝ Ⓢ
sideways		Ⓑ Ⓝ Ⓢ
sightsee (v.)		Ⓑ Ⓢ
sightseeing, **sightseer**		Ⓑ Ⓝ Ⓢ
sign-up (n., adj.), **sign up** (v.)		Ⓑ Ⓝ Ⓢ
single-handed, **single-handedly**		Ⓑ Ⓝ Ⓢ
sit-in (n.)		Ⓑ Ⓝ Ⓢ
-size, -sized Usually hyphenated: *life-size, bite-sized, pint-size.*		Ⓑ Ⓝ Ⓢ
skydive, skydiving, skydiver		Ⓑ Ⓢ
slow-cook, slow cooking, slow-cooking Punctuation Panel unanimously recommended hyphenating the verb form: *you should slow-cook the vegetables.* The panel split on whether to hyphenate the gerund form: *slow-cooking brings out the flavor/slow cooking brings out the flavor.* For the adjective form, standard hyphenation rules apply: *slow-cooked vegetables are her favorite.*		✚
slow motion (n.), **slow-motion** (adj.)		Ⓑ Ⓝ Ⓢ
small-business man, small-business woman Hyphenated as such to make clear that the business, and not the man or woman, is small.		Ⓝ

S

smartphone	Ⓑ Ⓝ Ⓢ
s'more, s'mores	Ⓑ Ⓝ Ⓢ
SMS Abbrev. for *Short Message Service*.	Ⓑ Ⓝ Ⓢ Ⓐ
so, commas with When used as a coordinating conjunction to link two complete clauses, a comma normally precedes *so*. But the writer can omit the comma if the clauses are short and closely related: *He has visitors from Seattle, so he didn't go to class. He was tired so he didn't go to class.*	Ⓑ Ⓝ Ⓢ Ⓐ
so-called, hyphenation of Hyphenate as an adjective: *my so-called neighbor.* (But no hyphen as a verb: *Judge Aaron, as he is so called.*)	Ⓑ Ⓝ Ⓢ
so-called, quotation marks with Do not put quotation marks around a term introduced by *so-called*: *My so-called life. This so-called god particle.*	Ⓑ Ⓝ Ⓐ
socioeconomic	Ⓑ Ⓢ
socio-economic	Ⓝ
soft-spoken	Ⓑ Ⓝ Ⓢ
-something *See* twentysomething	
SOS	Ⓑ Ⓝ Ⓢ Ⓐ
sourced Do not use hyphen to attach to an *ly* adverb: *Locally sourced ingredients. Globally sourced materials.*	
Spanish-American War	Ⓑ Ⓝ
species's Correct for both the singular possessive and the plural possessive.	Ⓑ Ⓝ Ⓢ Ⓐ
spell-checker	Ⓑ Ⓝ Ⓢ
Spider-Man	
spin-off (n.)	Ⓑ Ⓢ
spinoff (n.)	Ⓝ
spin off (v.)	Ⓑ Ⓝ Ⓢ
spring *See* seasons	
square feet, square miles, square yards, etc. Not hyphenated except as an adjective: *The house is 1,800 square feet. It's an 1,800-square-foot house.*	Ⓑ Ⓝ Ⓢ Ⓐ

Sr., commas with	Do not set off from a proper name with commas: *Lawrence Carlson Sr. was commemorated that day.*	Ⓑ Ⓝ Ⓢ
	Set off with commas: *Lawrence Carlson, Sr., was commemorated.*	Ⓐ

stand-alone (adj.)	Ⓑ Ⓝ Ⓢ
standard-bearer	Ⓑ Ⓝ Ⓢ
standby (n., adj.), **stand by** (v.)	Ⓑ Ⓝ Ⓢ
stand-in (n., adj.), **stand in** (v.)	Ⓑ Ⓝ Ⓢ

Term	Description	Styles
standoff (n., adj.), **stand off** (v.)		B N S
standout (n., adj.), **stand out** (v.)		B N S
standstill (n., adj.), **stand still** (v.)		B N S
stand-up (n.) *He is the only stand-up in the show.*		B S +
stand-up (adj.) *He is a stand-up comedian.*		B S
standup (adj.) *He is a standup comedian.*		N
stand up (v.)		B N S
Starbucks		
Starbucks's Singular possessive.		B S A
Starbucks' Singular possessive.		N
Starbuckses' Plural possessive: *those two Starbuckses' managers both run top-rated stores.*		B N S A
"The Star-Spangled Banner" Note hyphen. In book, news, and academic styles, song titles are placed in quotation marks.		B N A
start-up (n.)		B S
startup (n.)		N
start up (v.)		B N S
state of the art (n.)		B N S A
state-of-the-art (adj.)	Usually hyphenated before a noun: *state-of-the-art technology.*	B N S A
	Do not hyphenate after a noun unless hyphen aids clarity or readability: *this technology is state of the art.*	B
	Hyphenate after a form of the verb *be*: *this technology is state-of-the-art.*	N
states, commas with A state name after a city name is both preceded and followed by a comma: *they have lived in Madison, Wisconsin, for nine years.* (See also "Commas in Location Addresses," page 42.)		
states, periods in abbreviations of	Book style usually spells out states. (See also "Abbreviation of States," page 145.)	B
	News style usually uses abbreviated forms, which take periods, as opposed to postal codes, which do not: *they have lived in Madison, Wis., for nine years.*	N
states' rights		B N S
St. Patrick's Day		B N S A
steely-eyed (adj.) Because *steely* is an adjective, not an adverb, it is not exempt from hyphenation: *steely-eyed determination.*		B N S A
step- Not hyphenated when indicating family relation: *stepbrother, stepmother, stepsister, stepparent,* etc.		B N S

S

stepping-stone		Ⓑ Ⓢ
steppingstone		Ⓝ
stickup (n.), **stick up** (v.) *He plans to stick up the bank. She sticks up for him all the time.*		Ⓑ Ⓝ Ⓢ
stickup (adj.) *He is a stickup artist.*		✚
stockbroker		Ⓑ Ⓝ Ⓢ
stock-in-trade (n.)		Ⓑ Ⓢ
stock in trade (n.)		Ⓝ
stomachache		Ⓑ Ⓝ Ⓢ
stopgap		Ⓑ Ⓝ Ⓢ
stopover (n.), **stop over** (v.)		Ⓑ Ⓝ Ⓢ
story line		Ⓑ Ⓢ
storyline		Ⓝ
storyteller		Ⓑ Ⓝ Ⓢ
story telling (n.)		Ⓑ Ⓝ Ⓢ
streetwalker		Ⓑ Ⓝ Ⓢ
streetwise		Ⓑ Ⓢ
street-wise		Ⓝ
strong-arm (v., adj.)		Ⓑ Ⓝ Ⓢ
-style	In compound adjectives, standard rules of hyphenation apply.	
	Hyphenate before a noun: *a gladiator-style contest.*	Ⓑ Ⓝ Ⓢ Ⓐ
	Do not hyphenate after a noun unless it aids readability: *the contest was gladiator style.*	Ⓑ Ⓢ Ⓐ
	Hyphenate after a form of *be: the contest was gladiator-style.*	Ⓝ
	In compound adverbs, Punctuation Panel split on whether to hyphenate: *The combatants fought gladiator-style./The combatants fought gladiator style.*	✚
sub- Standard rules for hyphenating prefixes apply. In general, do not hyphenate unless affixed to a proper noun or necessary to prevent awkward or confusing compound.		Ⓑ Ⓝ Ⓢ
subbasement		Ⓑ Ⓝ Ⓢ
subcommittee		Ⓑ Ⓝ Ⓢ
subculture		Ⓑ Ⓝ Ⓢ
subdivide, subdivision		Ⓑ Ⓝ Ⓢ
subgroup		Ⓑ Ⓝ Ⓢ
submachine gun		Ⓑ Ⓝ Ⓢ Ⓐ

subprime	Ⓑ Ⓝ Ⓢ
subtotal	Ⓑ Ⓝ Ⓢ
subzero	Ⓑ Ⓝ Ⓢ
such as, commas with A comma often precedes *such as* but no comma should come after: *The store is having a sale on many items, such as clothes, books, and electronics. The store is having a sale on items such as clothes, books, and electronics.*	Ⓑ Ⓝ Ⓢ Ⓐ
suffixes, hyphenation of Most compounds formed with suffixes are not hyphenated. The most common exceptions are compounds that would triple consonants (*bill-less*) and compounds formed with proper nouns (*Austin-wide*). (For more, see "Suffixes," page 115.)	Ⓑ Ⓝ Ⓢ Ⓐ
summa cum laude	Ⓑ Ⓝ Ⓢ
summer *See* seasons	
super-, hyphenation of When forming a compound adjective not found in the dictionary, the writer can choose open, hyphenated, or closed forms: *I've been super busy. I've been super-busy. I've been superbusy.* A majority of the Punctuation Panel preferred open forms: *I've been super busy.* (See also "Compound adjective with *super*," page 98.)	✚
supercharge, supercharged	Ⓑ Ⓝ Ⓢ
super-duper	Ⓑ Ⓝ Ⓢ
superhero	Ⓑ Ⓝ Ⓢ
superimpose	Ⓑ Ⓝ Ⓢ
Superman, superman One word, no hyphen for both the proper name of the character and a generic noun.	Ⓑ Ⓝ Ⓢ
supermodel	Ⓑ Ⓝ Ⓢ
supernatural	Ⓑ Ⓝ Ⓢ
supernova	Ⓑ Ⓝ Ⓢ
superpower	Ⓑ Ⓝ Ⓢ
supersonic	Ⓑ Ⓝ Ⓢ
superstar	Ⓑ Ⓝ Ⓢ
superlatives, hyphenation of	Standard rules for hyphenating compound modifiers apply. In general, hyphenate whenever doing so aids clarity or readability.	Ⓑ Ⓝ Ⓐ
	In science style, superlative adjectives—forms ending in *-est*, such as slowest, fastest, longest—are not hyphenated before or after a noun: *The slowest burning fuel. The fuel that is slowest burning.*	Ⓢ
supra- General rules for hyphenating prefixes apply. In general, no hyphen except with a proper noun or as necessary to prevent awkward compound such as a double vowel: *supra-articulate*.	Ⓑ Ⓝ Ⓢ Ⓐ
surface-to-air missile	Ⓑ Ⓝ Ⓢ

S

suspensive hyphenation Suspensive hyphenation refers to any series of compounds that share a single element, such as a root word: *a Grammy- and Emmy-award-winning actor.* (For more, see "Suspensive Hyphenation," page 105.)

SWAT Acronym for Special Weapons and Tactics.

takeoff (n.), **take off** (v.)	B N S
takeout (n.), **take out** (v.)	B N S
takeover (n.), **take over** (v.)	B N S
tattletale	B N S

| **tax-free, tax free** | The adjective is hyphenated: *a tax-free investment.* | B N S |
| | The Punctuation Panel split on whether to hyphenate the adverb: *you can donate tax-free/tax free.* | ✢ |

T-bone	B N S
Teamsters union (See also "Possessive vs. Adjective Forms," page 16.)	N

teachers college No apostrophe in news style. In other styles, writers can opt for *teachers college* if they interpret *teachers* as an adjective or *teachers' college* if they intend it as a possessive. (See also "Possessive vs. Adjective Forms," page 16.) — N

teachers union, teachers' union The Punctuation Panel split on whether to include an apostrophe, with news style experts preferring no apostrophe and book style experts opting for the apostrophe. (See also "Possessive vs. Adjective Forms," page 16.) — ✢

tearjerker (n.)	B S
tear-jerker (n.)	N
tear-jerking (adj.) *A tear-jerking tale.*	B S
teenage, teenager	B N S

television programs	Use italics for show titles: *I Love Lucy, The Nightly Business Report.*	B A S
	Use quotation marks for show titles: "I Love Lucy," "The Nightly Business Report."	N
	Use quotation marks for individual episode titles: "The Bubble Boy."	B N S A

television stations Television station call letters are in all capital letters with no periods: *the segment will appear on KTLA.* — B N

telltale	B N S

temporary compound A temporary compound is any compound adjective, adverb, noun, or verb not found in the dictionary. For example, *well-spoken* is listed in the dictionary, making it a permanent compound, but *well-spent* is not in the dictionary. So *well-spent* is a temporary compound. In determining whether to hyphenate a compound, the writer should first check the dictionary to see if the term is listed. If the term is hyphenated in the dictionary, the writer should hyphenate accordingly. If it is not hyphenated in the dictionary, the rules of hyphenation described in this book apply. For the reader's convenience, many common temporary and permanent compounds are also listed here.

tenfold	🅑 🅝
test-drive (n., v.)	🅑 🅝 🅢
	Punctuation Panel book style experts split on whether to hyphenate noun form: *The customer took the car for a test drive. The customer took the car for a test-drive.* ✚
tête-à-tête	🅑
Texas Hold'em	🅑 🅢
Texas Hold 'em	🅝
Tex-Mex	🅑 🅝 🅢
thank you, commas with Set off with commas when used parenthetically as a phrase: *I'd love some, thank you.* No commas when integrated as a verb into the sentence: *I'll thank you not to call me that.* In neither of these uses is *thank you* hyphenated. ✚	
thank-you, hyphenation of When used as a noun, *thank-you* is hyphenated: *what a gracious thank-you!*	🅑 🅢
that, introducing quoted text, no comma with The word *that* before a quotation precludes the comma. He said, "There's profit to be made." He said that there's "profit to be made."	🅑 🅝 🅢 🅐
that, relative clause, commas with As a relative pronoun, *that* introduces only restrictive clauses, which are not set off with commas: *the car that I was driving was red.*	🅑 🅝 🅢 🅐
theatergoer	🅑 🅝 🅢
theirs Never takes an apostrophe.	🅑 🅝 🅢 🅐
there'd Contraction of *there had* or *there would.*	🅑 🅝 🅢 🅐
therefore, commas with *Therefore* may or may not be set off with commas, depending on whether the writer judges it to be a parenthetical insertion or well integrated into the sentence: *The solution, therefore, is simple. The solution is therefore simple.*	🅑 🅝 🅢 🅐
there's Contraction of *there is* or *there has.*	🅑 🅝 🅢 🅐
they'd Contraction of *they had* or *they would.*	🅑 🅝 🅢 🅐
they'll Contraction of *they will.*	🅑 🅝 🅢 🅐
they're Contraction of *they are.* Do not confuse the contraction *they're* with the possessive adjective *their* or the adverb or pronoun *there.*	🅑 🅝 🅢 🅐
they've Contraction of *they have.*	🅑 🅝 🅢 🅐
III Not set off from a proper name with commas: *Robert Ableman III attended.*	🅑 🅝 🅢
3-D Abbrev. of *three-dimensional.*	🅑 🅝 🅢
three Rs	🅑
three R's	🅝

T

'til Contraction of *until*. This form is discouraged by news, business, and book styles, which say to use *till* or *until* instead.	Ⓑ Ⓝ Ⓢ Ⓐ
till Synonym of *until*. Note no apostrophe.	Ⓑ Ⓝ Ⓢ Ⓐ
time-consuming	Ⓑ Ⓝ Ⓢ
time-out	Ⓑ Ⓢ
timeout	Ⓝ
tip-off (n.)	Ⓑ Ⓢ
tipoff (n.)	Ⓝ
tip off (v.)	Ⓑ Ⓝ Ⓢ
titled When used before the name of a written or produced work, no comma should follow, regardless of whether the name is in quotation marks or italics: *I read about it in an article titled "A Weekend in Big Bear."*	✚
'tis Contraction of *it is*.	Ⓑ Ⓝ Ⓢ Ⓐ
to go (adv.) *I'll take that to go.*	Ⓑ Ⓝ Ⓢ Ⓐ
too, commas with The major styles do not give express instructions on whether commas should set off *too*. A majority of the Punctuation Panel preferred a comma in: *I like it, too.* The panel split on whether to use a comma in: *I too saw that movie./I, too, saw that movie.*	✚
toothache	Ⓑ Ⓝ Ⓢ
Top 40 (adj.) *They had a Top 40 hit.*	Ⓑ Ⓢ
Top-40 (adj.) *They had a Top-40 hit.*	Ⓝ
topcoat	Ⓑ Ⓝ Ⓢ
top dog (n.)	Ⓑ Ⓝ Ⓢ
top dollar (n.)	Ⓑ Ⓝ Ⓢ
top-down (adj.) *A top-down compensation structure.*	Ⓑ Ⓝ Ⓢ
topflight The adjective is one word, no hyphen in book and science styles: *a topflight operation.*	Ⓑ Ⓢ
top-flight Hyphenate in news style: *a top-flight operation.*	Ⓝ
top hat (n.)	Ⓑ Ⓝ Ⓢ
top-heavy (adj.)	Ⓑ Ⓝ Ⓢ
top-notch (adj.)	Ⓑ Ⓝ Ⓢ
top tier (n.)	Ⓑ Ⓝ Ⓢ Ⓐ
toss-up (n.)	Ⓑ Ⓢ
tossup (n.)	Ⓝ
touch screen (n.), **touch-screen** (adj.) *The computer has a touch screen. Use the touch-screen buttons.*	Ⓑ Ⓝ Ⓢ

Toys"R"Us The toy retailer takes quotation marks around the *R* and no spaces.	Ⓑ Ⓢ
Toys R Us Do not use quotation marks or apostrophes; put spaces around the *R*.	Ⓝ
trade-in (n.), **trade in** (v.)	Ⓑ Ⓝ Ⓢ
trade-off (n.), **trade off** (v.)	Ⓑ Ⓝ Ⓢ
trade show	Ⓑ Ⓝ Ⓢ
trans- Standard rules for hyphenating prefixes apply. In general, no hyphen except before a proper noun or to avoid awkward compounds.	Ⓑ Ⓝ Ⓢ
transatlantic	Ⓑ Ⓢ
trans-Atlantic	Ⓝ
transcontinental	Ⓑ Ⓝ Ⓢ
transgender	Ⓑ Ⓝ Ⓢ
transoceanic	Ⓑ Ⓝ Ⓢ
transpacific	Ⓑ Ⓢ
trans-Pacific	Ⓝ
transsexual	Ⓑ Ⓝ Ⓢ
trans-Siberian	Ⓑ Ⓝ Ⓢ
Travel and Leisure Do not use a plus sign in the proper name of this travel magazine.	Ⓝ
Treasurys Shortened form for *Treasury notes* or *Treasury bonds* takes no apostrophe.	
T. rex Shortened form of *Tyrannosaurus rex*.	Ⓑ Ⓢ

trick-or-treat, trick-or-treating, trick-or-treater	Hyphenate the verb form: *They will trick-or treat tomorrow night. Last night the children were trick-or-treating.*	Ⓑ Ⓢ
	The gerund *trick-or-treating* and the noun *trick-or-treater* take hyphens: *our children love trick-or-treating.* The exclamation takes no hyphens: *"Trick or treat!" the children yelled.* The adjective form is also hyphenated: *playing cute was her trick-or-treat strategy.*	Ⓑ Ⓝ Ⓢ

trompe l'oeil	Ⓑ Ⓝ Ⓢ Ⓐ
troublemaker, troublemaking	Ⓑ Ⓝ Ⓢ
tryout (n.), **try out** (v.)	Ⓑ Ⓝ Ⓢ
T-shirt	Ⓑ Ⓝ Ⓢ
tune-up (n.)	Ⓑ Ⓢ
tuneup (n.)	Ⓝ
tune up (v.)	Ⓑ Ⓝ Ⓢ

T

Term	Styles
turned, in compound nouns, hyphenation of For compounds like *an accountant-turned-criminal*, the Punctuation Panel indicated that hyphens are necessary to show that the words are working together as a single noun.	✚
turnkey (n., adj.)	B N S
turn-on (n.)	B N S A
turn on (v.)	B N S
turned-on (adj.)	B S
'twas Contraction of *it was.*	B N S A
24/7 Uses a slash.	N
twentysomething Spell out.	B S
20-something Uses numerals and a hyphen.	N
'twere An archaic contraction of *it were.*	B N S A
two-door (n.) Hyphenate as a noun if hyphen aids readability or comprehension: *her car is a two-door.*	B N S A
two-door (adj.) Usually hyphenated before a noun: *a two-door sedan.*	B N S A
TV, TVs (pl.) No apostrophe in the plural except in all-capital contexts where an apostrophe is necessary to prevent confusion.	B N S A
TV stations *See* television stations	
über- Standard rules for hyphenating prefixes apply. In general, no hyphen unless necessary to prevent an awkward compound. Note that the preferred dictionaries for news and book styles indicate the umlaut should be used. Writers, especially in news style, can use their own judgment as to whether such foreign-language diacritical marks are appropriate.	B N
U-boat	B N S
UFO, UFOs (pl.) No apostrophe in the plural except in all-capital contexts where an apostrophe is necessary to prevent confusion.	B N S A
ultra- In general, do not hyphenate temporary compounds with this prefix unless it precedes a proper noun (*ultra-Republican*) or creates an awkward arrangement of vowels (*ultra-artistic*).	B N S
Exceptions: *ultra-leftist, ultra-rightist.*	N
ultramodern	B N S
ultrasonic	B N S
ultraviolet	B N S
un- Standard rules for hyphenating prefixes apply. In general, no hyphen except before a proper noun or to avoid awkward compounds.	B N S A
UN Abbrev. for *United Nations.*	B S
U.N. Takes periods (except in headlines).	N
un-American	B N S A

unarmed		B N S
under-	Under can be a prefix or a word. In forming compound modifiers not found in the dictionary, the writer can choose to hyphenate (*under-house plumbing*), to leave the compound open (*under house plumbing*), or to use a closed form according to the rules for hyphenating prefixes (*underhouse plumbing*).	B N
	For verb forms such as *undercook* and *underuse*, the Punctuation Panel recommends the closed form.	✚
underachieve, underachiever		B N S
underage		B N S
underbelly		B N S
underbrush		B N S
undercharge		B N S
underclass		B N S
undercook		N ✚
undercover		B N S
undercurrent		B N S
undercut		B N S
underdog		B N S
underestimate		B N S
underfoot		B N S
undergarment		B N S
underhand, underhanded		B N S
undernourished		B N S
underpants		B N S
underpass		B N S
underpay, underpaid		B N S
underperform, underperforming		B N S
underplay		B N S
underprivileged		B N S
underrate, underrated		B N S
undersell, undersold		B N S
undersized		B N S
undersecretary		B N S
understudy		B N S

U

under-the-table (adj.) *An under-the-table arrangement.*	Ⓑ Ⓝ Ⓢ
under the table, under-the-table (adv.) Punctuation Panel split on whether to hyphenate as an adverb: *He gets paid under the table. He gets paid under-the-table.*	✚
underthings	Ⓝ
underuse, underused	Ⓑ Ⓢ ✚
undervalue	Ⓑ Ⓝ Ⓢ
underwater (adj., adv.) *An underwater adventure. An underwater mortgage. Searching for treasure underwater.*	Ⓑ Ⓝ Ⓢ
underway (adj.) *The underway convention will end Tuesday.*	Ⓑ Ⓝ Ⓢ
under way (adv.) *The convention is under way.*	Ⓑ Ⓢ
underway (adv.) *The convention is underway.*	Ⓝ
underweight	Ⓑ Ⓝ Ⓢ
underworld	Ⓑ Ⓝ Ⓢ
undo, undid, undone	Ⓑ Ⓝ Ⓢ
unearned	Ⓑ Ⓝ Ⓢ
unfollow	Ⓑ Ⓝ Ⓢ Ⓐ
unfriend	Ⓑ Ⓝ Ⓢ Ⓐ
United States' Do not add an *s* after the apostrophe to form the possessive: *the United States' boundaries.*	Ⓑ Ⓝ Ⓢ
unnecessary	Ⓑ Ⓝ Ⓢ
unselfconscious	Ⓑ
unselfconscious, un-self-conscious Punctuation Panel split on whether to hyphenate.	✚
unshaven	Ⓑ Ⓝ Ⓢ
up- Do not hyphenate as a prefix except to avoid awkward combinations.	Ⓝ
up-and-comer	Ⓑ Ⓢ
up-and-coming	Ⓑ Ⓝ Ⓢ
up-and-down (adj.)	Ⓑ Ⓝ Ⓢ
updo	Ⓑ Ⓝ Ⓢ
upend	Ⓑ Ⓝ Ⓢ
up-front (adj.) *He has an up-front nature.*	Ⓑ Ⓢ
up front (adv.) *You two go up front.*	Ⓑ Ⓢ
upfront (adj., adv.) *He has an upfront nature. You two go upfront.*	Ⓝ
upgrade	Ⓑ Ⓝ Ⓢ

upkeep	Ⓑ Ⓝ Ⓢ
upload	Ⓑ Ⓝ Ⓢ
uppercase (n., adj.), **uppercased, uppercasing**	Ⓑ Ⓝ Ⓢ
upper class (n.), **upper-class** (adj.)	Ⓑ Ⓝ Ⓢ
upper crust (n.), **upper-crust** (adj.)	Ⓑ Ⓝ Ⓢ
uppercut	Ⓑ Ⓝ Ⓢ
upper hand	Ⓑ Ⓝ Ⓢ
uppermost	Ⓑ Ⓝ Ⓢ
uprise, uprising	Ⓑ Ⓝ Ⓢ
upshot	Ⓑ Ⓝ Ⓢ
upside	Ⓑ Ⓝ Ⓢ
upside-down (adj.), **upside down** (adv.) *An upside-down frown. Turn that frown upside down.*	Ⓑ Ⓝ Ⓢ
upstage (n., v., adj., adv.)	Ⓑ Ⓝ Ⓢ
upstart	Ⓑ Ⓝ Ⓢ
upstate	Ⓑ Ⓝ Ⓢ
upswing	Ⓑ Ⓝ Ⓢ
uptake	Ⓑ Ⓝ Ⓢ
uptick	Ⓑ Ⓝ Ⓢ
up to date, up-to-date Hyphenated before a noun: *an up-to-date report.* Usually not hyphenated after a noun, but can be hyphenated to aid clarity: *this report isn't up to date.*	Ⓑ Ⓝ Ⓢ
URL Abbrev. for *uniform/universal resource locator.*	Ⓑ Ⓝ Ⓢ Ⓐ

URLs (web addresses), punctuation after	URLs are punctuated like regular words in book, news, and academic styles. A comma, period, or other punctuation mark can follow the URL immediately without a space.	Ⓑ Ⓝ Ⓐ
	In science style, a period cannot immediately follow a URL. Science writers should avoid putting a URL at the end of a sentence because doing so would require writers not end the sentence in period: *a popular site with researchers is www.example.com* Scientific style prefers inserting a URL in parentheses within a sentence when possible: *the research site (www.example.com) is popular among scientists.*	Ⓢ

U

Term	Description	Styles
US, U.S.	Book style prefers no periods in the abbreviation for *United States* but allows periods.	Ⓑ
	News style uses periods in text but not in headlines.	Ⓝ
	Science style uses no periods in *US* when it's used as a noun: *he lives in the US*. But it requires periods in the adjective form: *he is in the U.S. Army*.	Ⓢ
	Academic style calls for periods in *U.S.*	Ⓐ
USA		Ⓑ Ⓝ Ⓢ Ⓐ
US Airways		
U.S.News & World Report, U.S. News Use periods and no space before the *n* when the full name of the magazine is used. But use a space before the *n* when it's shortened to *U.S. News*.		
USS No periods as part of a ship name.		Ⓑ Ⓝ Ⓢ
U-turn		Ⓑ Ⓝ Ⓢ
V-8 (n., adj.) An engine type: *he drives a V-8.*		Ⓑ Ⓝ Ⓢ
V8 Trade name for a vegetable juice.		Ⓑ Ⓝ Ⓢ
Valentine's Day, St. Valentine's Day, Saint Valentine's Day		Ⓑ Ⓝ Ⓢ Ⓐ
VCR		Ⓑ Ⓝ Ⓢ
V-E Day		Ⓝ
very, commas with Do not place a comma between very and an adjective that follows: *A very special day. A very overpaid man. However, place commas between multiple instances of very. A very, very special day. A very, very overpaid man.*		Ⓑ Ⓝ Ⓢ Ⓐ
very, hyphenation of Do not hyphenate very as part of a compound modifier: *A very nice day. A very well-known man.*		Ⓝ
Veterans Day		Ⓑ Ⓝ Ⓢ
vice-	Hyphenate in names of all positions and offices except *vice admiral and vice president.*	Ⓑ Ⓢ
	No hyphen in names of positions or offices: *vice president, vice mayor, vice admiral,* etc.	Ⓝ
vice versa		Ⓑ Ⓝ Ⓢ
VIP, **VIPs** (pl.) No apostrophe in the plural except in all-capital contexts where an apostrophe is necessary to prevent confusion.		Ⓑ Ⓝ Ⓢ Ⓐ
V-J Day		Ⓝ
V-neck		Ⓑ Ⓝ Ⓢ
vowels, words ending with, plurals of A word that ends in a vowel, like *ski,* forms the plural without an apostrophe: skis. This is also true for proper names: *the Micelis, the Corollas.*		Ⓑ Ⓝ Ⓢ Ⓐ
VoIP Abbrev. for *Voice over Internet Protocol.*		Ⓝ

Term		Style
vs Abbreviation for versus.		Ⓑ Ⓢ
vs. In running text, however, *versus* is often spelled out.		Ⓝ
wait list (n.), **wait-list** (v.) *I'm on the wait list. I wanted to enroll in the class, but they wait-listed me.*		Ⓑ Ⓝ Ⓢ
walk-in (n., adj)		Ⓑ Ⓝ Ⓢ
walk-through (n.)		Ⓑ Ⓝ Ⓢ
walk-through (adj.)		Ⓝ
walk-up (n., adj.), **walk up** (v.)		Ⓑ Ⓝ Ⓢ
Walmart, Wal-Mart Name for individual stores is one word, no hyphen: *we went to Walmart.* Corporation name has a hyphen: *we bought shares of Wal-Mart Stores.*		
warm-up (n.), **warm up** (v.), **warm-up** (adj.)		Ⓑ Ⓝ Ⓢ
Washington, DC, commas with	In book style, the abbreviation for the *District of Columbia* is normally set off with commas. But if the writer opts not to use periods in *DC*, commas to set it off are optional.	Ⓑ
	Right: *Washington, DC, gets hot in the summer.*	
	Right: *Washington DC gets hot in the summer.*	
	Right: *Washington, D.C., gets hot in the summer.*	
	In news style, D.C. is set off with commas: *Washington, D.C., gets hot in the summer.*	Ⓝ
Washington, D.C., periods with	Book style prefers no periods in *DC* but allows them in contexts in which the writer has chosen to use other US abbreviations with periods (as opposed to postal codes, which take no periods).	Ⓑ
	News style calls for periods in *D.C.*	Ⓝ
	Science and academic styles do not use periods in *DC*.	Ⓢ Ⓐ
Washington's Birthday		Ⓑ Ⓝ Ⓢ
wash up (v.), **washed-up** (adj.) *A washed-up actor.*		Ⓑ Ⓝ Ⓢ
watcher, as part of compound nouns Punctuation Panel members favored no hyphen in compound nouns formed with *-er* nouns, unanimously opting for no hyphen in *She is a regular market watcher.*		✚
watching, as part of compound nouns	When combining with another noun to create a term not found in the dictionary, do not hyphenate: *market watching can be lucrative.*	Ⓑ
	News style experts on the Punctuation Panel preferred no hyphen in compounds formed with gerunds such as watching: *market watching can be lucrative.*	✚
watchmaker, watchmaking		Ⓑ Ⓝ Ⓢ
waterborne		Ⓑ Ⓝ Ⓢ

watercooler, **water cooler**	One word as noun or adjective.	(B) (S)
	Two words, no hyphen as noun. Hyphenate as adjective: *a water-cooler program*.	(N)
waterlogged		(B) (N) (S)
water ski (n.), **water-ski** (v.), **water-skier** (n.)		(B) (N) (S)
water-skiing		(B)
water skiing		(N)
website		(B) (N)
Web site		(S) (A)
we'd Contraction of *we had* or *we would*.		(B) (N) (S) (A)
weekend		(B) (N) (S)
weeklong		(B) (N) (S)
week's, weeks' as in *one week's time, two weeks' pay*, etc. Treat as possessive, taking care to distinguish the singular possessive *one week's* from the plural possessive *two weeks'*. (See "Quasi Possessives," page 15.)		(B) (N) (S)

well, commas with When used as an interjection, *well* is often, but not necessarily, set off with commas. The writer can choose to omit commas if they do not aid readability or create the desired emphasis: *Well, you're the one who wanted to come here. Well you're the one who wanted to come here.*

well, **hyphenation of**	A compound adjective formed with *well* is hyphenated before a noun it modifies (*a well-considered idea*) but not after the noun (*That idea is well considered*).	(B) (S) (A)
	In news style, a compound adjective formed with *well* is hyphenated before or after the noun it modifies (*It's a well-considered idea. That idea is well-considered*).	(N)
	A majority of the Punctuation Panel preferred hyphenating *well* as part of compounds of three or more words, such as *a well-put-together woman*.	+
well-being		(B) (N) (S)
well-done, **well done**	Usually hyphenated as an adjective: *a well-done steak*.	(B) (N) (S)
	The Punctuation Panel, however, indicated no hyphen applies when *Well done!* is used as an exclamation or a freestanding term of praise.	+
well-known	Hyphenate before a noun: *a well-known conductor*.	(B) (N) (S)
	Hyphenate after a noun: *the conductor is well-known*.	(N)
well-off Hyphenate as an adjective in all contexts: *a well-off couple*. And use the hyphenated form as a noun (nominal adjective): *the well-off have people to handle their money*.		(B) (N) (S)

well-paying	Hyphenate as an adjective before but not after a noun: *A well-paying job. That job is well paying.*	Ⓑ Ⓢ Ⓐ
	Hyphenate before or after a noun it modifies: *A well-paying job. That job is well-paying.*	Ⓝ
well-spent, well spent	Hyphenate as compound adjective before but not after the noun it modifies: *It was well-spent money. It was money well spent.*	Ⓑ Ⓢ Ⓐ
	Hyphenate as a compound adjective before or after the noun it modifies: *It was well-spent money. It was money well-spent.*	Ⓝ

well-to-do Hyphenate as an adjective: *a well-to-do couple.* And use hyphenated form as noun (nominal adjective): *the well-to-do are on vacation this time of year.*   Ⓑ Ⓝ Ⓢ

well-wisher (n.), **well-wishing** (n., adj.)   Ⓑ Ⓝ Ⓢ

Wendy's The chain hamburger restaurant has an apostrophe in its name. To make plural, or to make singular or plural possessive, the Punctuation Panel unanimously favored using the singular name with no modifications.   ✦

we've Contraction of *we have.*   Ⓑ Ⓝ Ⓢ Ⓐ

whale watching (n.)   Ⓑ ✦

what it is is *See* is is

which, commas with When *which* is used as a relative pronoun, it most commonly introduces a nonrestrictive clause. Nonrestrictive relative clauses take commas: *spiders, which have eight legs, live in every region of the United States.* Less frequently, *which* heads up restrictive relative clauses, which are not set off with commas: *the house which we stayed in was nice.* (See also "Comma to Set off a Nonrestrictive or Parenthetical Word, Phrase, or Clause," page 32.)

whistle-blower   Ⓑ Ⓝ Ⓢ

whitewash (n., v.)   Ⓑ Ⓝ Ⓢ

whole grain (n.)   Ⓑ Ⓝ Ⓢ

whole-grain (adj.)   Ⓝ

wholehearted   Ⓑ Ⓝ Ⓢ

who's Contraction of *who is* or *who has.* Take care not to confuse *who's* with *whose,* which is used exclusively to show possession.   Ⓑ Ⓝ Ⓢ Ⓐ

who's who (n.) *A who's who of the entertainment industry was there.*   Ⓑ Ⓝ Ⓢ

wide-, as first word in compound modifiers Usually hyphenated unless closed form is listed in dictionary: *wide-angle lens, wide-eyed wonder, wide-body truck,* but *widespread problem.*   Ⓝ Ⓑ

| **-wide** (suffix) | Hyphenate compounds not found in the dictionary: *university-wide, office-wide,* but *worldwide.* | Ⓑ |
| | Do not hyphenate: *universitywide, officewide.* | Ⓝ |

wide-angle Hyphenate as an adjective (*a wide-angle lens*) but not as an noun phrase (*We viewed it from a wide angle*).		Ⓑ Ⓝ Ⓢ
wide-awake, wide awake	Hyphenate before a noun: *a wide-awake child.*	Ⓑ Ⓝ Ⓢ
	No hyphen after a noun: *the child was wide awake.*	Ⓑ
	Though news style suggests *wide awake* should be hyphenated after a noun, news style experts on the Punctuation Panel indicated they would not hyphenate *The child was wide awake.*	Ⓝ ✛
wide-eyed		Ⓑ Ⓝ Ⓢ
widely No hyphen as part of a compound modifier: *A widely renowned scholar. A widely held belief.*		Ⓑ Ⓝ Ⓢ Ⓐ
wide-open Hyphenate as an adjective in all contexts: *A It was a wide-open invitation. The invitation was wide-open.*		Ⓑ Ⓝ Ⓢ
wide receiver		Ⓑ Ⓝ Ⓢ
wide-screen (adj.) Hyphenate before a noun. Hyphen is optional after a noun.		Ⓑ
widescreen (adj.)		Ⓝ
widespread		Ⓑ Ⓝ Ⓢ
WiDi, Wi-Di Though Punctuation Panel was unanimous that Wi-Fi takes a hyphen, they split on whether to hyphenate *Wi-Di/WiDi.*		✛
widow's peak		Ⓑ Ⓝ Ⓢ
widow's walk		Ⓑ Ⓝ Ⓢ
Wi-Fi		Ⓑ Ⓝ Ⓢ
wildlife		Ⓑ Ⓝ Ⓢ
Wilkes-Barre, Pennsylvania		
windchill		Ⓑ Ⓢ
wind chill, wind chill factor		Ⓝ
wine tasting (n.)		Ⓑ Ⓝ Ⓢ
-winner, -winning Do not hyphenate noun forms with winner. *She is a Grammy winner.* Hyphenate adjectives with -winning: *she is a Grammy-winning artist.*		Ⓑ Ⓝ Ⓢ
winter *See* seasons		
win-win (n., adj.) *A win-win situation.*		Ⓑ Ⓝ Ⓢ
-wise	Standard rules for suffixes mean no hyphen in most temporary compounds: *dollarwise, slantwise, budgetwise.* Awkward or difficult-to-understand compounds can be hyphenated.	Ⓝ Ⓑ
	Punctuation Panel split on whether to hyphenate *cooking-wise/cookingwise, size-wise/sizewise,* and *driving-wise/drivingwise.*	✛

Term	Styles
WMD Abbrev. for *weapons of mass destruction*.	Ⓑ Ⓝ Ⓢ Ⓐ
women's The possessive of the plural *women*. Though some trade names may exclude the apostrophe, doing so is widely considered an error.	Ⓑ Ⓝ Ⓢ Ⓐ
word of mouth (n.) *People learned of the restaurant by word of mouth.*	Ⓑ Ⓢ
word-of-mouth (n.) *People learned of the restaurant by word-of-mouth.*	Ⓝ
word-of-mouth (adj.) *Word-of-mouth publicity can be the most effective.*	Ⓑ Ⓝ Ⓢ Ⓐ
words as words, plurals of In news and book style, words as words form the plural without an apostrophe: *no ifs, ands, or buts*. It's recommended that academic and scientific writers follow this style, but they may also opt for the apostrophe: *no if's, and's, or but's*.	Ⓑ Ⓝ
workers' compensation	Ⓑ Ⓝ
working class (n.)	Ⓑ Ⓝ Ⓢ
working-class (adj.) Hyphenate before or after noun: *A working-class family. The family is working-class.*	Ⓑ Ⓝ Ⓢ
would've Contraction of *would have*. This should never be written *would of*.	
write-down (n., adj.), **write down** (v.) The verb form is unhyphenated regardless of meaning: *Please write down what I'm telling you. The company had to write down its equipment depreciation.*	Ⓑ Ⓝ Ⓢ
write-in (n., adj.), **write in** (v.)	Ⓑ Ⓝ Ⓢ
write-off (n., adj.), **write off** (v.)	Ⓑ Ⓝ Ⓢ
write-up (n., adj.), **write up** (v.)	Ⓑ Ⓝ Ⓢ
wrongdoing	Ⓑ Ⓝ Ⓢ
Xmas	Ⓑ Ⓝ Ⓢ
X-Men	
X-ray	Ⓑ Ⓢ
x-ray	Ⓝ
Yahoo In news style, do not include exclamation point as part of proper name.	Ⓝ
y'all Contraction of *you all*.	Ⓑ Ⓝ Ⓢ Ⓐ
year-end Hyphenated as adjective or noun: *file the reports at year-end.*	Ⓑ Ⓝ Ⓢ
yearlong	Ⓑ Ⓝ Ⓢ
year old, year-old, years old, years-old, -year-old When not combined with a number, hyphenate only adjective forms before the noun: *a year-old newspaper, a years-old newspaper*. When combined with a number to form a noun or an adjective, hyphenate: *Quinn has a two-year-old and a four-year-old. Steve has a 2-year-old car.* (Note that news style always uses numerals with ages, while book and other styles usually spell them out. See also "Compound adjective indicating age with *year* and *old*," page 100, and "Numerals vs. Spelled-Out Numbers," page 140.)	Ⓑ Ⓝ

year-round, **year round** (adj., adv.)	Hyphenate as an adjective before a noun: *it's a year-round school.*	Ⓑ Ⓝ Ⓢ Ⓐ
	Hyphenate as an adjective after a noun or as an adverb: *This school is year-round. He plays golf year-round.*	Ⓝ
	Do not hyphenate after a noun or verb unless hyphen is needed for clarity: *This school is year round. He plays golf year round.*	Ⓑ Ⓢ Ⓐ

years, commas with Set off with commas in full dates: *March 22, 1968.* But do not set off with commas when paired with only a month: *March 1968.*	Ⓑ Ⓝ Ⓢ
years, apostrophe with For a single year as possessive, use an apostrophe: *1975's top films.* An apostrophe may also stand in for dropped numerals: *They visited in '75. That was '75's top hit. See also* decades	Ⓑ Ⓝ Ⓢ Ⓐ
year's, years' In *one year's time,* and *two years' pay,* etc., treat as posses-sive, taking care to distinguish the singular possessive *one year's* from the plural possessive *two years'.* (See "Quasi Possessives," page 15.)	Ⓑ Ⓝ Ⓢ

yes, **commas with**	*Yes* is often, but not necessarily, set off with commas. The writer can choose to omit commas if they do not aid readability or rhythm: *Yes, there is a Santa Claus. Yes there is a Santa Claus.*	Ⓑ
	The Punctuation Panel unanimously preferred a comma in *Yes, thank you.*	✚

yes, plural of The plural form, *yeses,* takes no apostrophe.	Ⓑ Ⓝ Ⓢ
you'd Contraction of *you had* or *you would.*	Ⓑ Ⓝ Ⓢ Ⓐ
yours Never contains an apostrophe.	Ⓑ Ⓝ Ⓢ Ⓐ
YouTube	
you've Contraction of *you have.*	Ⓑ Ⓝ Ⓢ Ⓐ
yo-yo Noun and verb forms hyphenated and lowercase.	Ⓑ Ⓝ Ⓢ
zigzag	Ⓑ Ⓝ Ⓢ
zip line (n.)	Ⓑ Ⓝ Ⓢ
zip-line (v.) Hyphenated in book and science styles.	Ⓑ Ⓢ
zip line (v.) Two words, no hyphen in news style.	Ⓝ
z's for sleep, as in *to catch some z's.* Multiple *z's,* as in *zzzz,* are more com-monly confined to graphics such as cartoons to indicate a snoring sound.	Ⓑ Ⓝ Ⓢ

UNDERSTANDING GRAMMATICAL UNITS: PHRASES, CLAUSES, SENTENCES, AND SENTENCE FRAGMENTS

A basic understanding of phrases, clauses, sentences, and sentence fragments is important for good punctuation.

Phrases

In grammar, a phrase is any single word or group of words functioning as a single part of speech.

Jack the accountant was running very fast.

In this example, *Jack the accountant* is a noun phrase, *was running* is a verb phrase, and *very fast* is an adverb phrase.

Note that, because single words function the same way, they are also categorized as phrases for syntactical analysis.

Jack ran fast.

In this example, the noun phrase is the single word *Jack*, the verb phrase is *ran*, and the adverb phrase is *fast*.

In addition to noun, verb, and adverb phrases, there are also adjective phrases (*beautiful, extremely beautiful*) and prepositional phrases (*on time, with great dignity*).

Note that phrases can contain phrases within them: the adjective phrase *extremely beautiful* contains both an adverb phrase (*extremely*) and an adjective phrase (*beautiful*).

Clauses

A clause is any unit that contains both a subject and a verb. In *Jack ran*, the subject is *Jack* and the verb is *ran*. In *Jack was running*, the subject is *Jack* and the phrase *was running* is functioning as the verb.

An independent clause is any clause that can stand alone as a sentence. Independent clauses are distinguished from dependent clauses (also called subordinate clauses), which because they are introduced by a subordinating conjunction, cannot stand alone as a sentence.

> *Jack ran* = independent clause
>
> *Jack was running* = independent clause
>
> *If Jack ran* = dependent clause
>
> *Because Jack ran* = dependent clause

Subjects are often nouns, but not always.

> *To give is better than to receive.*

In this example, the infinitive *to give* serves as the subject, and the verb is *is*.

Identifying independent clauses is important for understanding how to use commas and especially for following the comma rule that calls for a comma between independent clauses joined by a conjunction.

> *Barbara saw what you did yesterday, and she is going to tell everyone who will listen.*

The comma is necessary because the units joined by *and* are both independent clauses. If the second clause were dependent, no comma would be used.

Barbara saw what you did yesterday because she was spying.

In this example, the second part of the sentence is rendered dependent by the word *because*, so no comma is used.

Sentences

A sentence is any unit that contains at least one independent clause and expresses a complete thought.

Aaron watched.

Aaron watched with great interest.

Aaron watched eagerly.

Aaron watched and learned.

Aaron watched as Carrie left.

A complete sentence ends with either a period, a question mark, or an exclamation point.

Sentence Fragments

A sentence fragment is any group of words that fails to meet the minimum requirements to be a sentence but nonetheless is punctuated as a sentence.

No.

Soda?

Confess? Not me.

Jerk.

Beautiful.

He is a great man. Was a great man.

Sentence fragments are sometimes considered errors, especially in academic writing. But more often they are used deliberately for effect, especially in literary writing, or whenever a complete sentence seems unnatural or unnecessary.

IDENTIFYING PARTS OF SPEECH FOR BETTER PUNCTUATION

The parts of speech are as follows: noun, verb, adjective, adverb, conjunction, and preposition.

Noun

A noun is a person, place, or thing. It's helpful to note that a certain form of a verb, known as a gerund, is also classified as a noun. A gerund is an *ing* form that, in the sentence, is doing the job of a noun. Gerunds should not be confused with present participles, which are identical in form but usually function as verbs in a sentence.

> Gerund: <u>*Walking*</u> *is good exercise.* (*Walking* functions as a noun and is the subject of the verb *is*.)

> Participle: *He was* <u>*walking*</u>*.* (*Walking* functions as a verb showing action).

Nouns are commonly subjects performing the action in verbs (*shoes are required*) or objects of verbs or prepositions (*he wore shoes; they only serve guests with shoes*). However, nouns can also function attributively as adjectives: *a shoe store, a milk crate, a broom closet.* This attributive function can factor into some hyphenation decisions. For example, when a verb that's two words in the dictionary has a corresponding noun that's just one word (such as the verb *shut down* and the noun *shutdown*), the writer can form an adjective by hyphenating the verb (*the nightly shut-down procedure*) or by just using the one-word noun form attributively (*the nightly shutdown procedure*).

✚ The Punctuation Panel prefers using the noun as an adjective in most cases.

Verb

A verb conveys action or being.

> Larry *left*.

> Sarah *is* nice.

> Kevin *wants* ice cream.

Verbs take different forms, called conjugations, to indicate when an action takes place and whether the subject is singular or plural.

> Brad *reads*.

> Brad and Jerry *read*.

> Brad *was reading*.

> Brad *had been reading*.

> Brad *will read*.

> Brad *will be reading*.

The ability to identify verbs is important for correct hyphenation. For many terms, the question of whether to hyphenate rests on whether the term is functioning as a verb or as another part of speech. For example, according to the dictionary, *trade-in* is a noun. But the verb form is not hyphenated: *he's going to trade in his car.*

Machine gun is two words as a noun, but when it's used as a verb, the dictionary indicates it should be hyphenated: *the gangsters planned to machine-gun their enemies.* In many such terms, proper hyphenation depends on the ability to identify whether the term is working as a verb.

Participles are a form of a verb used with an auxiliary verb. Past participles work with forms of *have.* They often end in *ed* or *en,* but there are many irregular forms as well, which are listed in the dictionary.

Ed has <u>written</u> a play.

That store has <u>closed</u>.

Marcia had <u>known</u> about the party.

I shouldn't have <u>eaten</u> so much.

Identifying past participles is important for following certain hyphenation rules. For example, in book, science, and academic styles, compound adjectives containing past participles are hyphenated before a noun: *a moth-eaten sweater, a little-known fact.* But in news style, they are hyphenated only when necessary for clarity: *a little known fact, a well worn sweater,* but *acid-washed fabric.*

Present participles, also called progressive participles, end with *ing.* They are verb forms commonly used with forms of *be.*

Beth is <u>walking</u>.

The dogs are <u>barking</u>.

However, they can also be used as modifiers, especially at the beginning of a sentence.

<u>Barking</u> fiercely, the dogs scared off the prowler.

Identifying present participles is important for following the rules for commas after introductory participial phrases, like *barking fiercely* in the example above.

Linking verbs, also called copular verbs, are forms of *be* and similar words that refer back to a subject.

He <u>is</u> nice-looking.

She <u>seems</u> well-intentioned.

This is important to hyphenation because it often means that the descriptor after the verb is not an adverb, as it is in *He sang happily*, but an adjective, as in *He was happy*. Thus, compound modifiers that follow a linking verb are hyphenated according to the rules governing adjectives. See chapter 11 for those hyphenation rules.

Adjective

An adjective modifies a noun. Often adjectives are single words: *a small house, a nice person*. However, hyphenated compounds often function as adjectives: *a small-animal hospital, a good-looking man*.

The question of whether to hyphenate compounds functioning as adjectives (either before or after a noun) is discussed at length in chapter 11. In general, compound adjectives that appear before a noun are hyphenated whenever the hyphen aids readability. Compound adjectives after a noun are often not hyphenated, with the notable exception of the news style stipulation that compound adjectives after *be* are hyphenated: *that man is smooth-talking*.

The question of when to put commas between multiple adjectives is covered in chapter 2. In general, coordinate adjectives—adjectives that would sound natural with the word *and* between them—can be separated by commas instead of *and*s.

> *a nice and intelligent and friendly man = a nice, intelligent, friendly man*

Adjectives between which the word *and* does not sound natural should not be separated by commas.

> Right: *a flashy red sports car*

> Wrong: *a flashy, red, sports car*

Adverb

Adverbs do not only modify verbs (*she exited gracefully*; *he dances well*), they also answer the questions *When?* and *Where?* They can also modify whole sentences or clauses, and they can modify adjectives and other adverbs.

> *He worked diligently* = *ly* adverb modifying an action.
>
> *He worked hard* = non-*ly* adverb modifying an action.
>
> *He sang today* = adverb answering the question *When?*
>
> *He sang outside* = adverb answering the question *Where?*
>
> *Unfortunately, he sang "At Last"* = adverb modifying a whole sentence.
>
> *He ruined a perfectly good song* = adverb modifying an adjective.
>
> *We met a very recently divorced couple* = adverb modifying another adverb.

Note that many words that function as adverbs can also be different parts of speech. For example, *today* can be a noun (*today was wonderful*) as well as an adverb (*I'm leaving today*). Its classification depends on its job in the sentence.

The ability to identify adverbs and other words functioning adverbially is especially helpful for proper hyphenation. For example, while the adjective *after-hours* would be hyphenated in *an after-hours club*, there would be no hyphen in *The club stays open after hours* because in this context it's an adverb and the dictionary does not hyphenate the adverb form. *As is, arm in arm, first class, full time, over the counter*, and *upside down* are other examples of terms that would be hyphenated in adjective form but often not hyphenated when functioning adverbially.

Distinguishing adverbs from nouns and adjectives that end in *ly* is important for correctly following hyphenation rules. In all the major editing styles, *ly* adverbs are not hyphenated as part of compound modifiers.

> *a happily married couple*

But the rule does not apply to nouns and adjectives ending in *ly*.

a family-friendly resort

a lovely-faced woman

Conjunction

For punctuation purposes, it helps to think of conjunctions in two categories: coordinating conjunctions and all the others. The primary coordinating conjunctions are *and, or,* and *but.* The others include many subordinating conjunctions such as *if, because, until,* and *when.*

Coordinating conjunctions and especially *and* can be replaced by commas between coordinate adjectives.

a nice and sweet and friendly man = a nice, sweet, friendly man

Coordinating conjunctions can join independent clauses.

I don't mind grocery shopping in the morning, but I hate going to the store during rush hour.

Bob likes the pancakes at the Sunrise Cafe, and he speaks highly of a lot of their other menu items.

When a coordinating conjunction joins independent clauses, a comma is placed before the conjunction as above (unless the clauses are very short and closely related, in which case the comma can be omitted).

But when one of the units joined by a coordinating conjunction is not an independent clause, a comma is not customarily used.

I don't mind grocery shopping in the morning but hate going to the store during rush hour. (Subject *I* is absent from second clause, so no comma.)

Bob likes the pancakes at the Sunrise Cafe and speaks highly of a lot of their other menu items. (Subject *he* is absent from second clause, so no comma.)

Subordinating conjunctions like *because, if, until,* and *while* can also link clauses. For detailed rules on how to use commas with subordinating conjunctions, see chapter 2. In general, most styles call for no comma when the subordinate clause follows the main clause.

Mark wanted to drive because Evelyn had been drinking.

When the subordinate clause precedes the main clause, the writer can often opt for a comma.

Because it was raining, Mark wanted to drive.

Preposition

Prepositions are often small words such as *to, at, with, until, in,* and *on*—but some longer words are also prepositions: *between, throughout,* and *regarding.* They usually take objects, forming prepositional phrases: *to the store, at John's house, with ice cream, until Thursday, in trouble, on time, between friends, throughout his lifetime, regarding work.* Prepositional phrases are not usually set off with commas.

ACKNOWLEDGMENTS

Thanks so much to the Punctuation Panel members; my agent, Laurie Abkemeier; my editor, Lisa Westmoreland; and the unsung talent who copyedited and proofread this book. Thanks, too, to Ted Averi, Stephanie Diani, Dr. Marisa DiPietro, Maxine Nunes, Treacy Colbert, Donna Stallings, and Josh Jenisch.

ABOUT THE AUTHOR AND PUNCTUATION PANEL

Photo: Stephanie Diani

JUNE CASAGRANDE is the author of the weekly syndicated "A Word, Please" grammar column and a copy editor for the custom publishing department of the *Los Angeles Times*. She has worked as a reporter, features writer, city editor, proofreader, and copyediting instructor for UC San Diego Extension. She is the author of *Grammar Snobs Are Great Big Meanies, Mortal Syntax,* and *It Was the Best of Sentences, It Was the Worst of Sentences*. She lives in Pasadena, California, with her husband. Visit www.junecasagrande.com.

MARK ALLEN took the *Associated Press Stylebook* approach to grammar and punctuation for more than twenty years as a newspaper reporter and editor. Once he was freed of the daily grind of the copy desk, he took a broader view of usage, examining the way people write along with what is suggested in usage guides. He now writes lengthy margin notes for his copyediting clients from his home office in Columbus, Ohio. Mark also posts daily editing tips on Twitter as @EditorMark and blogs at www.markalleneditorial.com. He was the first freelance editor elected to the board of the American Copy Editors Society.

ERIN BRENNER has been a publishing professional for almost twenty years, working in a variety of media. Erin is the editor for the *Copyediting* newsletter and writes for *Copyediting*'s blog. In addition, she edits for several clients through Right Touch Editing, writes regularly for *Visual Thesaurus*, and teaches for the copyediting program at UC San Diego Extension. She is on Twitter at @brenner and on Facebook at www.facebook.com/erin.brenner.

HENRY FUHRMANN is an assistant managing editor at the *Los Angeles Times*, where he oversees the copy desks and leads the editorial standards and practices committee. Since 1990 he has served all over the newsroom, working as an editor on the metro, foreign, calendar, business, and web desks. He is a numbers nerd as well as a word nerd, having studied engineering at Caltech and UCLA before entering the news business. Fuhrmann holds two degrees in journalism: a BA from Cal State Los Angeles and an MS from Columbia University. He is active in the American Copy Editors Society and the Asian American Journalists Association.

PAUL RICHMOND is employed by Elsevier Inc., the world's largest publisher of science, technology, and medicine journals and books. After twenty years working in all facets of production, his current capacity is as supplier development manager for language editing, monitoring performance of the company's host of global third-party suppliers. For the past thirteen years, he has also been an instructor within and advisor to the copyediting-certification program at University of California San Diego Extension. In his spare time, Paul is owner of and custodian to a weather station (Station Pabloco) within his community in support of the National Weather Service. He also enjoys long-distance swimming in pools and the ocean. He resides in La Mesa, California, with his wife, Barbara, and their two cats and dog.

INDEX

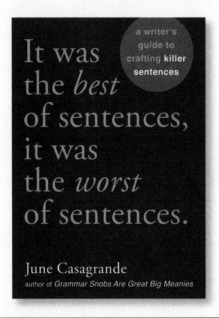